watergate

watergate

The Presidential Scandal
That Shook America

Keith W. Olson

 University Press of Kansas

Published by the
University Press of
Kansas (Lawrence,
Kansas 66049),
which was organized
by the Kansas Board
of Regents and is
operated and funded
by Emporia State
University, Fort Hays
State University,
Kansas State
University, Pittsburg
State University, the
University of Kansas,
and Wichita State
University

© 2003
by the University Press of Kansas
All rights reserved

Library of Congress Cataloging-in-Publication Data
Olson, Keith W., 1931–
Watergate : the presidential scandal that shook America /
Keith W. Olson.
p. cm.
Includes bibliographical references (p.) and index.
ISBN 0-7006-1250-5 (cloth : alk. paper) — ISBN 0-7006-1251-3
(pbk. : alk. paper)
1. Watergate Affair, 1972–1974.   I. Title.
E860 .O47 2003
973.924—dc21   2002038058

British Library Cataloguing in Publication Data is available.

Printed in the United States of America

10 9 8 7 6 5 4 3

The paper used in this publication meets the minimum
requirements of the American National Standard for
Permanence of Paper for Printed Library Materials
Z39.48-1984.

To the memory of David A. Shannon

Contents

Preface

My interest in Watergate dates from its beginning. Early in 1968 the three senior professors in my department who specialized in twentieth-century U.S. domestic history decided the department needed a new course that covered the postwar years because in their courses they never got beyond 1945. They assigned the course to me, a nontenured assistant professor. When Richard M. Nixon won the presidential election of 1968 I was teaching this new course, "The United States since World War II." The last week of the course I discussed the 1968 election. For the next fifteen or so years, the student response to this upper-level course, which I usually taught with three graduate assistants, was rewarding. Each time I taught the course the ending date advanced a year in time, so Watergate and Nixon's resignation gained prominent places in the syllabus. I based each new lecture on a close following of current events. As the years the course covered increased, I needed to eliminate a lecture topic when I added a new one. This meant I constantly rethought the entire Cold War era as I reconfigured lecture topics.

The University of Maryland and my home are in the northern suburbs of Washington, D.C. Each morning the *Washington Post* arrives in my driveway. For me, Watergate combined a professional interest, a current-events interest, and a local interest. The three times Nixon ran for president I voted for his Democratic Party opponent, although I cast my votes without enthusiasm. My research in newspapers that had supported Nixon, therefore, provided a perspective different from my own. Moreover, I had friends and colleagues who supported Nixon and his policies until early 1973.

At the various stages of my research and writing, professional friends have helped me with their critical analyses, their encouragement, and their readings of parts of the manuscript: Herman Belz, Michael Berry, Harry Blatt, Bob Buzzanco, Matthew Carnicelli, Lloyd Gardner, Jussi Hanhimaki, Bill Hoing, Mitch Horowitz, Harry Jeffrey, Joe Marcey, Steve Ochs, Don Ritchie, Whit Ridgway, Tim Sullivan, Sam Walker, and Matt Wasniewski. Wayne Cole read and commented on the entire manuscript near its final stage.

The two readers for the University Press of Kansas provided invaluable critiques that improved the manuscript substantively and stylistically. I am deeply grateful to them. For years Michael Briggs, editor in chief of the press, patiently and helpfully encouraged me. To him I also owe a lasting debt of appreciation.

As always, my greatest acknowledgment is to my wife, Marilyn, who read each of the various stages of the manuscript and has supported me in every other way.

Introduction

The Watergate scandal created a constitutional crisis second only to the Civil War of more than a century earlier and resulted in the first presidential resignation in U.S. history. Beginning in June 1972 and continuing to August 1974, the affair aroused increasing public interest and eventually dominated the national news. The event that served as Watergate's catalyst took place early on the morning of June 17, 1972, when metropolitan Washington, D.C., police arrested five burglars in the headquarters of the Democratic National Committee. That office was located in one of the three buildings of the Watergate complex, on the banks of the Potomac River in Washington. Watergate quickly became the term that stood for the events surrounding the break-in. Over time, Watergate took on a wider meaning, as media, judicial, and congressional investigations explored the background of the break-in and later the presidential cover-up and other related activities.

On April 30, 1973, President Richard M. Nixon presented a nationwide address, "About the Watergate Investigations," one in a series of climactic moments in the Watergate story. At the beginning of his address the president defined issues in "what has come to be known as the Watergate affair. These include charges of illegal activity during and preceding the 1972 presidential election and charges that responsible officials participated in efforts to cover up that illegal activity." The Watergate episode, as such, encompasses both of these phases.

An event as monumental as Watergate in the nation's history has stimulated a steady stream of books. Because of the author's insights and the book's rich detail, the most authoritative study remains Stanley I. Kutler, *The Wars of Watergate: The Last Crisis of Richard Nixon* (1990). A number of Watergate participants have also written books, including lawyers, journalists, politicians, and members of the White House staff and the Committee to Re-elect the President. Nixon's biographers and other scholars concerned with a wide range of subjects have also contributed to the large corpus of Watergate studies.

Rather than revisit the subjects of existing books, albeit with research in the new sources slowly becoming available, my purpose in this book is to write a brief analytical history to place Watergate into a broad context for persons too young to have lived through or to remember the years 1972 through 1974. In the first two chapters I summarize the events and attitudes that precipitated the June 1972 break-in. In the final, interpretative chapter I examine the extent to which Watergate, both the June 1972 break-in and its subsequent cover-up phases, fits into the broad Cold War mainstream framework of political values and rationalizations.

My second purpose is to analyze the unmasking of the cover-up, essentially from the public's perspective. The information the public received about Watergate and public reaction to this information provide the keys to understanding Nixon's resignation. Newspaper editorials from all corners of the country, news magazines, and politicians' statements document the changing national mood that steadily grew more negative toward the president's explanation and actions. To an important degree the politicians' positions and statements were both influenced by and a reaction to the media coverage of events. Unmasking the cover-up answers two fundamental questions: what role did Republicans and conservatives play in creating the atmosphere that led to resignation, and how strong and how widespread were the demands for Nixon to leave office? The ultimate failure of the cover-up, the role Republicans and conservatives played, and the strength of the movement to force Nixon from office form the narrative themes of chapters three through eight.

The six chapters concerned with unmasking the cover-up convincingly, and for the first time, document that Republicans and conservatives played indispensable roles in each of the four phases of the unmasking and that by August 1974 the overwhelming majority of Republicans demanded Nixon's removal from office. Public opinion polls and newspaper editorials showed impressive support for that demand. The documentation makes untenable the charge that liberal politicians and a liberal media drove Nixon from the White House.

Nixon arrived at the Watergate burglary, the cover-up, and the resignation by a journey on the main road of American politics. In the first post–World War II congressional election of 1946, veterans across the country won elections, including a young former naval officer, Richard M. Nixon. That year Republicans won control of both houses of Congress for the first time since 1928. Two years later Nixon won reelection, and in 1950 he won election to the U.S. Senate. Voters first in southern California and then throughout the state found the candidate Nixon appealing. Starting with his 1946 campaign against the incumbent H. Jerry Voorhis, Nixon used an aggressive campaign style. During his first term in the House he clearly established himself as an internationalist and an ardent anticommunist. His membership on the House Committee on Un-American Activities and his strong, effective participation in the Alger Hiss case elevated him to the level of a nationally known politician. As a campaigner and as a member of Congress, he projected a distinctive style and clear positions. Both the public and the politicians recognized his leadership.

In 1952 the Republican presidential nominee Dwight D. Eisenhower and his advisers selected Nixon as their party's vice presidential nominee. Nixon, they judged, was the Republican who would most help and least hurt Eisenhower's chances for victory. This meant, among other considerations, that both the moderate and conservative factions of a deeply divided Republican Party found him an acceptable compromise. In less than six years Nixon had climbed the political ladder from candidate for the House of Representatives to the second rung from the top of the national government. He was thirty-nine years old. As vice president, Nixon received special attention when Eisenhower endured a heart attack in 1955, underwent surgery for ileitis in 1956, and suffered a stroke in 1957.

Never politically or personally close to Eisenhower, Nixon nevertheless gained his party's nomination for president in 1960 but lost in one of the nation's closest presidential elections. Nixon's popular vote, though, exceeded the total vote of the 435 Republican candidates for the House of Representatives. Conversely, the popular vote for the Democratic Party's candidate, John F. Kennedy, was less than the total vote cast for his party's candidates for the House. In 1968 Nixon again won his party's presidential nomination, and this time he won the close election. Voters, however, elected Democratic majorities in both houses of Congress. As a presidential candidate, Nixon proved again that he was more popular than his party.

Nixon took the oath of office in January 1969, following a campaign in which he stressed law and order and a plan, with no specifics, to end the unpopular war in Vietnam. Four years later voters knew him and his public policies better and reelected him with the third highest percentage of popular vote in the nation's history. Nixon's Watergate behavior, therefore, was not the behavior of a political aberrant; rather, it was the behavior of a consummate politician who, for more than twenty years, had been among the nation's most important political figures. He rose to the top, step by step, within the system and, consequently, like most presidents, reflected the political values of the system.

CHAPTER ONE

Patterns from the Beginning

The climate of fear and suspicion . . . had grown up in the White House, an
atmosphere that started with the President himself and reached us through
Haldeman and Colson and others.
— *Jeb Stuart Magruder,* An American Life: One Man's Road to Watergate, *1974*

We had set in motion forces that would sooner or later make Watergate or
something like it, inevitable.
— *Charles Colson,* Born Again, *1976*

My reaction to the Watergate break-in was completely pragmatic. If it was also
cynical, it was a cynicism born of experience. I had been in politics too long, and
seen everything from dirty tricks to vote fraud. I could not muster much moral
outrage over a political bugging.
— *Richard M. Nixon,* RN: The Memoirs of Richard Nixon, *1978*

Richard M. Nixon intended to shape national policies according to
his political agenda and his personal likes and dislikes. To reach the White
House, a politician survives a grueling process that requires endurance, ability, good luck, and an incredible desire for power. Almost by definition a
president has a strong personality, and with the office comes tremendous
power, direct and indirect. In many ways, therefore, an administration is a
reflection of the president, his policies, his priorities, and his personality. The
historian Paul K. Conklin, for example, opened his influential book *The New
Deal* with his basic conclusion: "The New Deal was an exceedingly personal
enterprise. Its disparate programs were unified only by the personality of
Franklin D. Roosevelt."[1] "I Like Ike" buttons embodied the spirit of Dwight
D. Eisenhower's 1952 presidential campaign, and for eight years in office
Eisenhower maintained his popularity, based on a perceived public belief in
his honesty and decency. After John F. Kennedy's assassination, a federal
secretary unwittingly captured the strong feeling of action and enthusiasm
that ran through Kennedy's administration when she lamented that she still
did the same things every day but that the fun was gone.

Immediately and distinctly, Richard M. Nixon, like his predecessors, shaped his own presidency, even beyond the aides he selected to serve him in the White House and the politicians he asked to sit in his cabinet. From day one he demanded a daily "news summary" that reported commentary about him and his administration as well as national and world events. Some of the summaries reached fifty pages in length, with information drawn from perhaps forty magazines and fifty newspapers, television news, and even talk shows. Nixon then ordered his staff to remove eight of the nine television sets that his predecessor Lyndon B. Johnson constantly relied upon for news. Nixon did not like television newscasters and preferred his news in more detailed, written form. Following, but expanding, a practice from President Dwight Eisenhower, under whom he had served as vice president, Nixon directed Alexander P. Butterfield, his deputy assistant, to maintain a file of reports describing the substance, importance, and mood of every meeting and discussion in which the president participated, stipulating the exception only of Nixon's conversations with his top-level staff. Butterfield assigned White House staff members to attend presidential meetings according to the individual's primary area of responsibility and interest. James Keogh handled cabinet meetings, for example, and Patrick J. Buchanan Jr. summarized Nixon's meetings with legislative leaders. Butterfield explained to the note takers that Nixon wanted a detailed, written record that "should serve the purpose of triggering the President's memory, at a later date."

Nixon stamped his imprint in other ways. Often he categorically referred to the press as "the enemy." His biographer Stephen E. Ambrose has pointed out that "Nixon was obsessed with his image at least as much as Johnson" and that he "hated leaks. But he loved to leak himself, and to threaten."[2] Such strong feelings translated into a general White House atmosphere that aides absorbed, nurtured, and acted upon.

Nixon's attitudes and administrative procedures usually remained removed from public awareness although sometimes they became obvious during his public appearances and in the press coverage of his activities. Most Americans already had formed opinions of Nixon during his career as a member of the House of Representatives and of the Senate, as vice president, and during his two presidential campaigns. During his successful 1968 presidential campaign, moreover, Nixon had expressed positions, some more specific than others, on such issues as Vietnam, law and order, school busing, and federal appointment of judges.

By the time of the June 17, 1972, burglary of the Democratic Party's National Committee headquarters in the Watergate office building in Washington, D.C., Nixon had been in office almost three and a half years. Americans knew his public views and actions regarding major issues and recognized characteristics of his administration such as its relationship with the press and with Congress. Nixon, again like his predecessors, kept some actions removed from public scrutiny. By necessity certain aspects in the conduct of foreign relations logically fell under this category. Surveillance and information gathering also took place under secrecy, at times bending or breaking the law. Often, congressional oversight existed more in name than in reality. The June 17 burglary and subsequent cover-up took place within the broad context of the Nixon administration and its record of surveillance, information gathering, illegal actions, and cover-ups. That context is fundamental to understanding the entire Watergate affair.

During his first six months in office Nixon indicated a special interest in gathering information about his critics. To pursue this interest, he found at his service an impressive group of federal intelligence agencies, including the Federal Bureau of Investigation (FBI), the Internal Revenue Service (IRS), the National Security Agency (NSA), the Central Intelligence Agency (CIA), and the Defense Intelligence Agency (DIA). Nixon, however, believed these agencies often responded too slowly to his presidential orders, periodically leaked information to the press, and most important, sometimes refused to conduct illegal activities.

Nixon also knew that his predecessors placed a high value on intelligence gathering and that they often directed federal agencies to exceed the legal limits of their charters. As a candidate early in 1968, Nixon had hired John Ragan, a former FBI electronics expert, to inspect his law office, his hotel rooms, and his headquarters trailer at the Republican National Convention, as well as the rooms of his key aides, to guarantee that he and his aides were free of telephone taps and electronic receivers. During the presidential campaign later that year, Ragan performed similar services for Nixon.

Nixon's concern about intelligence information emanated from his understanding of politics. The week following his election, for example, while on his way from Key Biscayne, Florida, to New York City, the president-elect stopped at the White House to discuss the transition of administrations. As part of the orientation, one of President Johnson's assistants routinely showed Nixon and his staff the Johnson taping system and demonstrated how it worked. The system recorded conversations in the Oval Office and in the cabinet room. On the trip between Washington and New York, Nixon remarked to Robert Finch, his longtime friend and adviser, that he disliked the idea of a secret taping system in the president's office and intended to have it removed. After settling into office, Nixon ordered the Army Signal Corps to remove the system, an assignment carried out less than a month after inauguration day.

Once in office, the new president learned, if he did not already know, about the numerous instances of transgressions by the intelligence agencies. The FBI, for example, in 1956 initiated a counterintelligence program, COINTELPRO, under which its agents perjured documents, planted false stories in the press, and encouraged violence during protest rallies. In 1967 the CIA, despite its constitutional limit to overseas operations, instituted a domestic spying program, Operation CHAOS, under which CIA agents burglarized offices, tapped telephone lines, opened mail, and bugged rooms. Founded on the subterfuge that it needed to learn if foreign governments supported antiwar groups, the CIA fed 300,000 names into its computer and established dossiers on more than 7,000 Americans without their knowledge. Soon after the 1968 election, furthermore, the FBI director J. Edgar Hoover told Nixon that a few weeks earlier President Johnson had had the FBI investigate Nixon and vice presidential nominee Spiro T. Agnew. Many Washington journalists and politicians knew that recent presidents and Hoover had used FBI information to discredit persons with whom they disagreed. Hoover, for instance, repeatedly tried to get newspapers to publish information that the FBI had obtained from its electronic bugging of the civil rights leader Martin Luther King Jr.'s extramarital affairs.

Hoover and the CIA director Richard Helms, however, both had limits to how often and for what reasons they would break the law. The limits stemmed not from principles but from fear of the reaction if the public learned of the lawlessness. Once Hoover passed the federally mandated retirement age and continued in office by special presidential dispensation, he felt especially vulnerable and became more cautious regarding illegal activities. He realized that only public exposure of wrongdoing could drive him from office. Because of his popularity and because of his private files on indiscretions of presidents, members of Congress, and prominent persons who opposed him or his policies, Hoover operated the FBI much as he pleased, even in defiance of the attorney general, his nominal superior, and of the president.

Within Nixon's first month in office, Helms made known his fear of public disclosure of the CIA's illegal conduct. In sending a report to Nixon's national security adviser Henry Kissinger, Helms admitted, "This is an area not within the charter of this Agency, so I need not emphasize how extremely sensitive this makes the paper. Should anyone learn of is existence," he continued, "it would prove most embarrassing for all concerned."[3]

Nixon viewed Hoover and Helms as problems. The former operated beyond the president's control, and the latter just personally annoyed him.

Educated in Switzerland, Helms earned a Phi Beta Kappa key from Williams College and had been involved with intelligence since World War II. To Nixon, Helms had too much of a patrician manner and ran the CIA with too much of an old-school-tie atmosphere. The new president also judged the CIA less than competent because the agency could not prove the antiwar movement received support from foreign communists. Early in 1969, moreover, the CIA refused to place surveillance on Donald Nixon, whose supposed susceptibility to criminal influence might embarrass his brother, the president.

By March 1969, Nixon, disappointed with Hoover and Helms, wanted a small intelligence organization immediately responsive to his orders and outside the federal bureaucracy. He turned over the assignment to John D. Ehrlichman, his personal counsel and reliable aide. Ehrlichman remembered the New York City police detective John J. Caulfield, who had served as that city's police liaison to Nixon's 1968 campaign headquarters and whom Attorney General John Mitchell considered, but rejected, for appointment as chief marshall of the United States. Caulfield declined Ehrlichman's suggestion of setting up a private agency that would contract to carry out special investigations for the White House. Instead, he wanted to join the White House staff. Ehrlichman agreed and gave him the job description of liaison officer with the federal law enforcement agencies. In reality, Caulfield would conduct investigations as Ehrlichman directed.

Caulfield assumed his duties on April 8, 1969. The next month he gained an assistant. Upon Caulfield's advice, Ehrlichman flew to New York City and interviewed and hired Anthony T. Ulasewicz, a former Caulfield colleague. But whereas Caulfield's name appeared on the federal employees payroll roster, Ehrlichman arranged private, political funds to pay Ulasewicz's salary. The money came from surplus 1968 campaign contributions under the control of the president's private lawyer, Herbert Kalmbach. Ulasewicz immediately learned he would take orders from Caulfield and would not meet Ehrlichman again. When he reported to Caulfield, moreover, he would do so only verbally.[4]

Irritating as Nixon may have found some of the attitudes of the FBI and CIA directors, the agencies certainly were not one of his major concerns during the first months of his administration. Nixon's top priority went to foreign affairs, a field that had long commanded his foremost attention. Throughout early 1969 the new president worked to develop and launch his new diplomacy. His objectives included peace in Vietnam, eased tensions with the Soviet Union and China, limitations on nuclear arms, and stability in the Middle East. Much of the diplomatic groundwork for such major foreign policy initiatives required privacy from public awareness. Journalists and radio and television reporters, on the other hand, constantly probed and searched for bits of current news and for information about emerging policies. For decades, politicians, journalists, and scholars have analyzed, without resolution, the opposing objectives of the legitimate need for secrecy in the conduct of foreign affairs and the need to maintain a press free of government censorship.

Nixon's 1968 campaign assertion that he had a plan to end the Vietnam War only heightened reporters' natural eagerness to learn what the new president intended for the country. Reporters always have been able to glean information from a president's circle of advisers, cabinet members, and staff. Every president has experienced the phenomenon known as news leaks. Nixon's reaction to the inevitable leaks, however, not only exceeded in degree the responses of his predecessors under similar situations but also broke the law and offered a grave portent of events to come.

The problem as Nixon saw it originated with the *New York Times*'s coverage of the Vietnam War. On April 6 the paper reported that Nixon proposed a gradual withdrawal of U.S. troops. A month later the paper published a front-page story, written by its Pentagon correspondent William Beecher, reporting that for several weeks B-52 bombers had been raiding areas in Cambodia where the North Vietnamese and their South Vietnamese allies, the Viet Cong, had concentrated troops and supplies. The National Security Council (NSC) director Henry Kissinger read the article while spending the weekend at Nixon's Key Biscayne vacation house. Kissinger immediately telephoned Hoover and asked him to find out the identity of the person or persons responsible for leaking the supposedly secret information to Beecher. Obviously agitated, and obviously concerned about keeping the investigation secret, Kissinger telephoned Hoover twice more that day. Shortly after 5:00 P.M., Hoover telephoned Kissinger with a report that the leaked information probably flowed from a staff member of the NSC or from anti-Nixon personnel in the Pentagon. Hoover's prime suspect was Morton H. Halperin, chief of the NSC planning group and a Harvard graduate with Democratic leanings.

Kissinger moved quickly. The next day, after expressing faith in Halperin's innocence, Kissinger told his aide that he no longer could have access to sensitive material, reasoning that if the leak continued Halperin would be above suspicion. On the following day Kissinger dispatched his deputy, army colonel Alexander M. Haig Jr., to FBI headquarters with a request to install wiretaps on three members of the NSC, including Halperin, as well as the senior military assistant to the secretary of defense. A week later Kissinger asked the FBI to add the names of two more NSC members. On June 4, within hours after the *New York Times* published a story reporting a forthcoming announcement of the first withdrawal of U.S. troops from Vietnam, Kissinger requested Hoover to tap the telephone of the reporter who wrote the article. Before this wiretapping program ended, it had lasted twenty-one months and included seventeen persons.

The tapping originated in the name of national security, to preserve the secrecy of sensitive discussions and actions. Ironically, the motivation behind the desired secrecy in this instance was to keep information from the American public in fear of its opposition. Certainly the Cambodians and the Vietnamese upon whom the bombs fell knew of the new Nixon action. And in time such news also reached to North Vietnam and to the Soviet Union.

Aspects of the tapping program, moreover, indicated a large component of political opportunism rather than concern about national security. One of the first NSC members whose telephone Kissinger wanted tapped, Daniel Davidson, resigned on May 29, 1969, two and a half weeks after Kissinger's request. The tap continued on Davidson's telephone until September 15. He was a friend and former assistant to W. Averell Harriman, President Johnson's chief negotiator on Vietnam. Halperin, who like Davidson became increasingly unhappy with Nixon's foreign policy, left the NSC in September. Until the next March he held the title of consultant to Kissinger but worked only a single day. Halperin then became an unpaid adviser to Senator Edmund Muskie, the front-runner for the Democratic presidential nomination. Although Halperin had no access to sensitive information after May 9, 1969, although he had worked only one day for Kissinger after September 1969, and although he had no affiliation with Kissinger after March 1970, the tap remained on Halperin's telephone until February 10, 1971. Defense of the tap as necessary for reasons of national security would have been impossible. The usefulness of the tap as a source of information about the Muskie campaign, on the other hand, seemed obvious.

Anthony Lake's experience exhibited a similar pattern. A member of the NSC, Lake opposed the U.S. invasion of Cambodia early in May 1970 and resigned in protest. Kissinger immediately ordered a tap on Lake's telephone. Lake soon joined Muskie's staff. For the next seven months the tap remained, providing Nixon's staff with a second source of information from within the Muskie circle of advisers. From the start, moreover, Nixon ordered the tap reports sent only to H. R. Haldeman, whose responsibilities did not include national security.

Other cases also demonstrated that the tapping program, whatever its initial motivation, quickly became political in nature. On July 23, 1969, Attorney General John Mitchell requested a tap on John P. Sears, deputy counsel to Nixon. Sears had no access to national security matters, but he maintained a friendly relationship with reporters at a time when Nixon and his closest aides tended to view reporters with suspicion. Two weeks later the FBI installed a tap on the telephone of William Safire, Nixon's urbane speechwriter, who also had no authority to handle security information but who, to the disdain of Nixon's inner circle of advisers, enjoyed Georgetown dinner parties. Wiretapping for political reasons, of course, violated the law.

The FBI tapping of the journalist Marvin Kalb, which Nixon ordered on September 10, 1969, indicated the president's distrust of Kissinger himself to keep secrets. Kalb, one of Kissinger's closest friends within the newspaper world, had served as CBS correspondent in Moscow and was writing a biography of Kissinger. Any information Kissinger leaked might logically go to Kalb. Mitchell directed the FBI to send to him all transcripts and reports from the Kalb tap.

In his position as president, Nixon could order to have anyone tapped if he deemed it necessary for the general welfare of the nation. The list during his first twenty-five months in office included seven members of the Kissinger NSC staff, three White House staff members, two officials in the State Department, one in the Defense Department, and four newspaper reporters. By way of contrast, Nixon's three predecessors during the previous dozen years together had wiretapped a total of two government officials and no news persons, other than those working for the communist *Daily Worker*.

Despite such an unprecedented tapping program, Nixon found it inadequate in the case of the Washington journalist Joseph Kraft. In May 1969 Kraft wrote in his nationally syndicated column that the president's Vietnam plans would not work and the war would not end as Nixon projected. Kraft and Kissinger were friends. Once Nixon wanted to reach Kissinger on the telephone and found him at Kraft's Georgetown house for dinner. Nixon told Ehrlichman to arrange a tap. Ehrlichman turned to his special intelligence unit headed by Caulfield. In reply to Caulfield's logical question of why the FBI did not tap Kraft, Ehrlichman explained that the FBI leaked information. Much later, counsel to the president John Dean maintained that Nixon told him that Hoover simply would not tap Kraft. Caulfield recruited John Ragan, who previously had ensured that Nixon's campaign staff remained free of bugs and taps. In June, Caulfield's team, with telephone company credentials obtained under false pretenses, placed the tap, providing information from Kraft's telephone to Nixon.

The Kraft tap constituted the first major assignment for Caulfield's small intelligence unit. A month later Ehrlichman gave it another. Within hours after Senator Edward M. Kennedy drove off a bridge on the Massachusetts resort island of Chappaquiddick with his female passenger, who remained trapped in the submerged car, Caulfield's assistant, Ulasewicz, rushed to Chappaquiddick and spent four fruitless days investigating. Caulfield's unit made numerous attempts to learn more about Kennedy's private life. On one occasion in August 1969, for example, Caulfield spied on Kennedy while he stopped for a long weekend in Hawaii on a return trip from India. Caulfield also carried out such assignments as investigating the Quakers who held a vigil outside the White House; the comic Richard M. Dixon, who imitated the president; and the Democratic Speaker of the House Carl Albert, who became involved in a drinking incident at a Washington nightclub.[5]

By the end of summer 1969 the Nixon administration had in operation a program of intelligence gathering that paid scant respect to the law. The president and his assistants had attempted to involve the CIA more deeply in domestic surveillance, where it had no legal authority; had established a private, secret unit to carry out special assignments that rightly would belong in the purview of federal agencies; and had used FBI taps for political purposes. Furthermore, the administration had withheld from the American public vital information about U.S. foreign policy, information already known to the enemy. Nixon's first year in office foreshadowed the values and attitudes his administration would display in subsequent years.

As Nixon's first year in office ended and his second began, the war in Vietnam continued its relentless domination of the news, arousing passions among a growing number of Americans and contributing to an increasingly ugly mood within the Nixon administration. Mindful of these trends, the president struggled to shape the war effort so as to minimize its effect on the nation. The war pressed upon the sensibilities of Americans with an intensity rarely equaled in American history; and Nixon, like Johnson before him, failed to convince the nation of the necessity and righteousness of the war. Consequently, the United States entered a new decade divided and with an antiwar movement increasing in numbers and including such prominent leaders as the former marine corps commandant David M. Shoup. From the time he entered office, Nixon realized that the fabric of society could pull apart if he did not end the war. In June 1969 he started a periodic withdrawal of U.S. troops from Vietnam; simultaneously he escalated certain aspects of the fighting. That policy, he hoped, would lessen opposition to the war at home and thereby buy him time to make South Vietnam militarily self-sufficient. In spring 1970 the implementation of one component of this policy led to civil protests that shook the nation.

On April 20 the president announced that he had completed the withdrawal of 115,000 U.S. troops from Vietnam and that he planned to bring home 150,000 additional troops by the next spring. Ten days later he spoke to the nation on television during prime evening time to report that "in an age of anarchy, both abroad and at home," he had ordered a short-term American invasion of Cambodia in cooperation with South Vietnam, designed "to clean out major enemy sanctuaries on the Cambodian-Vietnam border," including "the headquarters for the entire Communist military operation in South Vietnam."[6] This invasion, he asserted, was "indispensable" for his withdrawal-of-troops program, which he acknowledged a majority of Americans favored. Nixon compared his Cambodian decision with the wartime decisions of Presidents Woodrow Wilson and Franklin D. Roosevelt.

In explaining his actions Nixon stated, "For five years, neither the United States nor South Vietnam has moved against these enemy sanctuaries because we did not wish to violate the territory of a neutral nation."[7] Actually, during the previous thirteen months the U.S. B-52s had carried out approximately 3,600 bombing missions against Cambodian targets, with Nixon's specific approval. In the Pentagon, the highest officials falsified records so that Cambodian missions appeared as routine missions over South Vietnam. Only pilots and navigators, not B-52 crews, knew their bombs fell on Cambodia. It was this bombing that the *New York Times* had reported in May 1969 and that led to the wiretapping program to determine who in the administration gave the information to the press. In direct contradiction to Nixon's April statement to the country, U.S. military intelligence teams had carried out more than 600 prior ground missions inside Cambodia. Keeping the increased military involvement in Cambodia secret from the American public constituted the first major cover-up in the Nixon administration. Some of the anxiety within the administration arose from fears that the public would learn of this cover-up.

Reaction to the Cambodian invasion spurred the antiwar movement to a new peak on the campuses of the nation's colleges and universities and attracted increased support from all segments of society. Louder and uglier than in their previous activities, students occupied buildings, blocked streets, boycotted classes, and vandalized property. They also continued to prevent military, CIA, and Dow Chemical Company (makers of napalm) personnel from recruiting on campuses. On May 4, 1970, National Guard troops on Ohio's Kent State University campus fired into a crowd of protesters, killing four and wounding nine. Ten days later, police at Mississippi's Jackson State College fatally shot two more students. The character and number of antiwar protests and especially the reaction to the killings at Kent State forced hundreds of campus administrators from coast to coast to suspend classes for varying periods. More than 130 campuses canceled the remainder of the spring term.

On May 8 Nixon, recognizing "the profound concerns that are rending many of our campuses today," appointed a special advisory committee on campus unrest. At 10:00 P.M. that evening the president held a news conference during which twenty-one of the twenty-four questions from the press related to the war or to the protests against it. Protesting students, meanwhile, camped around Washington's monuments and parks while sixty empty buses, parked bumper to bumper, formed a protective circle around the White House. Stationed in the basement of the Executive Office Building a battalion of airborne soldiers waited in combat gear for immediate deployment.

After his news conference, Nixon could not relax. At 10:35 P.M. he started telephoning aides, friends, and family, in a few instances returning calls. During the next three hours and twenty minutes he made forty-five calls, including one to New York's governor Nelson A. Rockefeller at 12:58 A.M. and another at 1:31 A.M. to Thomas E. Dewey, twice the Republican Party's presidential nominee. Six times Nixon telephoned his chief of staff Haldeman and seven times he telephoned his national security adviser Kissinger. The president hung up his telephone at 2:15 A.M. and went to bed. In a little over an hour he started making more calls, including another one to Kissinger at 3:38 A.M. At 4:22 A.M. Nixon telephoned his valet, Manolo Sanchez, and invited him to join the president on a visit to the Lincoln Memorial. In less than fifteen minutes they were on their way, much to the apprehension of the secret service members, who had no forewarning.

Once inside the monument, Nixon and his valet read Lincoln's words inscribed on the walls. Then the president moved to a group of about eight college students, in town for a protest demonstration, and started a conversation. He asked and answered questions that covered a range of subjects, permitted a bearded young man to take pictures, seemed reasonable and understanding, and shook hands upon leaving. After his visit with students, Nixon took Sanchez on a partial tour of the Capitol. By the time they left, Haldeman, Press Secretary Ron Ziegler, and Appointments Secretary Dwight Chapin had arrived, and at 6:40 A.M. the group headed for the Rib Room of the Mayflower Hotel, where Nixon ate his first meal at a Washington restaurant since becoming president.

Nixon's inability to sleep, his multitude of telephone calls throughout the night, and his impromptu 4:45 A.M. visit to the Lincoln Memorial suggested a troubled president. The ring of buses surrounding the White House and the battalion of combat-ready troops reflected uncommon concern for personal safety, but the visit to the Lincoln Memorial contradicted that concern. Press conference questions indicated a hostile press relentlessly focused on the war. Antiwar protests on and off campuses revealed a deeply divided nation. These conditions contributed to a defensive mentality within the White House, a reflex to strike out at opponents, and a penchant for secrecy.[8] The antagonisms between the president and his opponents nourished and incited one another. Illustrative of the depth and nature of this mood during summer 1970 was the proposed Huston Plan and Nixon's approval of it.

On June 5 the president summoned to his office the directors of the FBI, the CIA, the Defense Intelligence Agency, and the National Security Agency. He also called to the meeting Haldeman; Ehrlichman; Robert Finch, counselor to the president; and Tom Charles Huston, a White House aide with an ambition to gain control of all domestic intelligence. The summons stemmed from Nixon's long-standing dissatisfaction with the intelligence agencies. In addition to wanting quicker and less questioning responses to his directives, he wanted the work of the intelligence agencies coordinated with and reflective of White House concerns. Foremost on his mind was obtaining more information about the threat of domestic radicalism. The president appointed Hoover as chair of the group, newly named the Interagency Committee on Intelligence (ICI), and assigned Huston as White House liaison with authorization to call meetings.

Huston, an Indiana native and a graduate of Indiana University, held a law degree and had been national chair of the conservative organization Young Americans for Freedom. Born in 1940, he joined the Nixon administration early in 1969 upon completion of military service with an army intelligence unit. He was in charge of internal security and domestic intelligence. On his office wall he hung an oil portrait of John C. Calhoun, the nineteenth-century champion of states' rights and defender of slavery. Although Huston championed law and order, during summer 1969 he demanded that the Internal Revenue Service conduct intelligence operations that exceeded statutory limits. William Safire, with an office one door from Huston's office, later recalled that Huston frequently commented in summer 1970, "we're in a state of siege."[9]

Huston, working closely with Hoover's assistant William C. Sullivan, proved to be the dominant force behind a forty-three-page report completed in less than three weeks. To accompany the report, Huston wrote a top-secret memorandum to Nixon recommending the selection of the most severe, and illegal, options the official report presented. "Use of this technique is clearly illegal," Huston told the president in one instance; "it amounts to burglary."[10] The Huston proposals also urged illegal electronic surveillance and opening of mail. In mid-July Nixon ratified the proposals and had them incorporated into the document that became known as the Huston Plan.

When the directors of the four intelligence agencies received copies of the Huston Plan, only Hoover, who had cautioned restraint regarding illegal methods in the pursuit of domestic intelligence, objected. He did so not from constitutional principle but because he feared exposure by the press, by congressional investigation, or by a hostile attorney general. Hoover sought and gained the support of Attorney General John Mitchell to pressure Nixon to rescind the Huston Plan. Mitchell agreed when Hoover said he would demand a written order before carrying out an illegal activity. Like his predecessors, Nixon avoided a showdown over a matter about which Hoover expressed strong opinions. The directors of the CIA, the NSA, and the DIA, however, seemingly accepted as routine the commission of crimes along with their constitutionally assigned responsibilities. Later in 1970 and again during 1971, several of Nixon's aides urged implementation of at least some provisions of the Huston Plan.[11] Because Hoover and Mitchell both opposed the plan, Nixon transferred Huston's responsibilities for internal security and domestic intelligence to the attorney general, in reality to Mitchell's assistant John Dean, a young lawyer as ambitious as Huston. Soon thereafter the concerns about internal intelligence shifted to what became known as the Pentagon Papers.

On June 13, 1971, the *New York Times* published the first installment of a compilation of key documents detailing why and how the United States became involved in Vietnam. Four years earlier Secretary of Defense Robert S. McNamara had commissioned a study and directed that the report be "encyclopedic and objective." The result produced more than 4,000 pages of documents, supplemented by approximately 3,000 pages of narrative, all of which Presidents Johnson and Nixon intended to keep secret.

Daniel Ellsberg, a Pentagon bureaucrat who worked on the project and who, during the process, changed from a supporter to an opponent of the war, copied one of the fifteen copies of the report and gave it to the *New York Times.* The newspaper planned to publish a series of articles based on the report. After the first three articles appeared, the Justice Department stopped further publication by obtaining a temporary restraining order from a federal district court. The Justice Department contended that the publication of the Pentagon Papers would cause "immediate and irreparable harm" to national defense. On June 30 the Supreme Court ruled in favor of the newspaper, citing that the First Amendment guarantee of a free press overrode the government's claim.

Ellsberg's action and the subsequent publication of the Pentagon Papers infuriated Nixon. The documents revealed that four successive presidents, especially Johnson, had misled and deceived the public about Vietnam. Because the Pentagon Papers stopped with Johnson, Nixon initially reacted moderately but became more agitated by Kissinger's livid response. The publication, moreover, disturbed the secrecy Nixon believed essential in the conduct of foreign affairs: regarding Vietnam, to prevent Americans from learning about policies and actions most of them opposed; and regarding China and the Soviet Union, to explore possibilities of détente.

Nixon's reaction to the case had much to do with his state of mind and little to do with national security. Late in June and again six months later a Los Angeles grand jury indicted Ellsberg for violation of the criminal code. The government prosecutor, David Nissen, admitted at the time that after investigation the government had no evidence to substantiate a charge of espionage against Ellsberg. Publication of the Pentagon Papers tarnished the reputation of officials; it did not compromise national security.

From the beginning of the Pentagon Papers case, Nixon showed a lack of faith and trust in the FBI's competence to investigate and in the court system to dispense justice. He wanted more than a conviction of Ellsberg for breaking the law; he wanted to discredit him and thereby discredit the antiwar movement; he wanted to set an example of what happens to an insider who leaks information to the press. To accomplish his objectives, Nixon appears to have knowingly broken the law. Instead of turning to the FBI, the president turned to Ehrlichman's political intelligence unit.

Ehrlichman gave the job of supervising the unit jointly to White House aides Egil Krogh Jr. and David R. Young Jr. Like Ehrlichman and Haldeman, Krogh was a Christian Scientist, and like Ehrlichman he had been an Eagle Scout. While a law student at the University of Washington, Krogh had worked part-time for Ehrlichman's law firm. Young, who at thirty-two was a year older than Krogh, also held a law degree. Before this new assignment, he had been a member of Kissinger's National Security staff. Their nickname, "Plumbers," evolved because Krogh and Young planned to stop the unauthorized leaks of government information. They had a basement office in the Executive Office Building and listed one of their telephone numbers under the name of their secretary, who lived across the Potomac River in Alexandria, Virginia. Along with Ehrlichman, Charles Colson, another presidential assistant, also could command the service of the Plumbers.

Soon the Plumbers added two staff members. Colson transferred from his office E. Howard Hunt, whom he had recruited earlier from a public relations firm in part because of their mutual dislike of Kennedy politicians. Hunt previously had spent more than twenty years with the CIA, including close involvement with the overthrow of the elected government of

Guatemala in 1954 and with the Bay of Pigs invasion of Cuba in 1962. For four years during the 1960s he served as chief of CIA covert actions within the Domestic Operations Division. Throughout these years Hunt drew on his experiences and imagination to publish a steady stream of novels, especially ones with spy themes.

The addition of G. Gordon Liddy completed the Plumbers operational staff. Liddy had earned his law degree from Fordham University and spent five years with the FBI before starting a private law practice in the Hudson Valley, north of New York City. Four years later he became assistant district attorney for Dutchess County, New York. After the 1968 election, Liddy's congressman helped him gain federal appointment as special assistant to the assistant secretary of the treasury. Liddy cultivated a macho image, championed law and order, and glorified guns. Once during a jury trial he pulled a gun and fired into the ceiling; he liked to describe how to kill a person with a pencil.

The Plumbers group was not a new concept for Nixon's inner circle but an expanded version of the Caulfield intelligence unit that Ehrlichman had set up early in 1969. Hunt and Liddy added a more aggressive element to operations, and Krogh and Young improved the quality of administration and provided greater coordination within the White House. Although the Plumbers concentrated primarily on the Pentagon Papers case and other leaks to the press, they also spent time on different and unrelated projects, like declassification of World War II and Korean War documents. Hunt, for example, devoted time during summer 1969 to investigating Senator Ted Kennedy's accident at Chappaquiddick and John Kennedy's role in the Bay of Pigs and in the assassination of the Vietnamese leader Ngo Dinh Diem but found nothing to tarnish President Kennedy's reputation. Two years later, in another attempt, Hunt constructed fake government cables to implicate the president in Diem's assassination. Colson leaked the faked cables to a friendly journalist.

Nixon conveyed to Colson, Ehrlichman, and Krogh his intense desire to discredit Ellsberg publicly and pressured his assistants to find something damaging. The president was unhappy that the FBI investigation had found nothing useful except the fact that for two years Ellsberg had seen a psychiatrist. With only that information to act upon, Young requested the CIA's medical services to prepare a psychological profile of Ellsberg. Hunt obtained from the CIA a camera, disguises, and false identification papers. Colson solicited cash from a public relations man who represented the Associated Milk Producers, a lobby anxious to maintain good relations with the White House. Hunt recruited three Cubans living in Miami. With approval from Ehrlichman and Krogh and with hope of finding defamatory material, Hunt, Liddy, and the three Cubans flew to Los Angeles and burglarized the office of Dr. Lewis Fielding, Ellsberg's psychiatrist. The team ransacked the office but found nothing suitable for their purpose. One of the reasons for the later Watergate cover-up was the fear that Watergate would lead to the Fielding burglary.

Late in 1971 the Plumbers attempted to identify the individuals supplying government information to the columnist Jack Anderson. Nixon and his staff were concerned and annoyed by Anderson's repeated ability to base columns on secret material. During the 1971 Indian-Pakistani War, for example, Nixon publicly declared U.S. neutrality. Anderson documented the opposite; Nixon's actions supported Pakistan. The White House had Anderson followed, tapped his telephone, audited his taxes, and investigated his associates. Hunt made plans to assassinate Anderson but stopped short of implementation. Despite these activities, the Plumbers failed to find Anderson's source of information. Instead, they found that navy yeoman Charles E. Radford, a stenographer assigned to the Joint Chiefs of Staff (JCS) as a liaison with the National Security Council, regularly, under naval orders, stole "top secret 'eyes only'" material from the NSC and passed it to three admirals who, in turn, gave it to Admiral Thomas H. Moorer, the chairman of the JCS. The NSC had determined that national security required withholding certain material from the JCS. Denied access, the JCS arranged to steal the material. Nixon took no action when he learned that the nation's top-ranking military officer had resorted to espionage against his own government. Instead, the president covered up the crime, and Kissinger, Haig, and Ehrlichman went along. Later, Nixon reappointed Moorer to a second term as chairman of the JCS, despite his having received stolen secret security documents. Radford found himself transferred to a recruiting office in Oregon.[12]

During his first three years in office, Nixon routinely and repeatedly employed illegal activities within the executive branch of the federal government. Some of these activities he inherited; others he initiated. In one way or another all related to information about opponents and concern about information leaks in the context of foreign policies and opposition to those policies. Nixon accepted these illegal activities as an inherent power, risk free since secrecy would prevent discovery. After all, the director of the FBI, the director of the CIA, the chairman of the Joint Chiefs of Staff, and some of the top Pentagon officers had participated. When the head of the FBI balked at implementing the Huston Plan, Nixon transferred many of its projected activities to the Plumbers, already operating from within the White House but outside the law. Moreover, Mitchell and Dean established, despite Hoover's resistance, the Intelligence Evaluation Committee (IEC) within the Department of Justice to coordinate and direct intelligence gathering from the various agencies. Although limited in value, the IEC continued until Nixon dissolved it in June 1973. The aborted Huston Plan illuminated the changes that had evolved within the intelligence agencies during the Cold War and that Nixon had pushed to their culmination.[13]

To carry out his policies, Nixon resorted to illegal wiretapping, burglary, and cover-ups. Foreign and domestic policies were integrated rather than being separate spheres. The cover-up of the secret bombing of Cambodia, for example, led to illegal telephone taps and persistent lying to the public for domestic advantage. In June 1972 Nixon recalled he had "protected" Helms many times. Only if Helms had exceeded his authority would he have needed presidential protection.[14]

Almost all presidents have stretched their powers, broken laws, and lied if they believed circumstances justified such actions. Wartime imperatives usually offered such justification. During the Cold War, anticommunism and national security gave presidents ample circumstances to rationalize a wide range of illegal actions they kept from public awareness. Nixon accepted this interpretation of events and exercise of presidential power. During his first three years in office he developed programs and took actions that politically and ethically fit comfortably under the broad pattern he had inherited and expanded. The number of wiretaps he sanctioned, and Hoover directed, far exceeded those of his predecessors, but the practice of wiretapping was a continuation of past policy.

Keeping in mind this inheritance and exercise of power is indispensable in understanding the pattern of actions that led to the burglary of the national headquarters of the Democratic Party on June 17, 1972. To Nixon and his closest aides, the burglary seemed commonplace because such behavior fell within familiar patterns of activities they already had established. So, too, did the primary and presidential campaigns of 1972.

CHAPTER TWO

Context of the Break-in

Motives and Primaries

The first priority is to trip up Muskie in the primaries.
— *Pat Buchanan to Jeb Stuart Magruder; Magruder to John Mitchell, July 28, 1971*

McGovern has a long shot at the nomination, a very long shot. But if he wins, we win. Let's let him have his run at the nomination, and assist him in every way we can.
— *Pat Buchanan and Ken Khachigian to John Mitchell and H. R. Haldeman, April 12, 1972*

If we are running 50–50 with George McGovern in the polls election day — he could conceivably beat us by four to six points, on the basis of his first-rate get-out-the-vote machinery.
— *Pat Buchanan to H. R. Haldeman, June 8, 1972*

The American presidency is a political office. Location and timing of presidential speeches, selection of federal judges, and almost all other decisions have a political dimension. With his cabinet and other appointments, Nixon, like his predecessors, kept in mind the diversity of his party and the need to build broad-based support for his legislative and policy proposals. Perhaps equally important, this support, in turn, would enhance the prospects for a president's reelection; and ensuring this reelection remained ever present in the work and thoughts of Nixon and his staff. For Richard Nixon, this was especially true because of his political personality and his belief that he faced a close election in 1972.

Nixon's defeat in 1960 and his victory eight years later were two of the closest elections in American history. After his 1960 defeat in Texas and Illinois, Nixon examined some of the evidence regarding allegations of fraud and concluded that "there was real substance to many of these charges."[1] Had he carried those states, he would have won the election. In 1968, during the last week of the campaign, public opinion shifted markedly away from Nixon and reduced his once comfortable lead over the Democratic candidate Hubert H. Humphrey. Many observers believed that had the campaign lasted another week, Humphrey would have won. The Democrats, moreover, easily maintained control of both houses of Congress. Nixon won the election with only 43.4 percent of the popular vote, in part because the third-party candidate, George C. Wallace, captured 13.5 percent. Nixon had valid reasons to worry about reelection in 1972.

Nixon's drive for reelection exhibited the same characteristics that shaped his approach in other aspects of his administration: concern about public image; desire for knowledge about the plans and activities of opponents; and heavy reliance on public opinion polls, both to gauge public reactions and to guide future decisions. Similarly, there was a predilection for secrecy and deniability and a reliance on subordinates to assume responsibility for illegal activities. The existence and activities of the Plumbers, the illegal telephone tapping, the tolerance of spying (the case of the chairman of the Joint Chiefs), and the protective cover-ups of subordinates (repeatedly, the director of the CIA) had their counterparts in the reelection campaign.

The congressional election campaign during autumn 1970, moreover, had aggravated and deepened the dangerous divisions within the country. Vice President Spiro Agnew, whom Nixon called "the cutting edge" of the campaign, emphasized law and order in a series of slashing verbal assaults in which he indicted Democrats for their permissiveness toward crime, riots, drugs, pornography, and radicals. On October 29, after leaving the auditorium in San Jose, California, where he had given a campaign speech, Nixon climbed on the hood of his limousine and, in an attempt to antagonize protesters, flashed the V sign. The demonstrators responded as he had hoped, by throwing rocks, eggs, and verbal insults at the president's motorcade as it drove away. The war in Vietnam and the protests against it dominated the media. Campaigns in the United States often are divisive; 1970 provided a prime example. The portent for 1972 seemed ominous.

The full story of the 1972 Democratic Party primaries and the 1972 presidential campaigns remains hidden away in the locked records of the Nixon Project in the National Archives, in the personal files of participants, and in the files that Nixon's aides and the Committee to Re-elect the President (CREEP) workers shredded after news of the June 17 Watergate break-in became public. Three decades later no one has been able to identify a person who coordinated all activities. Circumstantial evidence suggests, however, that Nixon himself orchestrated the primaries and the election campaigns.

Stephen E. Ambrose concluded in his acclaimed, multivolume biography that President Nixon "compartmentalized power and knowledge." That compartmentalization, plus Nixon's addiction to secrecy and his desire to share power and knowledge with as few persons as possible, distinguished his administration. In practice, Ambrose points out, "Nixon would be his own press secretary. Nixon also intended to be his own foreign secretary." Often he kept both Secretary of State William Rogers and National Security Adviser Henry A. Kissinger uninformed about negotiations with China, Vietnam, and the Soviet Union. Nixon also distrusted the federal bureaucracy, including the state department and the CIA.[2]

Nixon's relationship with his three senior speechwriters illustrates another dimension of compartmentalization in operation. Although close in age (forty-two, thirty-three, and forty-two in 1972), William Safire was Jewish, Patrick J. Buchanan was a Catholic, and Raymond K. Price Jr. was a Protestant. At that time Safire considered himself a centrist, Buchanan considered himself a conservative, and Price leaned toward liberalism. It would follow that their writing styles varied. Price was lyrical, Buchanan hard hitting, and Safire more of a story teller. Nixon never wanted his three distinctly different speechwriters to collaborate. Safire recorded that Nixon "would sometimes give a Price draft to Buchanan for toughening, or a Buchanan draft to Price for softening, or a draft of either to me for making more quotable." The president used Price when he wanted to project visions and compassion; Nixon turned to Buchanan when he wanted to attack an opponent; and he asked Safire to help him blend a touch of humor with political philosophy and economics. Above all, Nixon insisted that the three writers work independently of one another.[3]

Nixon's need to control coexisted with his predisposition to secrecy. "Over time," Kissinger later wrote, Nixon's personality "led to a fragmented Administration" and produced a "sense of isolation." In his sympathetic study of Nixon, the journalist Tom Wicker concluded that "for Nixon, in fact, secrecy was a high principle — congenial, not only to his guarded personality but to his perception of the world."[4]

Nixon's personality, its manifestation in the compartmentalization of power and knowledge, and the record of his political career to that point give credibility to the conclusion that he ran his own campaign. In his nationally televised address of April 30, 1973, he emphasized that "to the maximum extent possible, therefore, I sought to delegate campaign operations, to remove the day-to-day campaign decisions from the President's office and from the White House."[5] Such delegation seems logical, and Nixon's statement is undoubtedly accurate. However, he would determine broad campaign strategy. On July 21, 1972, for example, he met for two hours with his cabinet and Republican Party leaders. Three days later he spent one and a half hours with the writing staff of speechwriter Raymond Price. During these meetings the president explained the campaign guidelines he wanted followed: use the term "McGovernite" rather than Democrat; "never give away the moral ground" on Vietnam; and stress that George McGovern was an isolationist. Nixon also commented on campaign issues such as busing, welfare, the defense budget, and aspects of foreign policy and reviewed how his administration had dealt, and would continue to deal, with these issues. In August 1969, for example, he had proposed a comprehensive Family Assistance Plan, whose centerpiece provided a national minimum family income. After the 1972 Florida primary, which George Wallace won, Nixon proposed a "moratorium" on court-ordered busing. To Price's staff, the president described the campaign strengths of cabinet members and how best to use them. Secretary of Labor George P. Shultz, Nixon concluded, "is not a particularly good speaker, but is effective in smaller groups." Nixon called Secretary of the Treasury John B. Connally Jr. "a very potent speaker and TV performer" but cautioned that "we have to preserve his scarcity value."[6] No contradiction necessarily existed between the notes from these meetings and Nixon's April 30, 1973, statement, depending upon a narrow definition of "day-to-day decisions."

Nixon did listen to suggestions regarding politics from persons with whom he basically agreed and whom he respected. Pat Buchanan was such a person. When he proposed a two-part plan that offered broad strategy for the primary and presidential campaigns of 1972, it resonated well with Nixon.

The Nixon-Buchanan relationship dated from January 1966, when Buchanan left his position as editorial writer for the *St. Louis Globe–Democrat* to join Nixon as a researcher and speechwriter. Nixon liked Buchanan's quick mind, writing ability, and absorption with politics. During Nixon's 1966 campaign for Republican congressional candidates, the twenty-seven-year-old Buchanan traveled with the former vice president on some thirty-five of his campaign trips. The next June Nixon took Buchanan with him on a trip to Africa. From the first day of his presidency, Nixon had Buchanan take notes when the president met with congressional leaders and assigned to Buchanan the responsibility of preparing the daily news summaries. Buchanan recruited Mort Allin to edit them but remained in charge and often wrote some of them. Nixon found the summaries invaluable, and his comments scribbled on the margins capture the only long-term record of his spontaneity. Safire later wrote that when Nixon "was at his most elemental," he turned to Buchanan for a speech. Political campaigns revealed Nixon at "his elemental."[7]

Early in November 1969 Buchanan wrote Vice President Agnew's biting criticism of network television news coverage. Agnew's speech attracted considerable attention and pleased Nixon, who ordered more of the Buchanan-Agnew cooperation. In a note to Haldeman on December 1, Nixon called Buchanan one of his "top inside political analysts." Nixon and Buchanan shared a dislike of political opponents that bordered on resentment, especially those in the media, in the antiwar movement, in the counterculture, and in the Kennedy-McGovern wing of the Democratic Party.

Throughout 1970 Buchanan handled his responsibilities with dispatch, insight, and single-mindedness. In January 1971, reflecting the sentiments that Buchanan had earlier incorporated in Agnew's media bashing, the news summary office prepared a list of "hostile commentators." The list perhaps served as the genesis of the enemies list that Charles Colson later compiled and sent to John Dean.[8] Safire observed that Nixon "had a personal affection" for Buchanan. The president agreed with most of Buchanan's political analyses, and perhaps most of all, he liked Buchanan's initiatives.[9]

In late March 1971 a political vacuum existed in the Nixon reelection planning and organization. Still in a formative stage, CREEP planned for a May announcement of its creation. Although John Mitchell planned to direct CREEP, he remained as attorney general until March 1972. Jeb Stuart Magruder, meanwhile, as deputy director, ran the committee. He held the job because both Mitchell and Haldeman trusted him and because he understood his holding-action responsibilities. Contributing to a feeling of leadership vacuum was the steady decline of Nixon's popularity during the previous three months, largely because of two war-connected events: first, the South Vietnamese military operation into Laos failed to destroy the increased presence of the North Vietnamese, and second, the public reacted with horror to the crime that led to the trial of Lieutenant William L. Calley Jr., who commanded a platoon of American soldiers that had slaughtered approximately 130 nonresisting Vietnamese, including many women, children, and old men. Dropping from a 56 percent approval rating for Nixon early in 1971, Gallup Polls showed a 51 percent rating in February and then 50 percent in March. The Harris Poll recorded a similar decline in voter preference for Nixon compared to Edmund Muskie. In January 1971, when questioned about which presidential candidate they would support if the choice were Nixon and Muskie, 43 percent chose Muskie and only 40 percent Nixon. In the February poll, Muskie led Nixon 44 to 39 percent. On March 24 Buchanan sent Nixon an eight-page, single-spaced letter on proposed campaign strategy. With CREEP on hold and with Nixon's falling popularity, Buchanan's initiative arrived at just the right moment to fill a planning gap.

In his letter, Buchanan urged the president to create a MUSKIE WATCH to research and publicize to the press and to interest groups Muskie's positions on key issues such as abortion, race, Vietnam, and the environment. "We ought to go down to the kennels and turn all the dogs loose on Ecology Ed," Buchanan exhorted. He reasoned that Muskie "remains by far the strongest possible candidate against Nixon," with one poll reporting results of Muskie with 48 percent and Nixon 42 percent, compared to the previous month's poll of Muskie at 46 percent and Nixon with 44 percent. Buchanan recommended that the MUSKIE WATCH "be tied in with Colson's shop."[10] At that time Colson was working to gather intelligence about the president's political opponents.

With Nixon's approval, Buchanan started to monitor the potential Democratic Party presidential nominees. He borrowed one of Colson's assistants, Ken Khachigian, to help. In April, for example, Buchanan sent the president a ten-page report, "Subject: The Resurrection of Hubert Humphrey," in which Buchanan presaged his strategy for the 1972 Democratic primaries still a year away. With typical clarity, Buchanan wrote, "the more brutal the fighting within the opposition party the greater our advantage." In June Buchanan sent a five-page assessment of Ted Kennedy's possible candidacy and a four-page analysis of Senator Henry Jackson's possible candidacy.

By this time Buchanan wielded power. Late in July Magruder sent Mitchell "a memo by Pat Buchanan outlining a strategy for dealing with opposition contenders . . . establishing the direction and scope of our activities over the next several months." Buchanan's first priority was "to trip up Muskie in the primaries."[11] Buchanan concerned himself primarily with analysis. He had neither the staff, time, nor desire to expand his responsibilities into operations that were the domain of Haldeman, Ehrlichman, and Colson. Nixon himself determined the themes of his campaign speeches, the public side of the campaign.

A long Buchanan and Khachigian memo to John Mitchell, dated March 14, 1972, further reveals Buchanan's role in the campaign. The memo "Attack Organization & Strategy," opened with, "We have been called upon to compose a memorandum delineating the division of responsibility and the formation of the 'attack' strategy for the fall campaign. Herewith, our views and recommendations." These recommendations included the need of "a central point of authority and direction over the attack — holding veto power over what goes and what does not." In the section "Media Attack," Buchanan recommended making campaign issues of school busing and of the "Democratic votes to cut the space program."[12] By using the passive verb form, he avoided identifying the person who asked him to compose the memo. Buchanan's orders came directly from Nixon or from Nixon through Haldeman.

In his memo Buchanan borrowed from the Bible, John 14: 2, and opened the section the "Present Situation": "In my Father's house there are many mansions." Those mansions included the Republican National Committee (RNC), the "Speakers Bureau," the "Hill operation," the "political 'surrogates'" within CREEP who worked with primaries, and the political "line" within CREEP that dealt with "reporters and columnists." According to Buchanan, Colson at times "orchestrated" attack operations in the RNC, the "Speakers Bureau," and, intermittently, the "Hill operation." Colson, however, did not coordinate these activities or Buchanan would not have identified the need for "a central point of authority and direction." Buchanan furthermore concluded that "there are currently several quasi-independent attack operations running." Other participants and observers drew the same broad conclusion.

Years later, Robert Reisner, who had served as assistant to the deputy director of CREEP, recalled "the highly compartmentalized structure that was created — where Colson and Dean and Haldeman and the campaign all ran independent operations — they didn't tell one another what was going on." Reisner concluded, "There was no review process in the White House."[13] Magruder remembered that Haldeman and Mitchell kept pressing for information and that Colson "had all sorts of things going on" and that as director of CREEP he "couldn't stop these activities" because they "were all peers."[14]

Theodore H. White, the prize-winning chronicler of presidential campaigns, looked back from the vantage point of spring 1973 and concluded that "the campaign of 1972 from the Republican side was more like the backfield of a football team with no quarterback and four footballs to run with . . . and the coach . . . preoccupied with action elsewhere."[15] The compartmentalization of the campaign paralleled Nixon's compartmentalization of his administration in general. To date there is less than clear documentation of who, if anyone, directed the campaign from the top. Nixon, of course, was the one person to whom everyone reported, directly or through one of his closest aides. These aides, moreover, all characterized the president's need to control and emphasized his addiction to secrecy. Existing records provide some insights into the uncoordinated campaign projects that reveal much about the character of the campaign and the methods campaign workers used. Nixon's aides and campaign workers all believed they carried out his wishes and had acted only in a manner he would approve.

CREEP represented the public face of the campaign. In May 1971, when it started formal operations under the direction of Magruder, everyone understood that eventually Mitchell would take command of the campaign. Magruder, meanwhile, cleared all his appointments with Haldeman and important ones with Mitchell as well. The most significant reports and plans routinely went from CREEP to Haldeman and Mitchell. Another Haldeman assistant, Gordon C. Strachan, served as liaison between CREEP and Haldeman. Magruder opened the plush headquarters at 1701 Pennsylvania Avenue in the First National Bank building, half a block from the White House. Four of his initial five assistants came from the White House.

From the beginning, CREEP isolated itself from Republicans in Congress and from the Republican National Committee. It virtually ignored such prominent Republicans as Governor Nelson A. Rockefeller of New York and former senator Henry Cabot Lodge, Nixon's running mate in 1960 and later ambassador to South Vietnam under Lyndon Johnson. Mitchell later insisted that the position of campaign chairman for Nixon carried no responsibilities toward the Republican Party. CREEP belonged to the White House and existed solely to carry out the president's wishes. The practice of a presidential candidate separating himself from his party's organization, during both primaries and general election campaigns, dates from 1952. Candidates from both major parties had run their campaigns in this manner.

Demonstrations in spring 1971 indicated that the war would remain a major issue during the campaign. On April 23 almost 24,000 veterans marched in Washington in protest and threw their medals over a fence that kept them away from the Capitol. On May 3 and 4 officials arrested 7,000 of the more than 200,000 antiwar protesters and temporarily incarcerated them in a sports stadium and coliseum. Both Nixon and Haldeman believed communists funded the antiwar movement and dismissed as inept FBI and CIA conclusions to the opposite. The Harris Poll, meanwhile, reported that Muskie ran ahead of Nixon, 47 percent to 39 percent, in a projected 1972 presidential election.

After June 13, when the *New York Times* published the first installment of the Pentagon Papers, Nixon turned to Ehrlichman's Plumbers rather than to the FBI to learn the details of the efforts to prosecute the thief. Among other considerations, Nixon assumed that the perpetrator was a Democrat and believed exposure would help discredit that party. Nixon bypassed the FBI as easily as he had CREEP bypass the Republican National Committee.

The motives behind all campaign activity went beyond Nixon's mere re-election. His aides, most of whom had never held elective office, believed the welfare of the country hung in the balance. Nixon's chief of staff, Haldeman, illustrated this most vividly on February 7, 1972, on his first television appearance. While a guest on the NBC *Today Show,* he discussed anti–Vietnam War sentiment and accused critics of the president's latest peace plan of "consciously aiding and abetting the enemy of the United States." When the host,

Barbara Walters, pointed out that the critics included several of the most prominent members of the U.S. Senate, Haldeman repeated his assertion: "In this particular posture, I think they are consciously aiding and abetting the enemy." Haldeman's repeated phrase was the constitutional definition of treason.[16]

The timing of Haldeman's interview was critical. Early in January Muskie had called for the United States to withdraw completely from Vietnam, whatever the consequences. A few days later, when announcing his candidacy for his party's presidential nomination, Humphrey identified an immediate end to the Vietnam War as the country's most urgent need.

Considering critics as traitors or enemies and therefore as a threat to the nation was hardly new in February 1972. In March 1971 Buchanan had looked ahead to the 1972 campaign and written "If the President goes, we all go, and maybe the country with us."[17] A further example of this White House mind-set was the "enemies list" John Dean collected from his colleagues in 1971 and to which Colson, Buchanan, and others contributed. The list, which grew to more than 200, included movie stars such as Paul Newman, the professional football player Joe Namath, and college presidents, along with the expected newspaper and television figures, including Daniel Schorr of CBS. Democratic senators Kennedy, Muskie, and Mondale also made the list. Nixon's aides' portrayal of opponents and critics as enemies seemed to rationalize breaking the law. In an election year, both the mind-set and the rationalization for illegal activity intensified; after all, enemies were a threat to the nation. Before the national election came a series of Democratic Party primaries to select the party's presidential candidate. The Nixon White House planned to play a major role in those primaries.

"Dirty tricks" operations became perhaps the best known of the several Republican stratagems that characterized the primary and general election campaigns. The Nixon campaign ran at least three independent operations. The one that later became best known came from Haldeman's office. Soon after the formal opening of CREEP, Haldeman ordered two of his assistants, Strachan and Dwight Chapin, to hire someone to set up a covert program to disrupt the Democratic Party primaries. They turned to a University of California college friend, Donald Segretti, who held a law degree from the University of California, Berkeley. After working briefly he had spent more than four years in the army, including a year in Vietnam, and as a captain had served in the Judge Advocate General Corps at Fort Ord, California.

Chapin, who served as the president's appointments secretary, instructed Segretti to generate havoc and bitterness among the various Democratic contenders for their party's nomination so that the party could not mount an effective campaign after the primaries. The uppermost objective, Segretti later acknowledged, was "to discredit Muskie because he was at that time the front-runner."[18] Chapin impressed upon Segretti the need to carry out his duties in such a manner that they could not be traced to the White House. Nixon's personal lawyer, Herbert Kalmbach, met with Segretti to discuss salary. Segretti subsequently hired twenty-eight persons who worked in seventeen primaries. He submitted no regular written reports of his work.

As a supervisor of a covert program, Segretti displayed remarkably flawed judgment. Blunt and boastful, he sometimes used his own name in delicate situations. Allan Walker, chair of CREEP for New Hampshire, called Segretti a threat to the campaign and complained to Chapin. Segretti must have introduced himself to Walker because Magruder later claimed he never knew about Segretti during the campaign. The dirty tricks themselves resembled those of an overzealous, not-too-bright, unethical college sophomore. Segretti carried out his tricks to the fullest extent in Florida against Muskie because, as Buchanan told Mitchell and Haldeman on January 2, 1972, "clearly, the Florida primary is shaping up as the first good opportunity and perhaps the last good opportunity to derail the Muskie candidacy."[19] One of Segretti's infiltrators stole Muskie campaign stationery and mailed a fraudulent letter to 300 supporters of fellow contenders in the Democratic primary, Senator Henry Jackson of Washington State and Hubert Humphrey of Minnesota. The letter sought to make its readers "aware of several facts," among them that Jackson had fathered a child with an unmarried teenager, that twice police had arrested him on homosexual charges, and that police had arrested Humphrey, while in the company of a prostitute, for driving under the influence of alcohol. Segretti and his assistants also issued press releases on Muskie stationery misrepresenting the candidate's positions. On another occasion, Segretti distributed 1,000 cards that read, "If you liked Hitler you'll love Wallace" on one side and "A Vote for Wallace is a Wasted Vote. On March 14, cast your vote for Senator Edmund Muskie." Twice, stink bombs disrupted Muskie picnics, and twice, including the eve of the primary election, stink bombs upset Muskie campaign headquarters in Tampa. At a Muskie press conference, a Segretti agent released two white mice, and another time a naked girl ran through Muskie's hotel, shouting, "I love Muskie." Telephones rang late at night in the homes of voters, with the caller asking for support for Muskie. Bumper stickers endorsing Muskie appeared on top of stickers of his opponents.[20] On primary day Floridians gave George Wallace, who had emphasized his opposition to busing to achieve school integration, a surprising victory, with 42 percent of the vote. Humphrey came in second, with 18.6 percent; then Jackson with 13 percent. Muskie finished an unexpected fourth, with 8.9 percent.

It is impossible to measure the impact of Segretti's dirty tricks in the Florida primary. The advertising industry evaluates the effectiveness of its commercials by sales. If increased sales follow increased advertising, corporate executives assume a positive correlation. Segretti's dirty tricks rested on that simple assumption and more or less on random activities while the advertising industry relies on systematic research and planning. Voters and consumers alike, nevertheless, often cannot explain exactly why they prefer one candidate, or one product, over another.

In his best-selling book about the campaign, Theodore White dismissed Segretti's dirty tricks as having "the weight of a feather." Nixon's speechwriter William Safire shared that conclusion.[21] Nixon's assistants, however, spent tens of thousands of dollars in the belief that the dirty tricks would help determine the results on election day. Chapin, who hired Segretti, and Haldeman, for whom Chapin worked, both left an advertising agency to join Nixon's staff. The correlation between Segretti's intense effort in Florida and the primary voting results reinforced their belief that such tactics paid rich dividends.

To varying degrees, Segretti's dirty tricks were repeated in other primaries. In Wisconsin, for example, he distributed flyers among Milwaukee's black residents, inviting them to a free lunch and beer picnic at which they could meet Mrs. Martin Luther King and the television star Lorne Greene. Those who came to the picnic found no celebrities, no lunch, and no beer. To disrupt a Muskie rally at a Washington, D.C. hotel, Segretti ordered, in Muskie's name, food, liquor, and two magicians. Segretti also invited to the rally, again in Muskie's name, six ambassadors, who arrived in rented limousines, the bill arriving at Muskie's headquarters.

On April 4 Muskie finished a disappointing fourth in the Wisconsin primary; McGovern won, with George Wallace, following only a ten-day campaign, placing second. Muskie's campaign for his party's presidential nomination had failed. Three months earlier he had seemed unstoppable; he had had ample financial backing, name recognition, experience, image, endorsements, and top standing in the polls.

Buchanan relished Muskie's downfall. In mid-April he reported to Mitchell and Haldeman that "our primary objective, to prevent Senator Muskie from sweeping the early primaries . . . and uniting the Democratic Party behind him for the fall has been achieved."[22] Buchanan then recommended that they concentrate on McGovern, not to derail his drive for the nomination but to assist his bid for it "in every way we can." Although most observers and politicians realized Muskie's candidacy was over, he did not formally withdraw from the race until after he lost the Massachusetts and Pennsylvania primaries on April 25.

Segretti, meanwhile, shifted his emphasis from discrediting Muskie to generating bitterness among Democratic Party leaders without attacking McGovern. On April 29 Nixon echoed Buchanan's recommendation to assist McGovern. The president told Haldeman, who recorded it in his diary, that Nixon "made the point that the most effective way now for us to build McGovern is to get out some fake polls showing him doing well in trial heats." Nixon, again as Haldeman recorded, wanted "to knock down" Humphrey "and build McGovern up."[23] The dirty tricks remained much the same, and the bogus letters and scurrilous and false literature produced the desired effect. McGovern's campaign manager Frank Mankiewicz recorded that McGovern and the Humphrey camp "had become enemies, and I think largely as a result of this activity." Muskie expressed essentially the same sentiment.[24]

The impact of Segretti's tricks again cannot be accurately assessed, in part because other Nixon agents were simultaneously conducting other activities, with the objective of denying Muskie his party's nomination and creating discord within the Democratic Party. Nixon supporters have sought to lessen the gravity of this campaign sabotage by calling the activities dirty tricks, political hijinks, political pranks, or shenanigans. Whatever their name and whatever their impact, two facts remain obvious and ominous. First, the intention was crystal clear, and, second, approval and funding came from Haldeman and in many instances from Nixon through Haldeman, Colson, or CREEP.

In September 1971 Magruder initiated a second dirty tricks operation. He delegated Herbert Porter, CREEP's director of scheduling, to begin a campaign with the same objective as Segretti's operation: to deny Muskie the nomination and simultaneously to spread dissension within the Democratic Party. The CREEP dirty tricks never attained the dimensions of Segretti's, but the methods were similar. Porter used two major agents, first Roger Greaves of California and then Michael W. McMinoway of Kentucky. Sedan Chair I and II, Porter's code names for the agents, arranged for pickets at Muskie speeches, impeded distribution of Muskie campaign material, and, in a major project, disrupted Humphrey's telephone campaign in Wisconsin. Segretti performed his tricks in seventeen primaries; the Sedan Chairs concentrated on four primaries: New Hampshire, Florida, Wisconsin, and California. Porter disbanded his dirty tricks program in July 1972.[25]

Charles Colson, special counselor to the president, ran a third dirty tricks program. Joining the White House staff in November 1969, Colson served as a liaison with special interest groups and reported to Haldeman. Colson increasingly impressed Nixon and added staff accordingly. Eventually, he became an autonomous power within Nixon's inner circle, second only to Haldeman, and reported directly to the president. Much of Nixon's success from 1970 to 1972 with Catholics, ethnics, and unions stemmed from Colson's ideas and efforts. Indeed, from Colson came Nixon's concept of the silent majority, that the majority of Americans worked, paid their taxes, and supported their government without loud protesting on public issues. Nixon's aides later characterized Colson as "an evil genius," having "one of the most brilliant innovative political minds," a panderer "to the president's worst instincts," "a tough son-of-a-bitch," and "one of the meanest people I ever knew." Haldeman classified him "a true zealot."[26]

In his memo of March 14, 1972, "delineating the division of responsibility . . . for the fall campaign," Buchanan cited three programs, which Colson headed to some degree. Discussing dirty tricks years later, Magruder declared, "There was always some of this stuff going on, and Colson was involved; he had all sorts of things going on, himself."[27] Indeed, Colson had ideas, intelligence, autonomy, and direct access to Nixon. What he lacked was respect for the law and a sense of limits in the give-and-take of politics.

Colson's activities predate, and involved more than, the dirty tricks of the 1972 primaries and presidential election. During the 1970 congressional campaign, for example, he arranged for *Life* to publish a story charging Maryland's Democratic senator Joseph M. Tydings with influence peddling. The charges subsequently proved false, but Tydings had lost the election. Colson, nevertheless, thereafter took pride in having rid the Senate of a Nixon critic.

In February 1972 Colson won Nixon's support for a write-in vote campaign for Senator Ted Kennedy in the New Hampshire presidential primary. Kennedy was not a candidate, but Colson believed that a Kennedy write-in movement would cut into Muskie's vote and sow bitterness between the two Democratic senators. Colson had an aide draft an appropriate letter and obtained, by misrepresentation, the support of a Democratic politician, Robin Ficker of Maryland, active in a national Kennedy-for-President movement. Under Ficker's signature, CREEP dutifully mailed out approximately 165,000 letters to the names on its list of New Hampshire Democrats. CREEP financed the Kennedy write-in campaign, a fact withheld from Ficker and the public.[28]

On May 3, 1972, the antiwar movement held a long-planned rally on the Capitol steps, coincidentally the same day that J. Edgar Hoover's body lay in state inside the building. Colson believed he could exploit the natural antagonism between the groups attending the two different events to tarnish the antiwar image. With CREEP money, Colson hired counterdemonstrators to oppose the antiwar supporters, including several who would provoke fights.

Twelve days later, in Laurel, Maryland, Arthur Bremer shot George Wallace while the Alabama Democrat gave a campaign speech in a shopping center. The next day Colson instructed Howard Hunt to fly to Milwaukee at once, search Bremer's apartment, and plant McGovern literature.[29] Nixon liked the idea.[30] Initially, Hunt protested because he believed the FBI already would have sealed the apartment. Before Hunt could leave, Colson reconsidered and canceled the plan.

Colson once publicly commented that he would walk over his grandmother for Nixon's reelection. Persons who worked with him in the White House undoubtedly believed him. For that time, evil genius is an apt characterization of him. The rest of Nixon's staff may have lacked Colson's brilliance, but most shared his ethics.

The foundation of a presidential campaign is financing, and in this crucial area Nixon relied on two men. His chief fund-raiser, Maurice H. Stans, born in 1908, was a self-made millionaire who had been Eisenhower's director of the Bureau of the Budget. An investment banker during the 1960s, Stans served as finance chair of Nixon's 1962 gubernatorial and 1968 presidential campaigns. In January 1969 he became secretary of commerce; three years later he resigned to assume responsibility as the chair of the finance committee of CREEP. During the early months of 1972 he worked hard to obtain large contributions from persons who wished to remain anonymous, pointing out that the new Federal Election Campaign Act would go into effect April 7 and would require candidates to report the sources of their financial support. Stans's record in 1968 and 1972 established him at that time as the most successful political fund-raiser in American history.

Second to Stans in fund raising stood Herbert W. Kalmbach, with roots in southern California. A naval veteran of World War II, a graduate and law school graduate of the University of Southern California, Kalmbach first worked for Nixon in the 1960 presidential campaign. In 1968 he proved especially adept at soliciting money but declined Nixon's offer to appoint him undersecretary of commerce. A few months later he accepted Nixon's invitation to serve as his personal lawyer. For the next three years Kalmbach enjoyed a lucrative law practice in Los Angeles while handling special financial projects for the president.

As did many of his political aides, Nixon's financial aides maintained a secret, illegal operation as well as an open, public operation. Kalmbach in particular wore two financial hats. From the early weeks of the Nixon administration he kept a secret fund to finance covert operations. Haldeman authorized disbursements. Initially, the fund consisted of unspent 1968 campaign contributions, a total of $1,668,000, approximately two-thirds of it in cash in two safe-deposit boxes and the rest in a checking account. A few months into the new administration, Ehrlichman arranged for Kalmbach to use money from the fund to pay the salary and expenses of the secret investigator Anthony T. Ulasewicz. Kalmbach added to the safe-deposit boxes when a contributor offered cash and wished to avoid publicity if the contribution were spent openly. In summer 1971 Kalmbach made the first payment to Segretti from the safe-deposit money. On February 3, in preparation for an intensive burst of raising money, Kalmbach transferred administration of the secret fund to Hugh Sloan Jr., the young treasurer of CREEP.

Twelve days later Stans became finance chair of CREEP, and Kalmbach accepted the position of associate chair. Together they raised almost $20 million before April 7. Nineteen corporations, including such well-known firms as American Airlines, Goodyear Tire and Rubber, Minnesota Mining and Manufacturing, and Phillips Petroleum, made illegal contributions. The law strictly forbade corporate political contributions. Executives who illegally gave their corporation's money presumably did so in hopes of receiving special favors from the president or because they believed Nixon needed an unfair advantage to win reelection.

One and one-third million dollars of the pre–April 7 contributions came from persons Nixon later appointed as U.S. ambassadors. Kalmbach implied and at times promised appointment in return for an appropriate contribution. The correlation of a campaign contribution and later appointment as ambassador was common, but setting an explicit price tag for an ambassadorship was new. Federal law forbade the promise of federal employment in return for political contributions. When the new disclosure law went into effect, Kalmbach resigned as associate finance chair of CREEP.[31]

In addition to accumulating secret, illegal campaign funds and conducting at least three dirty tricks campaigns, the Nixon reelection operation placed a great emphasis on intelligence gathering. This emphasis lay behind the telephone taps to learn the sources of leaks and to gain information about critics of the administration; this emphasis lay behind the establishment of the Plumbers; and this emphasis lay behind the various recommendations of clearly illegal provisions of the Huston Plan. Haldeman, Colson, Mitchell, Kissinger, Nixon, and others shared a belief that obtaining secret information would help them deal with critics in the press, in the antiwar movement, in the Democratic Party, and even within the Nixon administration. With the current limited access to many records, scholars still have much to confirm about the intelligence component of the Nixon reelection campaign.

The most important intelligence operation in terms of its impact stemmed from a plan of Gordon Liddy. In several ways Liddy's plan resembled an earlier proposal put forth by John Caulfield, who ran the small surreptitious office under Ehrlichman. In summer 1971 Caulfield told John Dean, counsel to the president, about his plans to establish a private security firm and asked for Dean's help in obtaining CREEP as a client. Caulfield prepared a twelve-page outline of his plan, which called for covert as well as security services, and discussed the plan with Magruder and Ehrlichman. Dean also approached Mitchell on Caulfield's behalf. The plan, Sandwedge, intrigued everyone; but Mitchell, Ehrlichman, and Haldeman doubted Caulfield's ability to carry it out. Mitchell, who believed that demonstrators would be the major security problem during the campaign, told Dean to find a lawyer to serve as CREEP's general counsel and director of intelligence gathering. Dean asked Egil Krogh about the possibility of recommending David Young for the position. Krogh countered with the suggestion of Liddy. Respectful of Krogh, Dean met Liddy and sent his name forward.

Mitchell interviewed Liddy on November 24, 1971, and approved. Ehrlichman, Haldeman, and Magruder also found Liddy suitable, given his experience as a lawyer, an FBI agent, and a Plumber. He reported to work on December 13; within a month he had a security-intelligence plan of his own and had taken over supervision of existing CREEP intelligence programs.

On January 27, 1972, Liddy presented his plan to Mitchell, who held ultimate authority over CREEP's expenditures. Magruder and Dean also attended the meeting that morning in the office of the attorney general of the United States. Presenting six colored charts, Liddy spent thirty minutes discussing a $1 million program, Gemstone, that included break-ins, wiretapping, sabotage, kidnapping, mugging squads, and use of prostitutes for political blackmail. Mitchell responded with "not quite what I had in mind" and objected to the cost.[32] Eight days later the four men again met in Mitchell's office to hear Liddy's revised plan. He had eliminated the prostitutes, kidnapping, and muggings and concentrated on electronic surveillance and surreptitious photography. The new budget totaled $500,000. During discussions, the group agreed that the top three priorities were Lawrence F. O'Brien's office as chairman of the Democratic National Committee, with headquarters in Washington's Watergate complex; O'Brien's hotel suite during the Democratic convention; and the headquarters of whoever emerged as the Democratic presidential nominee.[33] Eventually, Dean commented, "I don't think this kind of conversation should go on in the Attorney General's office."[34] That ended the meeting, with Mitchell still concerned about the cost and still unconvinced about some aspects of the plan. The plan sat on the shelf.

On March 1 Mitchell resigned as attorney general and assumed official directorship of CREEP; Nixon nominated Richard G. Kleindienst as Mitchell's successor. Late that month Mitchell left for a Florida vacation but, before leaving, told Magruder to join him in a few days with CREEP projects that needed decisions. On March 30, Mitchell, his assistant Fred LaRue, and Magruder, after considering a pile of decision papers, discussed a third version of the Liddy plan. Magruder reported that Colson had pressured him for approval and that Haldeman would accept the plan if Mitchell approved. Mitchell finally agreed but limited Liddy's budget to $250,000. Mitchell and Magruder concurred that Liddy's first priority should be to wiretap O'Brien's office.

Liddy set his plan in motion, despite complaining that approval came too late for full implementation. He requested $83,000 from CREEP's treasurer Hugh Sloan, who, before payment, checked with Magruder and then with Stans, who in turn spoke with Mitchell. Stans and Sloan learned that Liddy would furnish campaign intelligence and security against demonstrations. Howard Hunt, whom Colson had loaned to Liddy in February, drew on his CIA experience and arranged for Miami-based Cubans to provide services on an ad hoc basis. The principal Cuban, Bernard Barker, once had been a member of Cuban dictator Fulgenico Batista's secret police. After Batista lost the Cuban Civil War Barker fled to Florida and became a CIA agent. Barker and Hunt became close friends during the 1961 CIA-directed Bay of Pigs operation. For electronics expertise, Liddy relied on James W. McCord Jr., chief of security for CREEP. Liddy preferred not to use a CREEP employee, but Hunt had not found an appropriate, experienced CIA agent for the job.

McCord's background appealed to Liddy. The Waurika, Oklahoma, native had served in World War II and had spent a total of twenty-three years in the FBI and CIA. He had advanced to the position of chief of physical security with the CIA, won the praise of its director, Allen W. Dulles, and retired in 1970 with the Distinguished Service Award for outstanding performance of duty. After retirement he formed McCord Associates, Incorporated, a firm that offered security services. Unlike their response to Liddy, personnel at CREEP and others who met McCord liked and respected the quiet, church-going Methodist. He insisted that he believed Liddy's assignment came from Mitchell and the White House. The cautious McCord purchased equipment in Chicago and New York to avoid arousing suspicions in Washington.

On Memorial Day weekend, Liddy's team broke into the Watergate office of the Democratic National Committee (DNC). McCord tapped O'Brien's telephone and the telephone of the executive director of the Association of State Democratic Chairmen. Barker, at this time, conducted a cursory search and photographed some documents. The other members of the team consisted of Virgilio Gonzalez, a locksmith; Eugenio R. Martinez, a former CIA agent with 354 missions to Cuba; and Frank A. Sturgis, a pseudonym for Frank Angelo Fiorini, an American who thought of himself as a soldier of fortune. While the five-member team was in the DNC, Hunt and Liddy remained in a Watergate Hotel room monitoring walkie-talkie communication with McCord's assistant, Alfred C. Baldwin, who watched the windows of the DNC from a Howard Johnson Motel room across the street from the Watergate complex of buildings. Liddy called his room the command post and Baldwin's room the observation post.

The mission proved a failure. One of the telephone taps produced little of political value but a great deal about the staff's social life. The copied documents contributed no useful information. Most important, the O'Brien telephone tap did not work. It was probably too close to a steel column that absorbed the signal and weakened the transmission to the Howard Johnson Motel room, where Baldwin monitored the taps. Magruder voiced his annoyance to Liddy and told him that Mitchell and Strachan shared that annoyance. Liddy plotted a return burglary to replace or move the faulty O'Brien tap and planned for a second camera to copy more documents. Liddy specifically told his team that Magruder wanted to learn whatever derogatory information O'Brien had about CREEP. When planning the Watergate return, Liddy also scheduled a break-in at McGovern's campaign headquarters the next night to install a telephone tap.

In *Silent Coup: The Removal of a President* (1991), Len Colodny and Robert Gettlin alleged without substantiation that Dean himself designed the DNC break-in to remove possible evidence from the desk of a secretary that might implicate Dean's girlfriend, and later wife, in a call-girl operation from within the office of the DNC. Dean and his wife filed a $250 million libel suit against the authors and the publisher who settled out-of-court. Liddy, nevertheless, continued to allege that the call-girl motive was behind the break-in.

The second Watergate break-in used the same organization as the first: command post, observation post, and entry team. Liddy paid his agents before the job in $100 bills that he had obtained from CREEP. Hunt gave Sturgis his own false identification, Edward J. Hamilton, and gave McCord another, Edward J. Warren, both provided by the CIA. Using a series of several doors to the garage, the team planned to enter the Watergate Office Building, which was separated from the Watergate Hotel housing the command post. During the evening McCord taped the door latches to hold back the locking device, thus permitting someone to open the doors without a key later that night. He also taped doors to provide later access to the stairwell and floor corridors.

McCord placed the tape horizontally, with the tape ends visible on each side of the door, as opposed to vertically taping the door's edge, a procedure that would have hidden the tape from view. Horizontal taping is used by maintenance persons, to save time by avoiding having to select the correct key from among many keys. Both Liddy and Judge John J. Sirica explained later that commercial door locks are too strong for effective vertical taping.[35]

About 1:00 A.M. on June 17, a Watergate security guard, Frank Wills, who had come on duty an hour earlier, noticed tape on one of the garage doors while making his routine inspection. He removed the tape on the assumption that a maintenance man had placed it on the door. Shortly thereafter the observation post reported to the command post that the last worker had left the DNC office. The entry team went into action but found the tape gone and the door locked; they checked with Liddy, who decided to continue the break-in. Gonzales picked the lock and replaced the tape; the team soon entered the building and the stairwell. The lock on the door to the DNC office was too rusty to pick, so the team hammered out the hinge pins and removed the door. About 1:50 A.M. Wills, while on another inspection tour, found tape on the same garage door a second time. He telephoned the police.

The police dispatcher taking the call radioed the information to Officer Dennis P. Stephenson. Stephenson begged off the assignment, pleading lack of gas and a stack of reports to finish. The dispatcher then requested a response from any tactical guard unit in the area. Cruiser 172, an unmarked car with three casually dressed officers, responded, reaching the Watergate Office Building three minutes later. The police instructed Wills to stay in the lobby while they searched the building. Before long, the three members of the tactical squad caught Liddy's entry team in the middle of the DNC office. Had Stephenson accepted the assignment from the dispatcher, driven to Watergate, and parked in front of the building, as cruiser 172 did, Baldwin would have seen the police from his observation post across the street. He would have radioed Liddy, who in turn would have radioed Barker. With sufficient warning, the Watergate burglars probably would have escaped. Police and lawyers realize that apprehending criminals and solving crimes often hinge on a seemingly small factor, such as whether a marked or unmarked car or uniformed or civilian-clad officers respond to a request for assistance. Early on the morning of June 17, two small factors, tape on a door and an unmarked police car, resulted in the arrests that eventually led to the greatest constitutional crisis the country had faced since the Civil War, more than a century earlier.

The break-in at the Watergate DNC formed an integral component of the Nixon campaign for reelection. More than a year earlier Pat Buchanan had set the agenda to disrupt the Democratic primaries, to weaken party unity, and to deny Muskie the nomination. A year earlier Donald Segretti had launched his dirty tricks to implement the campaign agenda. Maurice Stans and Herbert Kalmbach, meanwhile, had been raising campaign funds in secrecy and in violation of the law to give Nixon an unfair campaign advantage.

In fundamental ways the campaign merely reflected existing characteristics of the Nixon administration. Covert burglary, telephone taps for political advantage, and an emphasis on intelligence gathering had earlier precedents. From the start of his administration, Nixon had viewed critics as enemies.

Nixon and his aides feared a close election, a fear polls validated throughout the first half of 1972. Buchanan and the rest of the president's staff had good cause, moreover, to worry about Muskie. The results of a November 1971 Harris Poll showed that Muskie remained a strong candidate. Had an election been held at that time, 43 percent of Americans would have voted for Nixon and 39 percent for Muskie. On January 17, 1972, however, the next Harris Poll reported that Muskie had pulled even with Nixon: 42 percent supported each. By the end of January the Gallop Poll reaffirmed the Harris survey: 43 percent for Nixon and 42 percent for Muskie. For an incumbent president, especially one facing a Congress controlled by the opposition party, the public opinion polls forecast a difficult campaign.[36]

Once the dirty tricks had helped drive Muskie from the race, McGovern appeared as the front-runner among Democratic candidates for the nomination. The Harris Poll result of May found that 40 percent supported Nixon, 35 percent McGovern, and 17 percent Wallace. On May 18, Haldeman offered a less optimistic assessment: "We are even in California", "50–50" in New York, "almost even" in Ohio, and "within striking distance" in Michigan.[37] On June 8, Buchanan sent Haldeman an "Assault Strategy Memorandum — and the Assault Briefing Book," seventy-two pages long, and the following warning: "If we are running 50–50 with George McGovern in the polls election day — he could conceivably beat us by four to six points, on the basis of his first-rate get-out-the-vote machinery."[38]

Nixon's staff considered McGovern the most vulnerable possible Democratic nominee because of his position that if elected he would immediately withdraw from Vietnam. Nonetheless, in June 1972 they still projected a close race and possible defeat. The assassination attempt on Wallace on May 15, his permanent injury, and his subsequent withdrawal from the campaign added a measure of instability. With these conditions and with Colson, Haldeman, and Magruder pushing for additional campaign intelligence, Liddy implemented the plan Mitchell had approved and attempted to tap the telephone of Lawrence O'Brien, chairman of the Democratic National Committee.

At the time, Nixon and his aides viewed the illegal entry and wiretapping of the national headquarters of the opposition party as a bungled political operation and potential public relations problem. Several years later Haldeman reflected on the break-in, remarking on "the unimportance of it in our minds at the time it happened." The break-in, he continued, was "really only one of maybe fifteen things we were honing in on that day."[39] However routine such activity may have seemed to the Nixon White House, scholars have not found in other presidential campaigns the degree and extent of illegal activities that characterized the Nixon campaign. Scholars, politicians, and the general public agree, however, that the break-in itself, of which Nixon had no specific foreknowledge, never would have led to his forced resignation. Nixon's response to the break-in was another matter.

CHAPTER THREE

The Cover-up

The P was concerned about what our counterattack is, our PR offensive to top this.
— H. R. Haldeman, Diaries, June 20, 1972

We are doing everything we can to take this incident and to investigate it and not to cover it up.
— Richard M. Nixon, press conference, August 29, 1972

It has been kept away from the White House and of course completely from the President.
— Haldeman to Nixon, September 15, 1972

The initial reaction of the White House and CREEP to the Watergate break-in, from Nixon and John Mitchell down through the organizational structure, launched the administration on a course to commit additional crimes to hide CREEP's involvement. These cover-up crimes primarily involved obstruction of justice and soon included perjury, both more serious crimes than the break-in. The cover-up crimes involved an unwieldy number of persons and an ever increasing complexity that made permanent secrecy ultimately impossible. For a few hours, even for a day or two, however, the several persons who set the course of action had a choice other than a cover-up, but none considered that option. Between June and November the cover-up effort succeeded in keeping Watergate out of the presidential campaign.

The cover-up, Jeb Magruder later recorded, "was immediate and automatic."[1] An administration that emphasized law and order, a president with experience as an attorney, and a chairman of CREEP who had spent three years as attorney general of the United States viewed the break-in primarily as a public relations problem, not a crime of any importance. John Dean remembered that the strategy to deny knowledge of, or responsibility for, the planning and carrying out of the break-in as well as blocking the investigation of the crime "was instinctive, from the very top of the Administration to the bottom."[2] Nixon and his aides simply drew from their three and a half years of experience in the White House and the atmosphere of lawlessness that they had established there.

Just as the break-in fit into a familiar pattern of illegal activities, so, too, did the response when police made the arrests on June 17, 1972. Howard Hunt and Gordon Liddy, hearing Bernard Barker's voice in the walkie-talkie whisper, "they got us," stuffed James McCord's extra electronics gear into suitcases and rushed out of the room. Hunt went to the listening post in the Howard Johnson Motel room and told Alfred Baldwin to get rid of the equipment. Baldwin loaded McCord's van and drove to McCord's house. Hunt, in the interim, went to his office in the Executive Office Building and placed in his safe a briefcase filled with more of McCord's equipment. He then telephoned Doug Caddy, a lawyer he and Liddy had agreed to use in case of a problem. Hunt removed $10,000 from his safe to pay Caddy's retainer's fee.

After a few hours sleep, Liddy drove to CREEP's headquarters and started shredding everything in his Gemstone file. Using his White House pass, he moved to the Situation Room in the West Wing and telephoned Magruder, who was in California with Mitchell to attend a series of meetings and parties with prominent Republicans. Magruder relayed Liddy's information to Mitchell. Shortly thereafter, one of Mitchell's assistants telephoned Liddy and directed him to tell Attorney General Richard Kleindienst that Mitchell wanted McCord released from jail immediately, before the police could establish his identity. At noon Liddy found Kleindienst at the Burning Tree Country Club and, according to Liddy, told him that the break-in was a CREEP operation and transmitted Mitchell's directive. Kleindienst refused and, after Liddy left, instructed Henry E. Petersen, assistant attorney general in charge of the criminal division, to treat those arrested at Watergate the same as anyone else. He withheld, however, the information Liddy had given him. Liddy returned to CREEP and shredded more files. Magruder, meanwhile, telephoned CREEP and told his assistant, Robert Reisner, to remove sensitive political material from the files, especially the Gemstone files

The *Washington Post* learned of the arrests shortly after 8:00 A.M. The metropolitan editor Harry M. Rosenfield checked with the city editor Barry Sussman about assigning reporters to what appeared on the surface an extraordinary event. They agreed on Alfred E. Lewis, a *Post* veteran of thirty-six years who covered police work, and Bob Woodward, who had been with the paper nine months and who had written stories about such subjects as violations in restaurants and consumer frauds. Lewis went to the Watergate building, where his legendary friendship with police officers helped him obtain information while Woodward attended the court arraignment of the five suspects. Several factors immediately reinforced Woodward's initial impression that this was a special case. The five men wore business suits or quality sport coats; they had two lawyers representing them although none of the accused had made a telephone call; all recorded "anti-communist" as their profession; four of the five lived in Miami; and one of the defendants stated he had recently retired from the CIA.

Eight *Post* reporters, in addition to Woodward and Lewis, eventually covered the story that day. The next morning the *Post*'s Sunday edition carried three articles about the break-in. The first described the event; the second covered the security guard; and the third focused on the five accused burglars. One of the reporters who worked on the third story was twenty-eight-year-old Carl Bernstein, who regularly covered the state of Virginia. Because of Bernstein's interest in the story, Sussman asked him and Woodward to work on a follow-up story. The two young reporters had never collaborated before.

When arresting the burglars, police found a walkie-talkie, lock picks, electronic devices for picking up and transmitting conversations, almost $2,000, and keys to two Watergate Hotel rooms. The walkie-talkie operated on a channel that the Federal Communications Commission had authorized for the exclusive use of the Republican National Committee. When searching the two rooms, police found, among other things, approximately $3,500 in cash, including thirty-two $100 dollar bills, sequentially numbered. They also found a stamped, unmailed envelope addressed to the Lakewood Country Club in suburban Maryland. Inside was a check to the club signed by E. Howard Hunt. In addition, the police found Barker's address book and Eugenio Martinez's telephone directory. Both the book and the directory listed Hunt's name and telephone number, one with the side notation "W. House."

Liddy's break-in operation left a trail of evidence that a thorough investigator easily could trace to the White House and CREEP. Hunt's name and telephone number proved the most glaring because his name appeared on the White House payroll. The sequentially numbered bills provided another lead because federal law required banks to keep a record of such bills. Public records, moreover, identified McCord as director of CREEP security, which was why his arrest so unsettled Liddy, Magruder, Mitchell, and other CREEP officials. Attorney General Kleindienst later claimed he had not believed Liddy's story at the Burning Tree Country Club and thus had not acted on it. Had Kleindienst told Nixon and Mitchell, they might have had second thoughts about the cover-up.

Hunt's White House connection caused an immediate stir. Early in the evening of June 17, FBI agents appeared at his door. He acknowledged the check to the country club as his own but refused to comment further without his lawyer present. About the same time, the assistant chief of the Secret Service telephoned John Ehrlichman with the information, obtained from a police report, that two of the Watergate burglars had Hunt's White House telephone number and one had a personal check of his. Ehrlichman telephoned Charles Colson, having recalled that Hunt had once worked for Colson, one of Nixon's closest advisers. Colson replied that Hunt no longer had a White House affiliation. Ehrlichman next telephoned H. R. Haldeman, at the time in Florida with the president, who having just returned from a trip to the Soviet Union was spending the weekend in the Bahama Islands with his businessman friend Robert H. Abplanalp. Haldeman was out, so Ehrlichman briefed Ron Ziegler, Nixon's press secretary.

The news about the break-in soon gained another dimension. Later on the evening of June 17, one of Ehrlichman's special investigators, John Caulfield, telephoned his boss with the news that the police had learned of McCord's employment at CREEP. Reaching Haldeman in Florida, Ehrlichman brought him up to date. Early the next morning, after the lavish "Celebrities for Nixon" party ended on the West Coast, Magruder received a telephone call from Haldeman, who told him to return to Washington at once to take charge of the situation. Magruder rushed to Chicago on a commercial flight and then chartered a plane for the rest of the trip when no airline had an available seat.

On Sunday, while Magruder was en route to Washington, Mitchell responded to an Associated Press inquiry. In a prepared statement about the break-in and McCord, Mitchell declared, "We have just learned from news reports that a man identified as employed by our campaign committee was one of five persons arrested. . . . The person involved is the proprietor of a private security agency who was employed by our committee months ago to assist with installation of our security system." Mitchell misrepresented both the manner by which he had learned of the break-in and the nature of McCord's work for CREEP. "We want to emphasize," Mitchell continued, "that this man and the other people involved were not operating either in our behalf or with our consent." He commented further that there "is no place in our campaign or in the electoral process for this type of activity and we will not permit it or condone it."[3]

Had Mitchell rejected Liddy's intelligence plan on three occasions, as he later claimed, he could have used the break-in to fire Magruder and to transform CREEP thoroughly into his own organization. Magruder, who once had worked in the White House, remained in constant touch with Haldeman. Hunt's involvement suggested a potential embarrassment for Colson. Thirty-five officials at CREEP had moved there from the White House, many of whom had worked with Colson and Haldeman. Mitchell disliked and distrusted both Ehrlichman and Colson and believed that a Mitchell-dominated presidential campaign would conduct an operation superior to the one Haldeman and Colson conducted.

Because Mitchell's wife, Martha, knew McCord and liked him, Mitchell had his aides try to isolate her from newspapers and friends. The aides once forced sedation on her; another time one aide ripped her telephone from the wall during a conversation; and they spread gossip about her drinking problem. Mitchell also refused to permit the police and the FBI to interview his wife. On the whole, the attempt to silence and discredit Martha Mitchell worked. When friends whom she managed to reach by telephone publicized some of her accusations, the charges seemed so bizarre that the rumors about her instability gained credibility.

On Monday morning, June 19, Magruder went to CREEP headquarters and talked first with the treasurer, Hugh Sloan. Magruder wanted to know if the police and the FBI could trace to CREEP the several thousand dollars in $100 bills that the Watergate burglars had with them when arrested. To Magruder's and his own discomfort, Sloan replied that investigators probably could trace the money to CREEP.

The money had arrived at CREEP just before the new campaign-financing law went into effect on April 7, the date when campaign organizations had to begin to record all contributions. The money that Sloan had given Liddy came from two pre–April 7 contributions: $89,000 from a group of Texas oilmen who presented four cashier's checks from a Mexican bank, and $25,000 from a Minnesota businessman, Dwayne Andreas, who gave cash to Kenneth Dahlberg, the Midwest chair for the Finance Committee of CREEP. Dahlberg converted the cash into a cashier's check before giving it to Maurice Stans. Sloan checked with Magruder and Stans and then gave the five checks to Liddy. Before approving the transaction, Stans first checked with Mitchell.

Liddy, in turn, gave the five cashier's checks to Bernard L. Barker, a Miami businessman and sometime CIA agent, who deposited the checks in his bank in mid-April. Barker then withdrew the money in $100 bills over several weeks and in mid-May gave the cash to Liddy, who then gave it back to Sloan. Ironically, and by chance, when Sloan gave Liddy money to finance the Watergate break-in, Sloan reached in his safe and picked up several packages of the $100 bills from Barker's bank. Had Barker taken $50 bills for his withdrawals, or if Sloan had given Liddy another stack of money, the Watergate investigation would have followed a different road and perhaps would have arrived at another destination.

By dealing in cash and cashier's checks, through different banks, the contributors and CREEP officials intended to prevent anyone from learning the source of the money. During the Watergate era, the media and the public popularized calling this procedure "laundering" money. Such a procedure was not foolproof because banks kept the serial numbers of $100 bills disbursed. Once investigators traced the $100 bills to Barker's withdrawals, that would have located the deposit record of Dahlberg's and the Mexican bank's cashier's checks.

Magruder also talked briefly with Liddy and then with Gordon Strachan, who served as Haldeman's liaison to CREEP. Magruder urged Strachan to destroy whatever documents he had that might tie the burglars to the White House. Then Magruder talked with Sloan again. He asked if CREEP had reported the disbursements made to Liddy, as the new campaign finance law required. Sloan replied he had not and that he had already filed reports covering the period with the Government Accounting Office. When Magruder suggested that Sloan might have to fabricate an explanation to get around the violation, the treasurer grew dejected. Their conversation ended.

While Magruder worked to create a record and a public image that the break-in had no direct connection with CREEP, Ehrlichman worked at the White House to learn more about the break-in. He and Haldeman discussed the situation by telephone on Sunday and Monday, June 18 and 19, and agreed to have John Dean, Nixon's counsel, investigate Watergate. Ehrlichman met first with Dean on Monday and gave him the assignment. The thirty-three-year old Dean had been counsel for two years and owed his appointment to the recommendation of his friend, Egil (Bud) Krogh Jr., an assistant to Ehrlichman. Dean's experience working for John Mitchell in the Justice Department had enhanced Krogh's recommendation. After seeing Dean, Ehrlichman met with Kleindienst, who promised to keep Ehrlichman informed of the Justice Department's investigation. Kleindienst already had ordered L. Patrick Gray, acting director of the FBI, to keep Ehrlichman briefed.

On Monday afternoon, Ehrlichman, Dean, and Colson met in Ehrlichman's office, later joined by Ken Clawson, the White House deputy director of communications, and Bruce A. Kehrli, one of Haldeman's assistants. The group discussed Hunt's status. Ehrlichman ordered Hunt's White House safe forced open and told Dean to take charge of the contents. The group realized that the materials in Hunt's safe might embarrass the administration. To conceal, destroy, or tamper with potential evidence constituted an obstruction of justice, which the group also knew.

Late Monday afternoon Mitchell returned from California. That evening, at Mitchell's request and in his apartment, Dean and Magruder met with Mitchell and his two closest aides, Fred C. LaRue and Robert C. Mardian. At that meeting Mitchell suggested to Magruder that the CREEP Gemstone file documenting Liddy's activities should be burned.

Magruder left the meeting early to keep a tennis match appointment initiated by Vice President Spiro Agnew. At one point Agnew quietly asked Magruder to explain the break-in. Magruder replied, "It was our operation. It got screwed up. We're trying to take care of it." Agnew responded, "I don't think we ought to discuss it again, in that case."[4] Magruder's admission that the break-in reached to the top of CREEP compromised Agnew. As vice president, he had taken an oath to uphold the law, and as a lawyer, he knew the law concerning withholding information about a crime. Magruder went home and burned the Gemstone file in his fireplace.

At the time of the break-in Nixon was on the private island of Robert Abplanalp, 150 miles from Haldeman in Key Biscayne, where Nixon maintained a Florida White House. Nixon and Haldeman, who already had spoken with Ehrlichman, talked on the telephone nine hours after the police arrested the burglars. Between noon the next day, a Sunday, and noon on Monday, Nixon and Colson spoke on the telephone three times. Early Monday afternoon Nixon and Haldeman talked for approximately an hour and fifteen minutes at Key Biscayne. That evening, on the return flight to Washington, the two talked for fifty-five minutes. The participants appear never to have revealed fully the subject of their conversations or at what point Nixon learned of CREEP's involvement in the break-in. Before leaving Florida, the president's press secretary told reporters he would not comment on "a third-rate burglary attempt."[5]

At 9:00 A.M., June 20, the first day Nixon and Haldeman were back in Washington, Haldeman met for an hour with Ehrlichman and Mitchell to discuss the break-in. Dean joined them at 9:45 A.M. and Kleindienst ten minutes later. Kleindienst told the group that the FBI had assumed jurisdiction of the investigation from the metropolitan police. Kleindienst invited Dean to his office and then summoned Henry E. Petersen, the assistant attorney general in charge of the criminal division. During their discussion, Petersen announced that he had ordered investigators to limit their work to the break-in and not to stray into other areas.[6] From 11:26 A.M. to 12:45 P.M. Haldeman and Nixon met and, according to Haldeman's notes, discussed Watergate.

The same day Haldeman met with his assistant, Gordon Strachan, who showed his boss a copy of a memorandum from early April that recorded the approval of a "sophisticated intelligence system with a budget of $300,000." Strachan also showed Haldeman copies of documents concerning various primary campaign dirty tricks. Haldeman looked at the papers and then told Strachan to "make sure our files are clean."[7] Strachan went through the files and shredded whatever he deemed potentially embarrassing.

Dean, meanwhile, asked Ehrlichman what he should do with the contents of Hunt's safe, which included McCord's attaché case, fabricated State Department cables regarding Vietnam, memos about the Plumbers' operations, and other incriminating materials. When Ehrlichman replied to shred the papers and to "deep six" (throw into the river) the attaché case, Dean reacted cautiously because several persons, including a Secret Service agent, had watched a GSA technician open Hunt's safe. As a result, a week later Ehrlichman gave the FBI two boxes of nonsensitive material. The next day, however, Ehrlichman and Dean gave Gray, the acting director of the FBI, two folders and told him they contained classified materials from Hunt's safe. Gray left the meeting with the belief that the files contained "political dynamite" but that they involved national security and not Watergate. He also left with the distinct impression that two of the president's closest aides wanted the files destroyed. Although troubled by the situation, Gray eventually carried out what he interpreted as an order.

Within four days of the break-in, Nixon's staff completed the destruction of files that documented the origins and nature of the affair and who was responsible. Nothing incriminating remained in CREEP's files; Magruder, Reisner, possibly Mardian, and LaRue had seen to that. Strachan had cleaned Haldeman's files. Liddy and Hunt had shredded their own material. Ehrlichman had taken care of Hunt's safe. To protect himself, Colson had an assistant destroy the pages in White House directories that listed Hunt as Colson's consultant. Nixon and his aides, however, knew that eliminating evidence constituted only the initial stage of managing the problem created by the break-in. They also deemed important a public relations strategy.

Nixon's first public statement about the break-in came during his afternoon press conference on June 22. In the first and only question about the break-in, the president was asked if he had ordered "any sort of investigation" to determine the accuracy of the charge by Lawrence F. O'Brien, chair of the Democratic National Committee, that the burglars "had a direct link to the White House." The president repeated his press secretary's position that "this kind of activity . . . has no place whatever in our electoral process, or in our governmental process" and that "the White House has had no involvement whatever in this particular incident." He ended his brief remarks by noting that because the police and the FBI were investigating the matter, he would not comment further.[8]

This denial of White House participation and the moral stance that such activity "has no place whatever in our electoral process" established the positions that Nixon intended to maintain. These positions echoed those of John Mitchell, who had publicly denied CREEP's involvement and had categorized the break-in as outside the acceptable limits of political behavior. A public disassociation and a private destruction of evidence constituted the first phase of a cover-up that evolved as a matter of course and seemed so logical that no one ever questioned its legal propriety, its amorality, or its practical wisdom.

Nixon and his aides faced problems more serious and more complex than public posturing and destruction of evidence. They also had to block the FBI investigation. At first, the FBI performed conscientiously and effectively. Within five days the investigation had traced the $100 bills to Barker's account and to his deposit of the four Mexican checks and the Dahlberg check, for a total of $114,000. Gray, as he had promised, kept the White House fully informed of the progress of the FBI investigation. He informed Dean that one FBI theory was that the CIA might be implicated, considering the amount of money that was involved, that both Hunt and McCord were former CIA agents, and that Barker also had worked for the agency. Dean realized the FBI would soon trace the five checks to CREEP; he conferred with his former boss, Mitchell.

The next morning, June 23, Haldeman and Nixon met for an hour and thirty-five minutes and discussed, among other subjects, one of the suggestions that came from the Dean-Mitchell conversation earlier that week. After explaining the source of the idea, Haldeman stated that "the only way to solve this . . . is for us to have [deputy CIA director Vernon] Walters call Pat Gray and just say, 'Stay to hell out of this — this is ah, business here we don't want you to go any further on it.'" Haldeman told Nixon that the FBI could trace back to CREEP the money Sloan had given Liddy to finance the break-in. Nixon endorsed the plan to curtail the FBI investigation on grounds of national security and coached Haldeman to instruct Walters: "The President's belief is that this is going to open the whole Bay of Pigs thing up again . . . that [the CIA] should call the FBI in and say that we wish for the country, don't go any further into this case."[9]

Haldeman immediately summoned the CIA director Richard Helms and Walters. Ehrlichman joined the group. Helms stated that the day before he had told Gray that the CIA had no involvement in the break-in. Haldeman replied that the president wanted Walters to suggest to Gray to limit FBI inquiry to the break-in and not to investigate the Mexican money. Afterward, Haldeman reported to Nixon that the meeting had posed "no problem. . . . I just said that, that, uh, this thing which . . . they were exploring leads that led back into — to, uh, areas [that] will be harmful to the CIA, harmful to the government."[10]

Immediately after the meeting Walters told Gray that the FBI might uncover secret CIA operations if it pursued its investigation of the Mexican money and suggested that FBI activities should be restricted to the five men arrested. Gray obliged and stopped the planned FBI interview of Manuel Ogarrio, whose name appeared on the Mexican checks. Dutifully, Gray then reported to Dean about his conversation with Walters and the action he had taken as a result.

During the ensuing weekend, Walters developed scruples regarding the whole affair. He checked with the CIA's Latin American specialists, who reaffirmed his original conclusion that an FBI investigation would not jeopardize CIA activities in Mexico. Dean, meanwhile, asked Walters if the CIA would pay the bail and salaries for the five arrested burglars. Walters replied that he would resign before implicating "the agency in this matter."

Gray felt caught between his desire to carry out the White House directive and the desire of his subordinates to continue their investigation. He waffled. On June 28 he ordered the Ogarrio and Dahlberg interviews but later the same day reversed the decision after talking with Dean. Then, a week later, Gray advised Walters that the FBI would complete the interviews unless the CIA submitted a written request to stop. Walters reaffirmed that the CIA was not involved and had nothing to hide or fear. The next day, Walters gave Gray a memorandum stating the CIA had no involvement with Ogarrio and Dahlberg. Walters and Gray wanted to protect the integrity of their agencies against what they believed were some middle-level presidential assistants who were responsible for the break-in. The two officials decided that one of them should express their assessment to Nixon.

On July 6 Gray telephoned the president, then in San Clemente at his California White House, and told him that he and Walters believed that some of the president's staff were trying to use the FBI and the CIA, which ultimately would "mortally wound" him. To Gray's surprise, Nixon asked no questions but replied, "Pat, you just continue to conduct your aggressive and thorough investigation."[11] Gray's message alerted Nixon, Haldeman, and Dean to the failure of their attempt to manipulate the CIA and the FBI into limiting the investigation.

Mitchell and Magruder moved on another front to contain the investigation; they plotted to cut the line of criminality at Hunt and Liddy. From the time the news of the arrests reached them, Mitchell and Magruder had tried to separate CREEP from the crime. They soon surmised that the investigation, because of the $100 bills and Hunt's telephone number that the burglars possessed, would eventually ensnare Hunt and Liddy. Their first step to maintain this separation was to destroy evidence. The next, open-ended step was coaching, pressuring, and rewarding individuals to withhold information and even to lie under oath. Mitchell's closest assistants (LaRue and

Mardian) and Dean shared in plotting and implementing the plan to place blame on Liddy, to claim he exceeded his authority. Liddy's sense of loyalty made him the perfect fall guy; from the start he repeated that the arrests were his fault and that he would never talk. In the short run, through the presidential campaign of 1972, this stratagem worked, but the number of persons involved made a permanent cover-up unlikely.

Money led to the unraveling of the cover-up. Liddy's intelligence operation was budgeted at $250,000, and numerous persons knew that only Mitchell could approve such a large campaign expenditure. CREEP's treasurer Hugh Sloan had given Liddy approximately $199,000. Magruder tried to persuade Sloan to tell the FBI that he had disbursed only $75,000 to $80,000 to Liddy. Sloan refused to perjure himself. Later, Sloan testified that Magruder told him, "You may have to."[12]

The same day he talked with Magruder, Sloan learned the FBI wanted to question him. Troubled by Magruder's visit, Sloan sought guidance from Mitchell. To the young treasurer's surprise, Mitchell merely replied, "When the going gets tough, the tough get going." The FBI's questions to Sloan, however, concerned only Alfred Baldwin's employment record with CREEP. Overwrought, Sloan unburdened himself to Dwight Chapin, Nixon's appointments secretary, and to Kenneth R. Cole Jr., Ehrlichman's assistant. Chapin recommended a vacation, but Cole set up an appointment for Sloan to talk with Ehrlichman. On June 23 Sloan expressed his concern to Ehrlichman and suggested an investigation of CREEP by someone not a member of the organization. The president's chief adviser on domestic affairs told Sloan that "he didn't want to know the details, that his position personally would be to take executive privilege on this matter until after the election."[13]

Following his talk with Ehrlichman, Sloan submitted to his boss, Maurice Stans, a final report on expenditures of funds that CREEP had received before the new campaign finance law went into effect on April 7. The report showed that CREEP had disbursed $199,000 to Liddy. At the insistence of Herbert Kalmbach, the former associate chair of the Finance Committee of CREEP, Sloan destroyed the cash book upon which he based his report. He also gave a copy of the report to Mardian, who urged him to take his scheduled vacation to Bermuda. The next day, June 24, Sloan and his wife left; they returned July 3.

On July 5 Magruder again tried, but failed, to convince Sloan to report to investigators that CREEP had paid Liddy a modest sum, this time only $40,000. Two days later Sloan told everything he knew about Liddy's operation to Paul L. O'Brien and Kenneth W. Parkinson, the Washington lawyers whom CREEP had hired to represent the organization in a civil lawswuit filed because of the break-in. The lawyers encouraged Sloan to leave the city, a suggestion LaRue reinforced a few hours later. Sloan complied and spent five days in California. When he returned he retained a lawyer, resigned from CREEP, and reported all he knew to the U.S. attorney's office. He offered shockingly damaging testimony but had no supporting documentary evidence. While Sloan privately agonized over the realization that the leadership of CREEP sponsored illegal activities and encouraged obstruction of justice and that some of Nixon's aides seemed indifferent, Magruder tried to circumvent the problem that the treasurer's uncooperativeness presented to the cover-up story.

Magruder called to his office Herbert Porter, whose father had served as a local chair in Nixon's first electoral campaign in 1946. At the time the younger Porter was eight years old and wore his first Nixon button. Like so many of his contemporary White House aides, he had attended the University of Southern California, a connection that led to his White House appointment in 1970. Soon thereafter he became director of scheduling for CREEP. Magruder asked Porter if he would be willing to swear to the FBI that CREEP had paid Liddy $100,000 to infiltrate radical groups that posed a safety threat to Porter's speakers program. Magruder correctly analyzed Porter's character. The ambitious, loyal supporter of the president agreed to commit perjury. Magruder intended to explain the remaining $150,000 of Liddy's authorized $250,000 budget line as funds earmarked for security at the presidential nominating convention and for handling any special problems that might arise. Porter's and Magruder's perjury pushed responsibility onto Liddy, who, the cover-up story clearly asserted, had used funds for illegal, unauthorized activities rather than for the purposes approved.

Liddy remained true to his vow of silence. On June 28, after finding his name in Martinez's address book, two FBI agents went to CREEP to question Liddy. After he refused to answer, Stans fired him.

Two days later Mitchell abruptly resigned as director of CREEP in order to appease his wife and to keep her from speculating about what she knew about McCord's duties there. Disillusioned with politics and embittered over the treatment she had received from her husband's aides, she threatened him: politics or me. Mitchell, concerned about his wife and chagrined that his campaign organization had embarrassed Nixon, publicly claimed that he lacked sufficient time to run a campaign and to fulfill his more important responsibilities as husband and father. Rather than returning to New York City, he remained in the Washington branch of his law firm, in an office directly across the hall from the door to CREEP's headquarters. His active participation in both the cover-up and the campaign continued; after the resignation, however, he conducted meetings in his law office.

The five men arrested at the time of the burglary, their boss E. Howard Hunt, and Liddy nonetheless presented a further problem for those who plotted the cover-up. Reflecting their familiarity with CIA procedures and traditional clandestine operations in general, the seven men expected higher-ups to post bail, provide legal services, and pay salaries. In their minds they had been on an anticommunist operation when the police arrested them. Liddy explained to CREEP officials the need to fulfill these expectations.

Nobody welcomed this task. On June 26, Walters emphatically rejected Dean's insistence that the CIA pay bail and salaries. According to Dean, who served as a bridge between the White House and CREEP regarding Watergate, Mitchell, Haldeman, and Ehrlichman then agreed that Kalmbach, Nixon's personal lawyer, should handle the operation. For the next three months Kalmbach secretly raised the money and gave it to Anthony Ulasewicz, Ehrlichman's assistant, who worked out the details. Ulasewicz negotiated with Hunt and with his wife, Dorothy, who at times served as an intermediary. The transfer of money involved actions worthy of a spy movie, complete with unmarked, brown envelopes and money left in telephone booths and airport lockers. Kalmbach, however, slowly reached the conclusion that paying the money was illegal. Consequently, on September 21, in Dean's office, he turned over the job to Mitchell's close associate, Fred LaRue.

John Dean's role and importance increased steadily as the continuing cover-up gained complexity. In addition to helping raise money for the seven men and coordinating cover-up stories, Dean also monitored the FBI and Justice Department investigations of the case. From the start, he found FBI and Justice officials especially cooperative. Both viewed the break-in in the narrowest of terms. During summer 1972, FBI officials even considered the break-in and the installation of the telephone wiretaps two weeks earlier to be two unrelated offenses. On July 10, Alfred Baldwin told the FBI about the telephone taps and about the equipment he had moved from the Howard Johnson Motel to McCord's house after the arrest. FBI agents never bothered to obtain a warrant to search McCord's house, never inquired about a transcript of the telephone conversations from the wiretaps, and never bothered to retrieve telephone taps from the Democratic National Committee's Watergate office. In August, FBI agents interviewed Haldeman's assistant Gordon Strachan, who later commented that he "was surprised that the FBI did not ask me more probing questions, even about Segretti."[14] The interrogators asked nothing about Watergate.

Earl Silbert, the assistant U.S. attorney in charge of the grand jury investigations, also failed to follow logical leads. When he and his fellow prosecutors interviewed Donald Segretti in private on August 22, preparatory to his appearance before the grand jury, they found no significance in that he had been hired by Nixon's appointments secretary and paid by Nixon's lawyer. The next day, before the grand jury, Silbert never asked a question about Chapin or Kalmbach. Silbert had subpoenaed Segretti because his name and telephone number appeared in Hunt's address book. Still, Silbert concluded that the Watergate break-in and the dirty tricks campaign against Democratic candidates were unrelated. Privately, he may have had doubts; if so, they were insufficient for him to challenge his boss, Henry Petersen.

Within the Justice Department, Petersen had overall responsibility for the Watergate investigation and played the key role in confining the investigations solely to the break-in. As late as March 21, 1973, Dean described Petersen to Nixon as "a soldier. He played — He kept me informed. . . . He believes . . . you." Dean added, "I don't think he has done anything improper, but he did make sure that the investigation was narrowed down to the very, very fine criminal thing which was a break for us."[15]

Petersen's actions were questionable. The day before a witness appeared before the grand jury, he or she would meet with the prosecutors, who would interrogate the witness more effectively and more intensively in private than they would before the jury. Whenever a CREEP employee met privately with the prosecutors, however, Petersen permitted a CREEP lawyer to accompany the employee. Grand jury rules forbade lawyers to accompany witnesses. Dean kept abreast of developments from the testimony of these witnesses because, as he told Nixon, Petersen "kept me informed. He told me when we had problems, where we had problems and the like."[16]

The last week in July Petersen again indicated his cooperativeness when Ehrlichman complained to him about the possible adverse publicity, should former cabinet members and high-ranking Nixon staff members appear before the grand jury. As a result, Kleindienst, Petersen, and Silbert met and decided that prominent White House officials would not have to appear; instead, an assistant U.S. attorney would interview them in Petersen's office. Questions from twenty or more members of a grand jury were naturally more effective and thorough than those coming from one attorney in a quiet office. Ehrlichman's complaint was triggered by his concern that Maurice Stans would have to go before the grand jury, but Kleindienst, Petersen, and Silbert extended this more private procedure to Colson and his secretary and to the two men who headed the White House Plumbers, Egil Krogh and David Young. In August 1972, the few courthouse reporters who might be hanging around the Justice Department building would not have been able to identify Colson's secretary or Young. Besides, the building had several entrances, including one in the basement for cars.

Gray was equally accommodating. He never challenged Mitchell when the former attorney general simply stated that the FBI could not interview his wife. Following Silbert's example, Gray allowed Dean or his assistant, Fred Fielding, to attend sessions whenever the FBI interviewed White House personnel. CREEP's lawyers O'Brien and Parkinson sat in when the FBI interviewed CREEP workers. Even after several of them complained to the FBI that they found the lawyers' presence intimidating, Gray continued the practice. When Kleindienst rejected Dean's request for the confidential FBI reports regarding its investigation, the White House counsel simply made the same request to Gray, who readily complied. Gray and Dean met throughout the summer. On July 28, for example, Gray personally passed eighty-two reports to Dean.

Dean used the information provided by Petersen and Gray to coach witnesses before they testified before the FBI or the grand jury. When Dean learned that the FBI planned to interview the White House secretary who worked for the Plumbers, he sent his assistant to London to bring her back from her vacation so that he could tell her not to answer questions that related to the Ellsberg break-in because it concerned "national security." The FBI's interest in her stemmed from Hunt's address book and its telephone number for the Plumbers.

Magruder carried out his role expertly when, on July 5, August 16, and September 6, he appeared before the grand jury. Petersen later recorded that he "could not refute" Magruder's story. "I did not like the story but I did not have any evidence. All I could say is it does not add up."[17] Even though he did not believe Magruder, Petersen never interviewed Magruder's administrative assistant, Robert Reisner. Neither did the FBI interview Reisner, although, like the grand jury, it considered Magruder a key witness. Magruder's consistent denial of prior knowledge of the break-in and his feigned insistence that CREEP hired Liddy to carry out legal activities pointed the arrow of responsibility at Liddy and protected White House aides and CREEP officials. A thorough investigation would have included questioning Reisner, to check Magruder's testimony. Magruder later commented that had either the FBI or the grand jury interviewed his assistant in summer 1972, "it might have blown the entire cover-up sky high. . . . Reisner didn't know the importance of the information he had, but if he'd been asked the right questions, his answers would have taken the wiretapping scheme directly to me and Mitchell."[18]

Because of Liddy's noncooperation, a thorough investigation would have included a more aggressive questioning of his secretary. Secretaries are usually well aware of the activities of their bosses. Liddy's secretary had typed the transcripts from telephone tapes and had given copies to Magruder. Like Reisner, she too "might have blown the entire cover-up sky high."

Petersen's and Gray's commitment to a narrow focus in their investigations and their willingness to keep the White House informed eased the difficulty of Dean's coordination of the cover-up. When briefing Nixon on the early months of the cover-up, in March 1973, Dean stated, "I was totally aware of what the Bureau was doing at all times. I was totally aware of what the Grand Jury was doing. I knew what witnesses were going to be called. I knew what they were asked."[19] Petersen and Gray, consciously or unconsciously, permitted their natural desire to please their boss to compromise their professionalism. On August 28, 1972, Kleindienst, who, as attorney general, served directly between Petersen and Gray and the president in the line of responsibility in enforcing the law, proclaimed that the Watergate investigation would be "the most extensive investigation since the assassination of President Kennedy."[20] This public pronouncement contrasted sharply with the actualities of Gray's and Petersen's investigations, but it reflected the gap between words and deeds coming from the White House.

The cover-up succeeded throughout summer and autumn 1972. Dean, Magruder, and Mitchell had cut the line of criminality at Hunt and Liddy. The press interested itself in other things. On June 29, when Nixon held a press conference, reporters asked twenty-two questions, none about the break-in. At his press conference a month later, Vietnam and the 1972 campaign dominated the questions. Once again, no reporter asked about the break-in. Then on August 29, at the third press conference since the break-in, a reporter asked the president what he thought about appointing a special prosecutor "to investigate the contribution situation and also the Watergate case?" The linking of the two issues was logical in light of a Bernstein-Woodward article revealing that campaign funds from CREEP had financed Watergate. Nixon noted that "the FBI is conducting a full field investigation" and that the Department of Justice "is in charge of the prosecution and presenting the matter to the grand jury." He added that a Senate Banking and Currency Committee and the Government Accounting Office also were conducting investigations about campaign spending. Nixon doubted that "adding another special prosecutor would serve any useful purpose." He pointed out that these investigations "had the total cooperation of the — not only the White House — but also of all agencies of the Government." He remarked that under his directions, "Counsel to the President, Mr. John Dean, has conducted a complete investigation of all leads which might involve any present members of the White House staff or anybody in the Government." Nixon then stated "categorically that his investigation indicates that no one in the White House Staff, no one in this Administration, presently employed, was involved in this very bizarre incident." He emphasized that "we are doing everything we can to take this incident and to investigate it and not to cover it up."[21]

Nixon's unequivocal statements reassured the public, especially when combined with Kleindienst's unqualified promise that the Watergate investigation would be "the most extensive investigation since the assassination of President Kennedy." Dean assessed the comments of Nixon and Kleindienst differently. He realized Nixon was lying and admired the performance. When Nixon's press secretary Ron Ziegler later asked Dean about the report, Dean replied that there was no report and that he was not working on one.

Nixon held only one press conference during the last nine weeks of the 1972 presidential campaign. On October 5, reporters asked him twelve questions concerning such subjects as the campaign, Vietnam, and welfare reform. One question related to Watergate. In response to the inquiry about what the administration was "trying to get done at the Watergate," Nixon answered, "One thing that has always puzzled me about it is why anybody would have tried to get anything out of Watergate." He pointed out that the break-in decision had "been made at lower levels, with which I had no knowledge." He then compared the FBI investigations of the break-in with its earlier investigation of the Alger Hiss case. The FBI, he continued, "did a magnificent job" in the Hiss case, but that investigation "was basically a Sunday school exercise compared to the amount of effort that was put into this." He then added that "it is now time to have the judicial process go forward," and with the seven burglars under indictment and awaiting trial, he would offer "no comment about the case." He reminded reporters that he had received vigorous criticism when he commented about the Charles Manson murder case at a similar point in the legal proceedings.[22]

Between the June 17 break-in and the November 7 election, Nixon held four press conferences at which reporters asked him a total of three questions about Watergate. Reporters who covered the president obviously considered the subject of marginal importance. Nixon's explicit language, his denial of prior knowledge, and his description of the intensity of the investigations seemed convincing. Gray and Petersen, on the other hand, must have discounted as politics Nixon's exaggeration of their investigations as more thorough than the Hiss case investigation. Two reporters, however, did doubt the accuracy of Nixon's statements and proved to be more thorough and effective investigators than Gray and Petersen. The articles that Bernstein and Woodward wrote during summer and fall 1972 mildly stirred the calm over Watergate that the cover-up had produced. Their investigations foreshadowed and contributed to the storm that broke early in 1973.

CHAPTER FOUR

Disclosures

I want you all to stonewall it, let them plead the Fifth Amendment, cover-up, or anything else.
— Nixon to Haldeman, Ehrlichman, Dean, and Mitchell, March 22, 1973

Even the old-line Republicans in the Senate are becoming aware of this situation, and are applying whatever strength they have on the White House to come clean and act as other people would be expected to act.
— George D. Aiken, Republican senator from Vermont, diary entry, week ending March 31, 1973

I condemn any attempt to cover up this case, no matter who is involved.
— Nixon, publicly, April 17, 1973

The Bernstein and Woodward articles posed a potential threat to the cover-up. One of these articles prompted the chair of the House Banking and Currency Committee to raise the possibility of an investigation, and inquiries by the director of the Federal Elections Division of the General Accounting Office presented Nixon with yet a third threat beyond the grand jury and FBI investigations. To parry these threats Nixon had initiated a public relations campaign and behind-the-scenes moves to control the Justice Department. The president's overwhelming reelection in November seemingly pushed Watergate out of the public mind until January, when the burglars stood trial. The presiding judge John Sirica concluded that the defendants withheld information and promised them stiff sentences unless they cooperated. One defendant, James McCord, lost resolve, bowed to Sirica's pressure, and wrote to him describing acts of perjury and the political pressure on McCord to remain silent. McCord's disclosures appeared during a ten-week period of disclosures that rocked the nation and led to the resignations of Haldeman, Ehrlichman, and Dean as well as the acting director of the FBI. The disclosures implicated the White House in the burglary and in obstruction of justice. By mid-May criminal actions and responsibility for the Watergate cover-up leaped over the Liddy stone wall and reached the door of the Oval Office. The disclosures also led to the appointment of a special prosecutor and the establishment of a Senate investigating committee; and, for all practical purposes, they destroyed the cover-up. By May the cover-up, with its obstruction of justice, had replaced the break-in as the center of attention.

While Jeb Magruder, John Dean, John Mitchell, Ron Ziegler, and others reinforced Nixon's statements with their own declarations of innocence and in some instances supported the cover-up with perjury, Carl Bernstein and Bob Woodward tenaciously investigated the affair. The amount of money involved, E. Howard Hunt's name on the White House payroll, and McCord's position as chief of security at CREEP aroused their suspicion that a high-level Nixon aide had ordered the break-in. They were supported by their editors at the *Washington Post,* especially the city editor Barry Sussman, although the fact that Woodward was the lowest paid regular reporter at the paper suggested the low priority the editors had initially placed on the story. The *Post,* largely due to the work of Bernstein and Woodward, eventually won Pulitzer Prizes for their coverage of Watergate.

Other than being young and single, and low on the totem pole at the *Washington Post,* the two reporters had little in common. The Jewish Bernstein, twenty-eight and separated from his wife, had dropped out of the University of Maryland. The Protestant Woodward, twenty-nine and divorced, had graduated from Yale. Bernstein was short, shaggy-haired, and rode a bike instead of driving a car. In contrast, his tall partner disliked manifestations of the counterculture, so popular at the time, and drove a late-model Karmann Ghia. Bernstein viewed both major political parties with antipathy; Woodward was a registered Republican. Although at the time neither of them, nor anyone else, realized it, Watergate presented an unparalleled journalistic opportunity.

Bernstein and Woodward focused their detective work on the burglars' money, where it came from and who controlled it. They telephoned and visited employees in the White House, at CREEP, and in the Justice Department. A few they knew; most they did not. Bernstein flew to Miami and talked with the Florida state attorney for Dade County and his chief investigator, who were investigating the bank records of the Watergate burglar Bernard Barker to determine whether or not he had broken Florida law. Before the reporters wrote a story containing an undocumented allegation, they required the testimony of two separate persons. Then before they published a story, one of the reporters would telephone the subject involved and offer an opportunity to comment. Their methods were based on sound journalistic practice.

Woodward had a friend, probably old enough to be his father, who, according to Woodward, held an "extremely sensitive" position in the executive branch of government and who "had access to information from the White House, Justice, the FBI . . . and CREEP." The friend, whom Woodward respected as "a wise teacher," proved willing to talk about Watergate but only would confirm information Woodward and Bernstein had obtained elsewhere. Woodward's friend also added "some perspective." This confirmation and perspective helped keep the two reporters on the right track. Equally important, the help reinforced the reporters' morale and convinced Woodward that he and Bernstein were working on a story of tremendous significance. This reinforcement, more than specific information, was Woodward's friend's real contribution to the reporters' pursuit of the Watergate story. Because only Woodward knew his friend's identity, one of the *Washington Post* editors named him "Deep Throat." The name came from combining the journalistic term "deep background," meaning without identification of source, with the widely known title of a pornographic film, *Deep Throat*.[1]

Three decades after Nixon's resignation, the identity of Deep Throat remains Woodward's secret.[2] The position he held and the access to information he enjoyed implies that he was a Republican. His demand to remain anonymous and to limit his contribution only to confirming Woodward's prior information or by adding perspective to his investigations suggests that he wished to remain in the executive branch and to remain a loyal Republican. The limits he placed on his conversations with Woodward meant, if necessary, that Deep Throat could tell the president, the media, and the Justice Department officials that he never leaked information and always supported the president.

Circumstantial evidence supports the conclusion that Deep Throat believed Nixon's public pronouncements that he wanted a clear, quick resolution to Watergate and knew nothing about a cover-up. Despite the president's disclaimers and assertions, anyone who observed at close range and knew some of the activities of Haldeman, Ehrlichman, Colson, Magruder, and their many assistants realized that Nixon's aides were managing a Watergate cover-up. Deep Throat believed the cover-up would destroy Nixon's presidency. By helping Woodward, a Republican, a navy veteran, and a person he had known "long before Watergate," Deep Throat perhaps hoped to expose the cover-up and save Nixon from the machinations of his aides in their attempt to give him an unfair campaign advantage.

Deep Throat, while possessing a long-held loyalty to Nixon, viewed Haldeman, Ehrlichman, Colson, and their principal assistants with a wary eye. Within the Nixon administration a bitter, suspicious, bipolarization existed between these aides and John Mitchell. Once, Deep Throat used the term "switchblade mentality" to characterize the attitude of many of Nixon's aides. "Numerous times," he reminded Woodward, "they are all under-handed and unknowable." Deep Throat once expressed obvious disappoint-ment to Woodward when remarking that Haldeman "slipped away from you." Deep Throat probably owed his appointment to Mitchell and, there-fore, had no qualms exposing Nixon's closest aides, all of whom had tried to diminish Mitchell's influence with Nixon and now apparently were dam-aging the president.

With the events at the end of April 1973, which included the resignations of Haldeman, Ehrlichman, and Kleindienst and Nixon's firing of Dean, Deep Throat may have realized Nixon's involvement in the cover-up. On May 16, when Woodward and Deep Throat met for the first time after Haldeman and Ehrlichman had resigned, Woodward concluded, "It was clear that a trans-formation had come over his friend." Between this meeting and late Febru-ary 1974, when Bernstein and Woodward completed the manuscript that became their best-selling book, *All The President's Men,* Woodward recorded only one additional meeting with Deep Throat. Regarding that meeting in November 1973, Woodward wrote, "Deep Throat's message was short and simple: one or more of the tapes contained deliberate erasures."[3] The trans-formation Woodward had clearly discerned in May 1973 seemingly marked the end of Deep Throat's cooperation in exposing the officials responsible for the cover-up. Ultimately, his loyalty to Nixon apparently overrode his com-mitment to a society based on due process.

Deep Throat played an important, and for the *Post* perhaps indispensable, role in unmasking the cover-up. Ironically, his motivation may well have come from a desire to save Nixon from the criminal actions of his aides. Equally ironic, to continue this conjecture, is that Deep Throat acted because he believed Nixon when the president denied any knowledge of the cover-up and wanted to identify the guilty persons involved. Deep Throat withdrew from further participation when he realized Nixon had been lying. No doubt, if this analysis is accurate, Deep Throat regretted his actions because they contributed significantly to Nixon's resignation. Deep Throat's importance emerged during the first stage of the unmasking of the cover-up. Bernstein and Woodward, encouraged by him, deserve the major credit for keeping Watergate alive as a public issue. Of these three, two were Republicans.

During the weeks between the June break-in and the November election, Bernstein and Woodward published several scoops. Each front-page story broad-ened the context of the break-in and implicated more persons within CREEP. An article of August 1 sought to link the financing of the burglary to CREEP through the cashier's check deposited the previous April in Bernard Barker's bank account. The check carried the name of Kenneth Dahlberg, Nixon's campaign finance chair for the Midwest. On September 17 Bernstein and Woodward disclosed that "funds for the Watergate espionage operation were controlled by several principal assistants of John Mitchell and were kept in a special account at CREEP." The account, the article continued, financed "sensitive political projects." Twelve days later, the two reporters revealed that Mitchell controlled the secret account and that Maurice Stans, Magruder, and two other unnamed persons also had authority to approve payments. Unlike the earlier scoops, the October 10 article was the lead story that day and carried pictures of Donald H. Segretti and Ken W. Clawson. It opened: "FBI agents have established that the Watergate bugging incident stemmed from a massive campaign of political spying and sabotage conducted on behalf of President Nixon's reelection and directed by officials of the White House and the Committee for the Re-election of the President." Bernstein and Woodward reported that Segretti and Clawson carried out some of the spying and sabotage, or dirty tricks, that had started in 1971 and that "represented a basic strategy of the Nixon reelection effort." Five days later, on October 15, another lead story reported that Segretti reported to Dwight L. Chapin, the president's appointments secretary and a close associate of Haldeman. Chapin issued a partial denial and resigned.

Ten days later the *Washington Post* carried a Bernstein-Woodward story that caused the reporters and the paper considerable discomfort. The article stated that the former CREEP treasurer, Hugh Sloan, in testifying before the grand jury, had charged that Haldeman had controlled the secret fund that bankrolled illegal political operations, including the break-in. Sloan, however, had not named Haldeman. The error resulted when Bernstein became confused whether the Justice Department lawyer's hanging up the telephone without comment meant that Haldeman was in charge or was not in charge, a subterfuge the two used so that the lawyer could truthfully say he had not discussed Sloan's testimony with a reporter.

The *Washington Post* covered Watergate more doggedly than any other newspaper. This was logical. The *Post* was on the scene; the story deserved attention, and the paper's owner and editors opposed Nixon politically. Nevertheless, the paper's coverage of Watergate during summer and autumn 1972 was modest at best. During the campaign, the sixteen leading news bureaus in Washington maintained 433 reporters, but only 14 received Watergate as a full-time assignment. Coverage also was uneven. The *New York Times* did seriously pursue the story, regularly carrying it on page one and sometimes breaking new ground. On July 31, for example, the

Times disclosed for the first time that the $89,000 deposited in Barker's Miami account came from a Mexico City attorney. The *Chicago Tribune*, on the other hand, never placed a Watergate-related story on page one until August 27, 1972.

The political preferences of the newspaper's editorial staffs, which mirrored those of the owners, explain much of the Watergate coverage, or lack thereof. In 1972, 71.4 percent of all newspapers endorsed Nixon for president; 23.3 percent remained neutral; and only 5.3 percent supported McGovern. The *Los Angeles Times*, which endorsed neither candidate, gave Watergate front-page treatment more than twice as often as the *Chicago Tribune* and more than four times as often as the *New Orleans Times–Picayune*, both of which championed Nixon's reelection.[4]

During the campaign the three television networks devoted greater attention to Watergate than did newspapers. Of all political items carried, Watergate constituted 20 percent of NBC coverage, 19 percent of CBS, and 17 percent of ABC. Watergate, in terms of airtime, compared favorably with Vietnam, the Paris peace talks, and the election campaign. Because television allotted only about seventy-five seconds to a news item, the information yield compares unfavorably with that of a front-page newspaper story. On October 27 and 31, however, CBS *Evening News* presented two long special reports on Watergate. Despite the lack of depth in television news, the three networks consistently and prominently spotlighted the Watergate story.[5]

By autumn 1972, television, and to a lesser extent newspapers and news magazines, had made Americans aware of Watergate, whatever their level of understanding. A mid-September Gallop Poll asked a national sample of persons, "Have you read or heard about Watergate?" Fifty-two percent replied they had, about the same percentage who, in a 1970 poll, could name their congressman. About the same time, the Harris Poll phrased the question differently: "Have you heard, or not, about the men who were caught trying to install wire-taps in the Democratic National Headquarters in Washington?" To this clearer question, 76 percent responded yes. A month later, a Summit County, Ohio, poll indicated that 87 percent of eligible voters knew of the "Watergate break-in." Regarding the legality of the "attempt to wiretap another party's headquarters," a national Harris Poll found that 84 percent believed such an attempt was a "basic violation of individual freedom." The results of these polls indicated that few Americans linked the president with Watergate. Despite public awareness and disapproval of the affair, Watergate played no perceptible role in the casting of votes in the 1972 election. Nixon won a stunning 61.1 percent of the popular vote, in part because as a candidate and campaigner, George McGovern had too many weaknesses.

Simultaneously with his public campaign to win reelection and to disassociate himself from Watergate, Nixon waged a secret campaign against individuals who might expose his role in the cover-up and reveal the dirty tricks his aides had perpetrated. The most serious threat came from the Democrat Wright Patman, chair of the House Banking and Currency Committee. On August 19, prompted by the Bernstein and Woodward article that sought to establish that CREEP money had financed the Watergate break-in, the seventy-one-year-old Texan ordered his committee staff to start an investigation of Nixon's campaign finances. For such an investigation, however, Patman's committee had to vote to give him the power to subpoena witnesses.

Once Patman announced his intentions, Haldeman coordinated a countermove to pressure committee members to deny Patman subpoena power. In New York, Mitchell worked to influence powerful constituents in Frank J. Brascoi's congressional district to pressure their congressman, who sat on Patman's committee, to vote against subpoena power. And Maurice Stans talked with the Republican House leader Gerald Ford.

After a meeting with Nixon and Haldeman, Dean telephoned John Connally Jr., the former Democratic governor of Texas and a Nixon supporter, asking for suggestions of "soft spots" in Patman's career that Dean could use to threaten the committee chair. Connally replied that Patman's most likely vulnerable spot involved contributions from an oil industry lobbyist. When Dean learned that Gerald Ford might have a similar problem, he dropped that particular approach. Dean, meanwhile, convinced Henry Petersen to send the Patman committee an official Justice Department letter protesting the hearings on the grounds that the resulting publicity would compromise the rights of the Watergate burglars for a fair trial. Dean also continued to remind William E. Timmons, the chief White House liaison with Congress, that he must pressure Ford to deliver the votes against Patman.

On October 3, Patman's committee met and voted twenty to fifteen against granting him power to subpoena. The next week Patman tried to hold public hearings, but Dean, Mitchell, Magruder, and Stans declined the invitation to testify voluntarily. Patman had no recourse and gave up the attempt to investigate campaign spending.

Bernstein and Woodward's story that CREEP funds financed the Watergate break-in sparked more than Patman's investigation. Soon after the article appeared, Philip S. Hughes, the director of the Federal Elections Division of the General Accounting Office (GAO), ordered a full-scale investigation for possible violations of the Federal Campaign Expenditures Act, which had become law on April 7, 1972. Before assuming the directorship, Hughes had spent more than twenty years with the Bureau of the Budget. During part of the Eisenhower administration he worked under Maurice Stans, when he had headed that bureau. Hughes read the reports his former boss had submitted, which contained no mention of Dahlberg's $25,000 check. As the investigating agency of the Congress, the GAO regularly conducted audits and usually issued reports within a few weeks from the inception of a project. The investigation of CREEP, the first initiated under the 1972 act, took less than a month. Both Stans and the former CREEP treasurer Hugh Sloan refused requests for interviews; the GAO had no subpoena power.

On August 26 the GAO issued a twelve-page report listing eleven "apparent and possible violations" of the new election law, including more than $100,000 laundered through Mexico, and recommended that the Justice Department consider prosecution. Stans replied publicly that any irregularities stemmed from the highly technical nature of the law; he labeled the report's conclusions "false and unwarranted." He also called for an investigation of McGovern's campaign records on the vague grounds that they "will be very revealing." The GAO, as part of the legislative branch of the federal government, lacked authority to prosecute. The Justice Department, under jurisdiction of the president, simply ignored the GAO recommendations until after the 1972 elections.

Yet another threat to the cover-up simmered among the seven Watergate burglars. On September 15, the federal grand jury announced an eight-count indictment against them, including unlawful entry, theft, and installation of electronic surveillance equipment. The indictment made no mention of who had financed the operation or how it was financed, despite the equipment and cash the defendants carried. When releasing the grand jury indictment, Attorney General Kleindienst nevertheless declared that the three-month investigation constituted "one of the most intensive, objective, and thorough investigations in many years." House leader Gerald Ford reiterated that no leadership in the Republican Party, CREEP, or the White House had anything to do with Watergate. Senator Robert Dole, chair of the Republican Party, and Clark MacGregor, chair of CREEP, attacked McGovern and "those who have recklessly sought to connect others with the case."[6]

The grand jury indictment meant that the seven defendants would be tried in federal district court. Chief Justice John J. Sirica designated himself as the presiding judge, rather than selecting one of the other fourteen judges on the court. Before doing so, he consulted several fellow judges because the case obviously had political overtones. Sirica believed that his background in Republican politics and the fact that a Republican president, Dwight D. Eisenhower, had appointed him to the bench would counter any charge of bias against the defendants. Sirica quickly set the trial date for after the elections; he also denied the motion to move the case out of the District of Columbia.

When Nixon, Haldeman, and Dean met late in the afternoon of the day the public learned of the grand jury action, the three seemed confident that they had events under control. In concluding a telephone conversation with John Mitchell that interrupted the meeting, Nixon admonished him, "Don't bug anybody without asking me, OK?" Nixon told Dean, who coordinated the cover-up, "The way you have handled all this seems to me has been very skillful putting your fingers in the leaks that have sprung here and sprung there." Several times during the meeting Nixon indicated that he expected "all the trouble" to pass, and, when it did, he would seek revenge. "We'll have a chance to get back one day," he once commented. Another time, he declared, "This is a war," adding, "I wouldn't want to be on the other side right now. Would you?" Dean replied that he had "begun to keep notes on a lot of people who are emerging as less than our friends because this will be over some day and we shouldn't forget the way some of them have treated us." The president wanted "the most comprehensive notes on all those who tried to do us in. . . . They are asking for it and they are going to get it." Dean expressed satisfaction that Watergate had not affected the president. Haldeman seconded the point: "It has been kept away from the White House and of course completely from the President."[7]

Events during the rest of September and all of October seemingly justified Nixon's, Haldeman's, and Dean's confidence. Watergate played no role in the campaign that ended on November 7 with Nixon's impressive reelection victory. Neither Patman, the GAO, nor the grand jury had connected any high-ranking official to Watergate. The seven defendants remained silent while the perjured testimony of Mitchell, Magruder, and Porter gave plausibility to the White House's and CREEP's explanations of Watergate. Behind the scenes, the FBI and the Justice Department had also interpreted the break-in in the narrowest way possible. Newspaper reporters and the public seemed only mildly interested.

Nixon's inaugural address on January 20, 1973, represented the high point of his presidency. With good reason he looked back and proclaimed that "1972 will be long remembered as the year of the greatest progress since the end of World War II towards a lasting peace in the world." During the year, to improve relations, he became the first president to visit the People's Republic of China and the first president since 1945 to visit the Soviet Union. Throughout the year he had steadily withdrawn American troops from Vietnam, and he had recently signed an accord that promised an end to American combat.

On the domestic front, the president started to implement his plan to make the executive branch more responsive to his orders. He cut back some welfare programs and impounded other funds Congress had authorized. As a national party, the Democratic Party seemed in disarray. From January 26 to 28, the Gallop Poll surveyed Americans and found that 68 percent of them approved the way Nixon was "handling his job as President." This rating matched his previous high of November 1969. On inauguration day the *Washington Post* printed a twenty-two-page section, "The Nixon Years," that made no mention of the Watergate affair. Forces beyond Nixon's control, however, already were in motion and would soon shatter his national preeminence.

The trial of the Watergate burglars opened on January 10, 1973, in the U.S. District Courthouse in Washington after two days devoted to jury selection. Earl Silbert, the principal assistant U.S. attorney, headed the prosecution and outlined the case in his opening presentation. He had been in charge of the investigation since its beginning. Although well prepared and aware that the break-in had been part of a wider program of political sabotage, Silbert never argued, or even suggested, the possible involvement of individuals more important than Liddy.

Following Silbert's opening statement, Howard Hunt changed his plea from not guilty to guilty. He explained that he wanted to avoid a long trial, in part because he wished to spend more time with his four children; his wife, with $10,000 cash in her handbag, had died in a plane crash just a month earlier. Hunt told reporters, "Anything I may have done I believe to be in the best interests of my country." The four Miami men, who had unquestioning trust in Hunt, fired their lawyer and also changed their pleas to guilty. A frustrated Sirica excused the jury and for an hour questioned the four defendants. They revealed nothing. To the question, have you ever worked for the CIA, Eugenio R. Martinez replied, "Not that I know of." In reality, he had been on a $100 monthly CIA retainer at the time of his arrest. The same week of their plea changes, *Time* reported that each defendant, if convicted, would receive up to $1,000 "for every month he spends in prison, with additional amounts to be paid at his release." To Sirica, the trial appeared to be turning into another step in the cover-up of a crime rather than a process to learn the truth about criminal responsibility.

Liddy and McCord maintained their not guilty pleas and stood trial. Sixty witnesses testified. Magruder, former director of CREEP, and Porter, CREEP's former scheduling director, perjured themselves by insisting that they knew nothing about Liddy's plans to obtain intelligence about the Democrats or how he intended to spend the $250,000 CREEP had given him for legitimate intelligence work. A skeptical Sirica asked Sloan, CREEP's former treasurer, forty-two questions in a futile attempt to learn more. On January 30 the jury of eight women and four men needed only an hour and a half to return guilty verdicts for McCord and Liddy.

Sirica's skepticism and his advice to the defendants to answer his questions shifted the focus of Watergate to the level of responsibility above the burglars. "Maximum John," a "law and order judge," set March 23 as the date for sentencing. Bernstein and Woodward continued their investigative reporting, but Sirica, the Republican appointee to the federal judiciary, ushered in a second stage in the unmasking of the cover-up.

Sam J. Ervin, North Carolina's seventy-six-year-old Democratic senator, had been waiting for the trial to end so that he could introduce for himself and for the Senate majority leader Mike Mansfield a resolution to establish a Select Committee on Presidential Campaign Activities to investigate the 1972 election. Before the trial had started, the Senate Democratic Policy Committee (DPC) had concluded that ample grounds existed for such an investigation. Wanting as objective a committee as possible, the DPC passed over Senator Ted Kennedy for appointment as chair. Kennedy, a member of the Judiciary Committee, served as chair of the Subcommittee on Administrative Practices and Procedure and already had conducted research on campaign financing as a follow-up to the GAO report. The DPC instead chose Ervin to chair the Select Committee, his honesty, ability, and nonpartisanship having earned him widespread respect among his colleagues. Ervin, moreover, was too old to harbor any presidential ambitions. He enjoyed his reputation as both a constitutional expert and a commonsense country lawyer.

On February 7, two days after its introduction, the Senate adopted Senate Resolution 60 by a vote of seventy-seven to zero. The resolution established a Select Committee composed of seven members (four Democrats and three Republicans) and gave it the broadest possible powers to subpoena; authorized the expenditure of $500,000; and ordered submission of a final report "no later than February 28, 1974." To ensure an objective investigation, the DPC added to the committee Democrats Herman E. Talmadge of Georgia, Daniel K. Inouye of Hawaii, and Joseph M. Montoya of New Mexico. The three men were low-key and unlikely presidential hopefuls. The Senate Republican leadership likewise named three men with low-profile national reputations: Howard H. Baker of Tennessee, Edward J. Gurney of Florida, and Lowell P. Weicker Jr. of Connecticut. Baker served as ranking minority member of the committee.

White House officials crafted their response to the creation of the Special Committee. On February 10 and 11, Haldeman, Ehrlichman, Dean, and the presidential assistant Richard Moore met at the LaCosta Resort Hotel, south of the president's house in San Clemente, California. Their basic strategy was to have Nixon publicly promise full cooperation but secretly to withhold as much information as possible and to prevent witnesses from testifying. At the same time, the White House would work behind the scenes to have the media portray the Senate committee as excessively partisan. A subsequent Haldeman memo to Dean documents their strategy: "We need to get our people to put out the story on the foreign or Communist money that was used in support of demonstrations against the President in 1972. We should tie all 1972 demonstrations to McGovern and thus to the Democrats as part of the peace movement." Haldeman suggested, for example, having two sympathetic journalists, the nationally known columnists Robert D. Novak and Rowland Evans Jr., publish a particular story. "In any event," Haldeman continued, "we have to play a very hard game on this whole thing and get our investigations going as a counter move."

Ervin picked Samuel Dash, a law professor and the director of the Institute of Criminal Law and Procedure at Georgetown University, as chief counsel for the committee. A graduate of Harvard Law School, Dash had distinguished credentials. Before becoming a professor, he had worked as a trial lawyer for the Justice Department, had served as district attorney of Philadelphia, and had spent almost a decade in private practice. In 1959 he published a highly acclaimed study of electronic surveillance, *The Eavesdroppers.* His honors included the presidency of the National Association of Criminal Defense Lawyers.

For minority counsel, Baker selected Fred D. Thompson, a Nashville lawyer who had managed Baker's 1972 reelection campaign. (Thompson, from 1985 to 1993, pursued an acting career in movies and on television before winning a Senate seat in 1994.) Unlike Dash, Thompson had been active in politics, including an unsuccessful attempt to win election to the House of Representatives. At age thirty, he was eighteen years younger than Dash.

Dash and Thompson both wanted their staffs to maintain separate identities and yet cooperate fully for a unified committee. Senate Resolution 60 authorized separate majority and minority budgets. Because of the massive volume of information generated, Dash ordered a new machine and a new procedure for Congress, a computer to keep the files in order; at its peak operation, the committee employed more than forty. Senate Resolution 60 identified three principal areas of investigation: the Watergate break-in and cover-up, the campaign dirty tricks and political espionage, and the illegal campaign financing. Dash appointed an assistant chief counsel to head each of the three areas. The media quickly dubbed the committee the Senate Watergate Committee, the Ervin Committee, or the Watergate Committee.

Weeks before the Watergate Committee held its first meeting, a different Senate hearing suddenly commanded national attention. On February 28, the Senate Judiciary Committee considered the confirmation of L. Patrick Gray as director of the FBI. In May 1972 Nixon had named Gray acting director, following the death of J. Edgar Hoover. Gray, a retired navy captain, included in his background experience private law practice and work in the Department of Justice. Above all, he had been an active, loyal political supporter of Nixon since the 1960 campaign.

To win confirmation, Gray had to give straightforward answers. In so doing, he inadvertently revealed the professional ineptitude of his supervision of the FBI's Watergate investigation. On the first day of the hearings, he admitted to having given John Dean unevaluated, or raw, investigative material and other FBI data. Gray offered to make the same files available to any member of the Senate Judiciary Committee or to the newly established Ervin Committee. Dean, Gray further testified, sat in during the FBI interviews of fourteen White House aides. As justification for his actions, Gray explained that Dean, after all, served as the president's counsel. Gray immediately undermined his explanation when he related that he insisted Dean pick up the Watergate files in person instead of having a Justice Department courier deliver the material. The testimony surprised senators because J. Edgar Hoover had never permitted anyone, including presidents, to read raw files.

On March 7 events took an even more dramatic turn when Senator Robert Byrd of West Virginia, a member of the Judiciary Committee and the Senate Democratic whip, made available to reporters copies of FBI documents that Gray had supplied to the committee in response to members' questions. One document carried the heading, "Interview with Herbert W. Kalmbach." In this interview Kalmbach said that, on instructions from Dwight Chapin, the president's appointments secretary and a close associate of Haldeman, he, Kalmbach, had paid Donald H. Segretti for undercover political activities. Kalmbach stated that Segretti had started his work in early autumn 1971. The Kalmbach information undercut the basic assertion of innocence that Nixon and his staff maintained. Moreover, the document added a large measure of credibility to Bernstein and Woodward's article of October 10, in which they identified Segretti as a central figure in an extended campaign of sabotage, spying, and harassment of Democrats. After release of the Kalmbach interview, according to Gray, Kleindienst ordered him to stop discussing Watergate.

Five days after Senator Byrd gave copies of "Interview with Herbert W. Kalmbach" to the press, Nixon released a statement about executive privilege. In it he promised the principle "will not be used as a shield to prevent embarrassing information from being made available" but would be "exercised only in those particular instances in which disclosure would harm the public interest." He explained that "constitutional doctrine" and "practical necessity" required that "a President must be able to place absolute confidence in the advice and assistance offered by the members of his staff." The possibility that this advice and assistance might someday become public would inhibit candor and weaken "the decision making process at the very highest levels of our Government."[8]

The next day the Judiciary Committee voted unanimously to invite Dean to testify about his relationship with Gray. Dean cited Nixon's statement and refused. In response, the *Fort Worth Star–Telegram* wrote that "in order to clear the air President Nixon ought to offer a compelling reason why Mr. Dean and other executive staff members with knowledge of the situation are not being allowed to appear before the committee or he ought to send them to testify."[9] The Judiciary Committee indefinitely postponed action.

Comparing the questioning at Nixon's press conferences of March 2 and March 15 documents the increased interest the Gray disclosures stimulated. Of the sixteen questions from reporters on March 2, only two concerned Watergate and executive privilege. On March 15, half, that is seven of the thirteen questions, dealt with executive privilege and Watergate, including a question about Segretti.

The start of the Gray hearings coincided exactly with the beginning of a series of intense meetings between Nixon and Dean. Dating from the previous summer, Dean had orchestrated the cover-up; he coached Magruder before he appeared before the grand jury or the FBI; he coordinated cover stories; and he supervised the payment of money to the burglars while they first awaited trial and then while they awaited sentencing. Although he discussed and planned with Nixon's closest aides on a regular basis, he had not met with the president since September 15. This changed abruptly as Dean began to report directly to Nixon. During the next twenty-five days, the two of them spoke thirty-one times in person or on the telephone. Often Haldeman and Ehrlichman joined the discussions. Dean later explained that "we were all worried that my claim of executive privilege might not hold up in court because I had had negligible contact with the President. This had to be remedied."[10] At one of the first of these meetings, Nixon advised, "Let's remember this was not done by the White House. This was done by the Committee to Re-elect, and Mitchell was the chairman."[11]

On March 19 Hunt presented the White House with another cover-up crisis. Paul O'Brien, the CREEP lawyer who had served as intermediary between Hunt and the White House, told Dean that Hunt demanded $132,000 for support money and legal fees to be paid before Judge Sirica passed sentence on March 23. If he did not receive the money, plus the promise of presidential clemency by December, he threatened to disclose the Plumbers operation that Ehrlichman had directed. After talking with Ehrlichman, Dean telephoned Mitchell. Dean then received a telephone call from Nixon, and they agreed to meet so that Dean could review for the president the entire Watergate affair. Unknown to Dean, however, Nixon had just completed a seventy-minute conversation with Haldeman, during which they reviewed the Segretti dirty tricks operation, the Watergate break-ins, the burglary of Dr. Lewis J. Fielding's office, and the secret $350,000 fund that Haldeman controlled through Gordon Strachan. Nixon knew much more than Dean suspected.

Dean spent an hour and forty-three minutes with Nixon and Haldeman on the morning of March 21. By this time Dean had developed doubts whether the cover-up could succeed. He told Nixon, "We have a cancer within, close to the Presidency, that is growing. It is growing daily." The basic problem, he explained, was that "we are being blackmailed" and persons "are going to start perjuring themselves very quickly" in order to protect others. Dean added that even with payoffs and perjuries, he could give no assurances because the grand jury could indict Mitchell, Haldeman, Ehrlichman, and Magruder. Dean also told Nixon that Chapin, Kalmbach, and Colson had hired criminal lawyers to represent themselves against Watergate charges. To lessen possible sentences, they might tell the truth and implicate others, just as Dean feared Magruder might. Several times Nixon returned to Hunt because his threat involved a time deadline. Dean estimated that it would require $1 million to keep the Watergate burglars content. Nixon believed that such a sum "would be worthwhile" and could "be arranged." He saw, moreover, no alternative but "to take care of the jackasses who are in jail." Hunt received the money before the deadline.

The next day, March 22, Mitchell joined the inner circle, and the discussion continued. At one point Nixon told them, "I don't give a shit what happens. I want you all to stonewall it, let them plead the Fifth Amendment, cover-up, or anything else, if it'll save it — save the whole plan. That's the whole point." Above all, Dean said, the critical objective was to get Nixon "up above and away from it."

The discussants analyzed the problem created by the negative public reaction to Gray's disclosures and to the president's blanket claim of executive privilege for the 2.5 million employees in the executive branch of government. As a countermeasure, Nixon suggested that Dean write a report explaining why he had received FBI files and sat in on interviews. "You were our investigator," Nixon advised; "you were directed by the President to get me all the facts. Second, as White House Counsel you were on it to assist people in the Executive Branch who were being questioned. Say you were there for the purpose of getting information." Nixon also pointed out that "at the President's direction you have never done anything operational, you have always acted as Counsel." Dean's report, Nixon continued, should conclude that neither the president nor any member of the White House staff had been involved in Watergate. The president proposed to send the report to the Ervin Committee along with the offer that the committee question White House staff members "on an informal basis."[12]

Dean was reluctant for good reason. The report would absolve Ehrlichman and Haldeman of all blame and provide the president with the perfect explanation for his claim to being uninformed about whatever disclosures surfaced in the future: Dean's report had withheld information. On Nixon's insistence, a reluctant Dean left for the weekend to write the report at Camp David, the presidential retreat in the nearby Catoctin Mountains.

The day Dean left for Camp David, March 23, was the date set by Judge Sirica to pass sentence on the Watergate burglars. That morning, however, Sirica read in open court a letter from James McCord in which he claimed that "there was political pressure applied to the defendants to plead guilty and remain silent," that "perjury occurred during the trial," that "others involved in the Watergate operation were not identified during the trial," and that "the Watergate operation was not a CIA operation." McCord also requested a private meeting with Sirica because "I cannot feel confident in talking with an FBI agent, in testifying before a grand jury whose U.S. Attorneys work for the Department of Justice."[13] McCord's belated decision to tell the truth ensured that he would receive a lighter sentence from the judge.

Sirica directed McCord to testify before the Ervin Committee and the grand jury. Two days later, at a Sunday afternoon press conference, the chief counsel of the Ervin Committee, Sam Dash, announced that he had interviewed McCord twice and tape-recorded the sessions. Dash disclosed that McCord "named names." The next morning the *Los Angeles Times* reporter Robert L. Jackson wrote that both Magruder and Dean had prior knowledge of the break-in.

McCord's accusation against Dean came six days after Gray had charged that Dean "probably" had lied to the FBI on June 22, 1972, when he said he did not know if Hunt had a White House office. Neither Gray nor Jackson supplied evidence to substantiate their charges. The implications of the charges, one by a high-level Nixon appointee and the other by a CREEP employee and former CIA agent, were explosive; the man Nixon asked to investigate the break-in may have been one of its planners. The White House immediately released a statement of "absolute and total confidence" in Dean. The statement made no mention of Magruder and thus indicated that Nixon was willing to let the former CREEP chief become the scapegoat. A troubled Dean was at that time working on the ordered report at Camp David. Gray's charge, McCord's letter, Dash's press conference, and Jackson's disclosures intensified Dean's perception that once he wrote the report Nixon wanted, he would suffer the same fate as Magruder.

Gray and McCord elevated Watergate into a major story since their accusations focused attention on Nixon's counsel. Television crews from the networks started to wait outside the houses of McCord, Dean, Haldeman, and Ehrlichman. The maverick Republican senator Lowell Weicker stated that he believed White House officials had participated in the break-in. The next day Martha Mitchell telephoned the *New York Times* and said, "I fear for my husband. I'm really scared. I have a definite reason. I can't tell you why. But they're not going to pin anything on him; I won't let them." Two days later two Republican senators, Robert Packwood of Oregon and Charles McC. Mathias Jr. of Maryland, demanded the appointment of an independent special prosecutor to investigate Watergate. In addition, Vermont's Republican senator George D. Aiken recorded in his diary that "the White House should be demanding an opportunity to testify" before the Senate Watergate Committee. "Even the old-time Republicans in the Senate," he wrote, "are applying whatever strength they have on the White House to come clean and act as other people would be expected to act. So far, no success."[14] On April 3, Senator Weicker escalated his charges and called for Haldeman's resignation. Charges and disclosures by Republicans and by Nixon's appointees meant the cover-up had started to unravel. Subsequent developments proved that once it started, Nixon would be unable to check the process.

After five days at Camp David, Dean returned to Washington at Haldeman's request. He had not written the report. Dean told Mitchell and Magruder in person what he had told Haldeman on the telephone, that he had been considering testifying before the grand jury. After their meeting Dean went home and arranged to meet with Charles Norman Shaffer, a criminal lawyer. Shaffer listened to Dean's lengthy story and arranged a meeting with Earl Silbert, Seymour Glanzer, and Donald Campbell, the grand jury's prosecutors. The group first met on April 8. At the next session, a day later, Dean continued his narrative and revealed that he had never made the report, as Nixon had announced to the nation on August 29, 1972. Dean also described the intricate raising and distributing of the secret payments to the burglars. Once, Shaffer interrupted and told the prosecutors that Dean had given them "a start on an obstruction case against half the White House staff." He emphasized that Dean was "a witness, not a defendant." He wanted the prosecutors to grant Dean immunity from prosecution. At that time, however, they refused to commit themselves.[15]

Throughout April the prosecutors and the reconvened grand jury harvested the testimony of a bumper crop of witnesses, especially of Magruder. Some of the substance of their testimonies reached the public; all of it reached Nixon, who spent hours almost every day planning countermoves with Haldeman and Ehrlichman, the only two aides he apparently trusted. On April 14, Magruder admitted complicity in the break-in and the cover-up in hopes of leniency from the courts. By the end of the month Secretary of State William Rogers and the former secretary of the treasury, John B. Connally Jr., two persons whom Nixon held in great respect, advised the president to fire Haldeman and Ehrlichman. Even the assistant attorney general, Henry Petersen, believed Nixon's two closest aides had broken the law and must leave the White House. The grand jury evidence was that damning.

Within the White House a mood of suspicion and an emphasis on self-interest prevailed. Haldeman taped conversations with his assistant Larry Higby and Magruder. Ehrlichman taped conversations with Colson, Kalmbach, Mitchell, and Magruder. Colson brought his lawyer when he met with Ehrlichman. Magruder did the same. Dean refused to meet Ehrlichman and sent his message to that effect through Higby.

During a lengthy meeting the morning of April 14, Nixon instructed Ehrlichman to meet Mitchell to tell him that "the President considers this of the highest urgency . . . , that this is the toughest decision he's made and it's tougher than Cambodia, May 8 [mining of Haiphong Harbor, naval blockade of North Vietnam, and drastic escalation of bombing], and December 18 [intensive bombing of Vietnam in 1972] put together" but "that he just can't bring himself to talk to you about it. Just can't do it." Nixon wanted Mitchell to "go in and say look I am responsible . . . and nobody else had — that's it.

Myself . . . this thing has got to stop." Finally, Nixon instructed Ehrlichman to tell Mitchell that the president "will not furnish cover for anybody."[16] Aware that the grand jury had sufficient evidence to indict Mitchell, Nixon realized that a confession might actually help him. The testimonies of McCord, Dean, Magruder, and others had destroyed the original White House claim that Liddy planned and carried out the burglary as part of his intelligence program and that he had done so without the knowledge or approval of his superiors in CREEP.

Ehrlichman met Mitchell that afternoon and explained Nixon's desire that Mitchell confess to being responsible for ordering the break-in. Mitchell refused. Ehrlichman reported back to the president that Mitchell considered himself "an innocent man in his heart and in his mind and he does not intend to move off that position." He hadn't been "keeping track of what was going on" within CREEP, Mitchell admitted, and "Colson and others were effectively running the Committee through Magruder and freezing him out." Nixon responded, "Throwing off on the White House won't help him one damn bit."[17]

Nixon, Haldeman, and Ehrlichman were not alone working weekends on Watergate. On Saturday evening of April 14, the grand jury prosecutors briefed Henry Petersen about the information furnished by Magruder and Dean. Petersen immediately telephoned Attorney General Kleindienst and shortly thereafter, about 1:00 A.M., arrived at the Kleindienst house with the chief prosecutor Earl Silbert and the U.S. attorney Harold Titus. The three visitors briefed Kleindienst until 5:00 A.M. After sleeping for three hours Kleindienst telephoned to schedule an appointment with the president. Following a White House church service, the two men talked for more than an hour, Kleindienst under the belief that Nixon was hearing for the first time the complicity of Mitchell, Dean, Magruder, Colson, Haldeman, Ehrlichman, and others in the break-in and cover-up. The grand jury, Kleindienst continued, would indict Mitchell, Magruder, and Dean, maybe Strachan, with at least a bit of taint touching Haldeman. Finally, the attorney general recommended that Haldeman and Ehrlichman should resign and the president should appoint a special prosecutor. Two minutes after Kleindienst left, Ehrlichman arrived and spent more than an hour with Nixon. The president spoke then with Haldeman on the telephone for fifteen minutes. Kleindienst subsequently returned with Petersen, who reported in more detail about the charges against Nixon's staff; Petersen also recommended Haldeman's and Ehrlichman's dismissal. Nixon urged caution before granting immunity in exchange for testimony.

While Nixon spent the day meeting with Kleindienst and the others, Dean continued to testify before grand jury prosecutors. Trying without success to exchange his cooperation for immunity, Dean revealed for the first time that Liddy and Hunt had burglarized the office of Daniel Ellsberg's psychiatrist, Dr. Lewis J. Fielding, in order to obtain information to discredit Ellsberg's reputation in the news media. Dean's lawyer also revealed that he withheld from the FBI the materials in Hunt's White House safe and that he had given the materials to Gray. The prosecutors immediately passed the revelation about Gray to Petersen, who dutifully relayed the information to the White House.

As the grand jury prosecutors acquired more and more evidence, the White House constantly had to change its explanation of events and the role individuals played. On Monday, April 16, for example, Nixon asked Haldeman, "How has the scenario worked out?" Haldeman replied, "Well, it works out very good. You became aware sometime ago that this thing did not parse out the way it was supposed to and that there were some discrepancies between what you had been told by Dean in the report." A minute later, Nixon wondered, "How do I get credit for getting Magruder to the stand?" Ehrlichman explained, "Well it is very simple. You took Dean off of the case right then." Next, the president asked, "Why did I take Dean off?" Haldeman answered, "The scenario is that he told you he couldn't write a report, so obviously you had to take him off."[18]

That same morning, the president tried to pressure Dean into signing both a letter of resignation and a letter requesting a leave of absence so that Nixon could use whichever letter seemed appropriate at a future time, depending on how events developed. Dean countered, "Well, I think it ought to be Dean, Ehrlichman, and Haldeman" and said he would write his own letter. Late that afternoon Dean read his letter to Nixon. It opened, "Inasmuch as you have informed me that John Ehrlichman and Bob Haldeman have verbally tendered their requests"; at this point Nixon interrupted and commented, "You don't want to go if they stay." Dean replied that he did not wish to be the one to become a "scapegoat." Nixon did not press the issue.[19]

Henry Petersen, meanwhile, continued to keep Nixon up to date about grand jury proceedings. The two met for almost two hours the afternoon of April 16 and talked on the telephone for sixteen minutes that evening. Petersen told Nixon that late in the afternoon Frederick C. LaRue had confessed to his role in the cover-up. Nixon thanked Petersen and added, "If anything comes up, call me even if it is the middle of the night."[20]

The next morning Nixon met Haldeman, who insisted that "the White House has got to move." Nixon agreed because events were "breaking so fast." That afternoon Nixon, Haldeman, Ehrlichman, and Press Secretary Ron Ziegler met for an hour and forty-five minutes. Nixon worried that if Dean gained immunity from prosecution in exchange for information he would implicate Haldeman, Ehrlichman, and even the president. "Petersen's the guy that can give immunity," Nixon remembered, and no doubt took some comfort from the fact that Petersen was such a loyal supporter.[21]

Late that afternoon Nixon read a short statement to the press. First, he reported that he and the Ervin Committee had agreed on "the ground rules" for the testimony of White House personnel that "would preserve the separation of powers without suppressing the facts." All staff members would appear if the committee requested; the first appearance could "be in executive session, if appropriate"; and witnesses could assert executive privilege to a particular question. Nixon's second announcement concerned Watergate directly: "On March 21, as a result of serious charges, which came to my attention, some of which were publicly reported, I began intensive new inquiries into this whole matter." He added that "there have been major developments in the case" but that "it would be improper to be more specific now." The president continued, "I have expressed to the appropriate authorities my view that no individual holding, in the past or at present, a position of major importance in the Administration should be given immunity from Prosecution." Nixon closed with the statement, "I condemn any attempts to cover up in this case, no matter who is involved."[22]

After the president left, reporters bombarded Ziegler with questions, especially about Nixon's earlier statements on the thoroughness of the Watergate investigation. Ziegler finally declared, "This is the operative statement, the others are inoperative."

Nixon's explanations resolved nothing. He had reversed his position regarding testimony by aides, but he maintained the right of executive privilege on specific questions. He still insisted that the White House should investigate Watergate. The grand jury and its prosecutors, meanwhile, continued to interview CREEP and White House personnel. By the end of April, the list (in addition to Dean, McCord, and LaRue) included Kalmbach, Porter, Colson, Hunt, Magruder, Mitchell, Strachan, and Chapin. Petersen kept the president informed as the evidence mounted against Haldeman and Ehrlichman. Nixon and Petersen often met twice a day and also talked on the telephone. Petersen, for example, told Nixon that Magruder had testified that he had given the Liddy intelligence budget and summaries of telephone tapes to Strachan for delivery to Haldeman and that Strachan had denied the transactions took place. Petersen reported further that Magruder passed a lie detector test and Strachan failed. When Petersen told Nixon that the prosecutors had evidence that Hunt and Liddy had burglarized the office of Daniel Ellsberg's psychiatrist, the president ordered the assistant attorney general to stay away from that case, as it pertained to national security. Petersen relayed the president's order to the grand jury prosecutors.

By this time, Dean presented Nixon with a serious problem. Two days after the president's public statement, Dean released his own statement. In it he expressed the belief that the Watergate "case will be fully and justly handled by the grand jury and the Ervin select committee." Then, in a comment aimed at Nixon, Haldeman, and Ehrlichman, Dean warned, "Some may hope or think that I will become a scapegoat in the Watergate case. Anyone who believes this does not know me, know the true facts nor understand our system of justice." This marked the first public glimpse of the tug-of-war between the president and his counsel.

The same day, April 19, the *Washington Post* devoted half of its front page to what had been learned about Magruder's testimony to prosecutors. Mitchell and Dean, the article opened, "approved and helped plan the Watergate bugging operation," and the two of them "later arranged to buy the silence of the seven convicted Watergate conspirators." Magruder's story, the *Post* stated, rested on "three sources in the White House and the Committee for the Re-election of the President." That same day the *New York Times* carried a five-column headline about Watergate and reported, among other things, that the grand jury had shifted emphasis from the break-in to the cover-up.

Interest in the cover-up increased after each testimony, especially after Mitchell acknowledged to reporters that he had been present at meetings when Liddy offered his plans to burglarize the Democratic campaign headquarters and illegally tap telephones. Yet as the nation's attorney general, Mitchell had taken an oath to uphold the law. On April 25 the *Arkansas Democrat* called Mitchell's admission "the most damaging event in the Watergate scandal" because "until last week, Mitchell had insisted that he knew nothing whatsoever about Watergate." The editorial writers doubted that Nixon knew about Watergate in advance but warned that "the American people can forgive a mistake but not a cover-up."

Appearing on *Meet the Press* three days later, Republican Senator Edward W. Brooke expressed his view that it was "inconceivable" that Nixon did not know in advance of the Liddy plan to tap the telephones in the Democratic headquarters. Two days after Brooke's stunning conclusion, the *Washington Star* described a previously unknown $500,000 fund that Herbert Kalmbach kept for political projects. The same day, Ken Rietz, an aide to the Republican's national chairman, George Bush, resigned after a Woodward and Bernstein article revealed that Rietz had taken part in dirty tricks as a CREEP official during the 1972 campaign.

On April 25, the day after the Kalmbach and Rietz stories, the *Washington Post* published a new account of fraud, detailing the manipulation of public opinion by CREEP and the White House, following the mining of the North Vietnamese harbor of Haiphong in May 1972. According to the article, CREEP placed an advertisement in the *New York Times* that suggested most Americans supported the mining, giving the appearance that a group of ordinary citizens had sponsored the advertisement. CREEP failed to identify itself as sponsor and, in violation of campaign disclosure laws, failed to report paying for it. At the same time, officials at CREEP had arranged for a flood of telegrams and postcards to reach the White House in support of the mining. In response, Ron Ziegler maintained that the public overwhelmingly supported the president's action.

A bigger story broke the next day. Senator Weicker informed the press that L. Patrick Gray had burned two folders of documents that had been taken from the safe in Howard Hunt's White House office. Weicker reported that Ehrlichman and Dean had given Gray the folders soon after the June 1972 break-in. One folder contained State Department documents that Hunt had doctored to implicate, falsely, President Kennedy in the 1963 assassination of Ngo Dinh Diem, president of South Vietnam. The other folder contained material Hunt had assembled about Senator Ted Kennedy's automobile accident on Chappaquiddick Island in 1969. Gray quickly withdrew his name for confirmation as director of the FBI.

Another disturbing development started to unfold on April 26. In a Los Angeles courtroom, federal Judge W. Matthew Byrne Jr. received material from the Justice Department, read it, announced that government prosecutors had withheld evidence, and dismissed the jury. Daniel Ellsberg was then on trial, charged with publicly disclosing the secret Pentagon Papers. In court the next day, Judge Byrne read aloud a document, and the public learned that Gordon Liddy and Howard Hunt, while employed at the White House, had burglarized the office of Dr. Lewis Fielding, Ellsberg's psychiatrist.

The rapid-fire succession of disclosures prompted Republican leaders such as Senator Robert Dole of Kansas, former party chairman, and George Romney, former secretary of housing and urban development, to demand action to clear up the Watergate affair. Senator Charles H. Percy (R-Ill.) proposed that a special independent prosecutor, rather than the Justice Department, should investigate Watergate.

This pressure from Republicans worried Nixon, especially because he feared more disclosures. The next day he expressed his fear to Petersen that

Dean already had made "statements to the prosecuting team, implicating the President. . . . Now, Henry, this I've got to know." Petersen left the president's office immediately, telephoned to check, returned, and reported that Dean's lawyer had indicated his client might accuse the president but had not yet done so. Petersen reiterated that he had told the prosecutors that "we have no mandate to investigate the President. We investigate Watergate." He then confessed, however, "I don't know where that line draws." In another conversation later that day, Nixon concluded, "It's his word against mine. Now for — who is going to believe John Dean?" He added, "Dean was the one who told us throughout the summer that nobody in the White House was involved when he, himself apparently, was involved, particularly on the critical angle of subordination of perjury."[23]

Petersen's constant supplying of information to Nixon, his insistence that the grand jury had "no mandate to investigate the President," and his close working relationship with Dean during summer 1972 convinced the grand jury prosecutors that Petersen was an inappropriate person with whom to communicate. The prosecutors, thereafter, stopped all contact with Petersen and the Justice Department.

A troubled Nixon spent the weekend of April 28 and 29 at Camp David, first in seclusion, then in a series of meetings with Secretary of State Rogers, Secretary of Defense Elliot L. Richardson, Ron Ziegler, and an aide, Leonard Garment. A tearful president also met with Haldeman, Ehrlichman, and Kleindienst to ask for their resignations. The next day he announced the resignations and called their acceptance "one of the most difficult decisions of my presidency."

The nation's newspapers continued to publish stories that added to Nixon's worries. On April 29 the *Washington Post* reported that Magruder and LaRue, according to "highly reliable sources," had both told prosecutors that Colson not only knew of the plans to bug Watergate but also had pressed to expedite the surveillance. Colson, who had resigned as Nixon's aide in March, had earlier denied advanced knowledge of the bugging plans. The *Post* also reported that the grand jury had started an investigation of Kalmbach for obstruction of justice in providing money to the Watergate burglars so they would remain silent.

That same day the Harris Poll released the results of its survey conducted April 18–23, before many of these disclosures. Of persons polled, only 9 percent replied "frank and honest" to the question, "Do you feel that the White House has been frank and honest on the Watergate affair, or do you feel they have withheld important information about it?" Sixty-three percent responded that they believed the White House had "withheld important information."

On Monday, April 30, Judge Byrne revealed that earlier that month, while presiding over the Ellsberg trial, he once met with Nixon and twice met with Ehrlichman. At the meetings, they discussed Byrne's possible interest in the directorship of the FBI. Because the president favored an Ellsberg conviction and had said so publicly, the meetings gave the appearance of a presidential attempt to influence a conviction.

On the same day of Judge Byrne's disclosure, Nixon announced one result of his weekend assessment of the impact of the various Watergate revelations: the resignations of Kleindienst, Haldeman, and Ehrlichman and the firing of John Dean. In the case of the first three, he released their letters of resignation. The attorney general stated that his "close personal and professional associations" with persons who "could be involved in conduct violative of the laws" compelled him to resign. Haldeman maintained he needed time "to clear up" the false "allegations and innuendoes" against him. Ehrlichman also expressed that the need for time to straighten out incorrect allegations prevented him from carrying out his official responsibilities. Nixon named Leonard Garment as counsel to the president and Elliot Richardson as attorney general.

At 9:00 P.M. that evening, flanked by a bust of Abraham Lincoln and a photographer's portrait of his family, Nixon addressed the nation. To the televised audience he said that the news of the June 1972 break-in had "appalled" him and the news that the burglars worked for CREEP "shocked" him. "Until March of this year," he continued, "I remained convinced that the denials were true and that the charges of involvement by members of the White House staff were false." On March 21, having received "new information," he reported that he "personally assumed the responsibility for coordinating intensive new inquiries into the matter." He called Haldeman and Ehrlichman "two of the finest public servants it has been my privilege to know" and identified Kleindienst as "a distinguished public servant, my personal friend for twenty years." The new attorney general, Nixon continued, would have "the authority to name a special supervising prosecutor for matters arising out of the case." In explaining how Watergate occurred, Nixon said he had delegated to others "the day-to-day campaign decisions." But he failed to blame those persons; "that would be a cowardly thing to do. . . . In any organization, the man at the top must bear the responsibility. . . . I accept it." Before concluding his address, the president added, "We must maintain the integrity of the White House. . . . There can be no whitewash at the White House."[24]

Newspaper editorials evaluating Nixon's speech ranged from the belief that he had resolved the problem to the position that he had accomplished nothing. The *Arkansas Democrat* concluded that the president's actions, explanations, and promises "will be good enough for everyone but those people who have always believed Mr. Nixon kicked dogs, and they will never be satisfied with anything he does."[25] The *Des Moines Register* thought that "the President ought to be eager to provide documentation and testimony that would support his assertions."[26] The *Virginian Pilot* asserted that "to accept the story that Mr. Nixon, ostrich like, was unaware of the implications of Watergate for many months requires the willing suspension of disbelief."[27] In Montana, the *Billings Gazette* commented: "The very thought of a United States President having to appear before the people who gave him such a mandate to admit he had been duped, shown bad judgment in the selection of his cohorts, and been too busy to watch the store does not make a strong case for credibility in his actions."[28] The *Philadelphia Evening Bulletin* also questioned Nixon's credibility: "The flaw to full disclosure with credibility in Watergate investigation all along has been that the Nixon administration has been investigating the Nixon administration and its appendage, the Committee to Re-elect the President. That flaw remains."[29] The *Twin City Sentinel* in Winston-Salem, North Carolina, took issue with the president: "He said he was 'appalled' when he first heard about the break-in and bugging at Democratic headquarters last June 17. But if he was really appalled, the record does not bear him out. Two days after the arrest his press secretary was authorized to belittle the crime as a 'third-rate burglary attempt.'" In the same vein, the editorial continued, "he gently praised the press for bringing the wrongdoing to light. But for ten months all of the power of the White House had been used to discredit what the press was reporting." The editors concluded that to believe that Mitchell, Kalmbach, Haldeman, Ehrlichman, and others never told Nixon about their Watergate actions "is to indict Mr. Nixon for absolute incompetence as an administrator."[30] The *New York Times* pointed out that Nixon conceded only what the country already knew, that he "failed to resolve" the crisis and that "the whole trend of future events remains in doubt."[31]

On balance, the editorials offered Nixon little comfort. He and his supporters could dismiss the *New York Times* as part of the biased anti-Nixon northeast, but sharp criticism from Virginia, North Carolina, Iowa, and Montana foreshadowed continued problems. The day after Nixon's address to the nation, Republicans in the Senate presented him with another threat, an independent investigation of Watergate.

Senator Charles H. Percy (R.-Ill.) introduced a "sense of the Senate" resolution, requesting the president to appoint a special prosecutor to head the Watergate investigation. Eleven Republicans and seven Democrats cosponsored the resolution. The handful of senators on the floor at the time approved the resolution by voice vote. Percy insisted that the executive branch should not investigate itself. The resolution called for Senate confirmation of the special prosecutor.

The same day, on the West Coast, Judge Byrne dropped another bombshell when he released a summary of the FBI interview with Ehrlichman made three days earlier. Ehrlichman stated that in July 1971 Nixon had directed him to investigate the Pentagon Papers case "independent[ly] of concurrent FBI investigation." Because the case focused on Ellsberg, Ehrlichman hired Hunt and Liddy to determine Ellsberg's "habits, mental attitudes, motives, etc." Ehrlichman said he never authorized the burglary of the office of Ellsberg's psychiatrist, and when he learned of it he told Hunt and Liddy "not to do this again." After Byrne released the FBI summary, Hunt described to one of the grand jury prosecutors the aid that he had obtained from the CIA for the Ellsberg burglary.

In yet another development the same day, the Justice Department, acting on a recommendation of the General Accounting Office, filed criminal charges against the Finance Committee to Re-elect the President. The charge accused the committee of concealing a $200,000 contribution from international financier Robert L. Vesco by not keeping records and by not reporting the contribution to the GAO as required by law.

The next week the CIA director James R. Schlesinger admitted before a Senate panel that his agency had been "insufficiently cautious" in loaning Hunt a miniature camera, a tape recorder, false identification papers, and disguises. The former deputy CIA director Robert E. Cushman Jr. testified that he had assisted Hunt because Ehrlichman had requested it. Although the 1947 law that established the CIA forbids the agency from carrying out internal security or law enforcement activities, and although Ehrlichman held the position of assistant to the president for domestic affairs, apparently no one at the CIA inquired about the nature of Hunt's assignment.

On May 11, Judge Byrne dismissed the Justice Department's case against Ellsberg. In his prepared statement, Byrne concluded that "governmental agencies had taken an unprecedented series of actions" and that "the totality of the circumstances of this case . . . offend 'a sense of justice.'"[32] The charges of burglary, bribery, and intentional withholding of information pointed directly at the office of the president. From upstate New York, the editors of the *Syracuse Herald–Journal*, who had supported Nixon in 1972, declared that "the tactics smack of Germany's Gestapo. And of stupidity." The *Nashville Tennessean* observed that "the Nixon administration's pretensions of concern for law and order in the nation are revealed as a monumental hoax on the American people."[33]

Three days after Judge Bryne's dismissal of the Ellsberg case, Senator Stuart Symington (D-Mo.) and chair of a Senate Armed Services subcommittee investigating the CIA's role in the Ellsberg case, released to the public information that outlined the White House attempt to get CIA assistance in the Watergate cover-up. Vernon Walters, who in April 1972 had become deputy director of the CIA, had submitted to the Symington subcommittee a memorandum he had written the previous summer recording his June 23, 1972, meeting with Ehrlichman and Haldeman, and as a result, his efforts to keep the FBI from investigating money laundering in Mexico and from questioning Kenneth Dahlberg. The Walters memorandum also included an account of John Dean's attempts to have the CIA post bond and make support payments to the Watergate burglars. Richard Helms, the CIA director during summer 1972, explained to the subcommittee that he and Walters had finally concluded that "some things" had gone "too far," and they had then stopped cooperating.

During the two a half months between the start of the Gray confirmation hearings at the end of February and the Helms appearance in mid-May, the various disclosures had destroyed Nixon's claim of White House noninvolvement and resulted in probable criminal indictment of most of his closest advisers. The involvement of Nixon's aides in the burglary of Dr. Lewis Fielding's office and of the Democratic Party's national headquarters enhanced the credibility of those investigating Watergate. Gray had compromised the FBI when he passed raw files to Dean and destroyed the Hunt records. The CIA, likewise, had compromised its professionalism. In the Ellsberg case, Ehrlichman and Nixon had so violated due process that Judge Byrne threw the case out of court. The public now knew that Nixon's appointments secretary, Dwight Chapin, and the president's personal attorney, Herbert Kalmbach, had hired Donald Segretti to perform "undercover activities" during the 1972 campaign. An ever increasing volume of incriminating testimony against Haldeman and Ehrlichman led top officials in the Justice Department, all of whom were Nixon appointees, to recommend the firing of the two assistants. Jeb Magruder, the director of CREEP, meanwhile had confessed to perjury and obstruction of justice. John Mitchell, Nixon's 1968 campaign manager, former attorney general, and head of CREEP until after Watergate, had admitted publicly that Liddy had submitted to him a plan to obtain "political intelligence."

During these ten weeks early in 1973 Nixon had sought to maintain control, despite a rising crescendo of devastating disclosures. First, the congressional, legal, and media reaction to his sweeping claim of executive privilege had forced him to retreat and to modify this claimed right to control information. Then, the reactions of Senate Republicans and those newspapers that had heretofore supported him compelled him to accept the future appointment of a special prosecutor. Moreover, the general mood of the country almost required him to acknowledge the positive role of the press in Watergate. In his address to the nation on April 30, Nixon paid tribute to the press for bringing "the facts to light." After his speech, he told White House reporters that "we have [had] our differences in the past, and I hope you will give me hell every time you think I'm wrong." The next day the White House apologized to the *Washington Post* for its consistent denunciations of its Watergate coverage. Six days later the newspaper won that year's Pulitzer Prize for journalism for its Watergate stories.

Public opinion polls added yet another pressure. The Gallup Poll periodically asked the same question to a systematically determined cross-section of voters: "Do you approve or disapprove of the way Richard Nixon is handling his job as President?" From his all-time high of a 68 percent approval rating at the end of January 1973, after he announced the treaty agreement ending American combat involvement in Vietnam, Nixon's rating steadily dropped as the public learned more and more about Watergate. By mid-May his approval rating stood at 44 percent. The mid-May poll results also indicated that 96 percent of Americans had heard or read about Watergate, 46 percent believed Nixon "knew in advance" about the break-in, and 56 percent believed that he participated in the cover-up. The Harris Poll the same month reported a 47 percent approval of Nixon's "overall job" as president. And from the Senate came two ominous forces that would present Nixon with his greatest challenge: the resolution calling for a special prosecutor and the Ervin Committee, both to investigate Watergate.

CHAPTER FIVE

The Senate Committee, Testimonies, and Butterfield Disclosure

Do you think President Nixon has participated in a cover-up of the Watergate situation, or not? Yes, 67 percent; No, 19 percent; No opinion, 14 percent
— Gallup Poll conducted June 1–4, 1973

The most important thing to this country was the reelection of Richard Nixon. And I was not about to countenance anything that would stand in the way of that reelection.
— John N. Mitchell, July 11, 1973

President Nixon had no knowledge of or involvement in either the Watergate affair itself or the subsequent efforts of a cover up of the Watergate. . . . I had no such knowledge or involvement.
— H. R. Haldeman, July 30, 1973

The unmasking of the cover-up moved into another stage on May 17, with the Senate Select Committee on Presidential Campaign Activities taking the central role. The nation's attention shifted away from the series of disclosures that began the end of February, involving McCord, Gray, Haldeman, Ehrlichman, Mitchell, Hunt, Magruder, and Liddy, among others. Each disclosure lessened Nixon's credibility concerning Watergate. Judge Sirica, catalyst for the second stage of the cover-up's undoing, and Bernstein and Woodward, catalyst for the first stage, continued to ferret out the truth about Watergate. Nonetheless, for two months the main spotlight shone on the Senate Watergate Committee.

Although the committee questioned thirty-three witnesses and television cameras covered the 237 hours of testimony, the most profound impact came from the appearances of the former presidential counsel John Dean and the former Haldeman assistant Alexander Butterfield. The committee carefully planned Dean's testimony to maximize its effect. Butterfield's disclosure of Nixon's taping system, on the other hand, surprised, even shocked, not only the public but even the persons involved in the Watergate investigations. Dean implicated Nixon in the cover-up, and Butterfield described the existence of a taping system that could resolve whether Nixon or Dean was telling the truth.

At 10:00 A.M. on May 17 Senator Sam Ervin called to order the Senate Select Committee. In his opening statement, Ervin declared that the committee began its work "in an atmosphere of the utmost gravity" and emphasized that "the purpose of these hearings is not prosecutorial or judicial, but rather investigative and informative." The vice chair of the committee, Howard Baker, reiterated these points and added that "any doubts that I might have had about the fairness and impartiality of this investigation have been swept away during the last few weeks. Virtually every action taken by this committee since its inception has been taken with complete unanimity of purpose and procedure." The Tennessee senator characterized the committee's preliminary work as "a bipartisan search for the unvarnished truth."

Room 318 in the Old Senate Office Building, known as the Caucus Room, had been the site of several earlier notable Senate investigations. The most recent included the Estes Kefauver investigation of organized crime (1950–1951), the so-called Army–McCarthy Hearings on communist infiltration of government (1954), and the J. William Fulbright investigation of the Vietnam conflict (1966). These and other hearings had been televised nationally, and public reaction played an important role in the future careers of the major participants. The Kefauver Hearings propelled the Tennessean into national prominence and into serious contention for the Democratic presidential nomination in 1952 and 1956. The Army–McCarthy Hearings eroded Joseph McCarthy's support and led to a Senate censure of his conduct. The Fulbright Hearings fueled opposition to U.S. involvement in Vietnam and made that opposition more respectable.

The Senate's decision to allow television coverage of the Watergate Hearings, therefore, constituted part of a pattern dating to the early years of television. For the first two weeks, the three networks — ABC, CBS, and NBC — carried the hearings live. Starting the third week, despite large audiences, the networks agreed to rotate live coverage so that at any time two networks could broadcast their regular shows. The new Public Broadcasting Service (PBS), meanwhile, taped the entire event and replayed the hearings in the evenings on approximately 150 to 160 PBS stations.

Television news summarized the day's highlights, and the newspapers did the same the following day. Few Americans could avoid the hearings. The average rating for the proceedings exceeded the average rating for entertainment aired at similar hours. An early August Gallup survey found that almost

90 percent of Americans had watched at least part of the hearings. At the end of May the hearings recessed for a week for the Memorial Day holiday; in June they recessed for another week when the Soviet leader Leonid Brezhnev visited Washington; and they recessed for ten days over the July 4 break. Brezhnev's visit and that of the Shah of Iran in July were low-key. During summer 1973 the international scene remained quiet; the Watergate Hearings dominated the news.[1]

Sam Dash and his staff, with crucial support from Ervin, planned the hearings carefully. They had spent weeks interviewing those involved in the break-in and cover-up and scheduled those witnesses so that their testimony and answers to questions would tell the story in sequence. The committee first wanted a clear understanding of how CREEP operated and its relationship to White House staff. Robert C. Odle Jr., former director of administration for CREEP, and Bruce A. Kehrli, special assistant to the president, the first two witnesses, elaborated on organization charts and transfer of personnel from the White House to CREEP. Three Washington, D.C. police officers who participated in the arrest at Democratic National Headquarters testified next.

On the second day of hearings, James W. McCord Jr. took the stand. In reply to Dash's questioning, McCord explained how he had burglarized the building and taped the door and that Liddy and Hunt had told him that John Mitchell, John Dean, and Jeb Magruder had approved the operation. McCord described how he had been pressured by the White House aide who had hired him, John Caulfield, to remain silent and had in turn been promised financial support, rehabilitation, employment, and presidential clemency. Caulfield, at this time a Treasury Department official, testified next and confirmed McCord's story. He related that Dean said the offer of clemency to McCord came from "the highest levels of the White House." McCord, Caulfield continued, "wanted his immediate freedom," and if he did not get it, he threatened to make a public statement about Watergate.[2]

President Nixon attempted to counter the interest the committee generated. The day before the hearings opened, he publicly proposed to Congress the establishment of a nonpartisan, federal election commission "to examine our laws and see what new ones are needed, but also to examine the observance and enforcement of our laws, and those campaign standards and practices not governed by law but rooted in common usage." Such a commission could produce "a set of proposals that will work and that will help to restore the faith of the American people in the integrity of their political process."[3] The Senate, of course, believed that it already had assigned the committee responsibilities identical to those that Nixon outlined for a newly formed commission.

McCord's testimony about the offer of clemency, moreover, spurred Nixon to reply. Because McCord testified on a Friday, the president had the weekend to draft a statement. Nixon's 4,000-word report went well beyond a denial. He explained that the "three security operations initiated in my Administration"—the 1969–1971 wiretaps, the 1970 Huston Plan, and the Special Investigations Unit in the White House — stemmed from national security needs. The president reiterated his position that he neither knew nor approved of illegal activities. Regarding Watergate, he considered it his "responsibility to see that the Watergate investigation did not impinge adversely upon the national security area." Once again, Nixon categorically denied having "prior knowledge of the Watergate operation," having taken part in a cover-up, offering clemency or funds, or authorizing "others to attempt to implicate the CIA in the Watergate matter."[4]

The media response to Nixon's lengthy explanation varied. The *Los Angeles Herald Examiner* concluded that "President Nixon's strong, comprehensive statement . . . clearly shows that the President himself was not involved." The *Washington Post* saw no such clarity. Between the two extremes, the *Wall Street Journal* found Nixon's statement about the break-in "a plausible and even persuasive explanation of events" but viewed his comments about the cover-up "far less persuasive" and "a pity" that he had not made them "long ago." Overall, the editorial concluded, "the President is acting like a man with something to hide."

In the midst of the Ervin Committee's opening and Nixon's response, the Office of Special Prosecutor was opened. Attorney General Elliot Richardson, at the time of his confirmation hearings, had promised to act promptly on the Senate's unanimous endorsement of Senator Charles Percy's resolution. Richardson's announced intention to retain "ultimate authority," however, was criticized by the president of the American Bar Association and drew rejections of Richardson's first four choices. Aware of what was at stake, Richardson retreated with his image slightly tarnished. He telephoned Harvard law professor Archibald Cox, offered him the position, and promised complete autonomy. Respected for his ability, experience, independence, and honesty, Cox had served the Kennedy administration as solicitor general, the official who represents the federal government before the Supreme Court. On May 21, Cox appeared with Richardson for questioning before the Senate Judiciary Committee; two days later the Senate confirmed his nomination by an eighty-two to three vote.

The sixty-one-year-old Cox immediately antagonized the Ervin Committee when he called a press conference to announce his opposition to public hearings and then petitioned Judge Sirica to postpone the hearings until the Special Prosecutor's Office made its own investigation and prosecuted any criminals it found. Ervin rejected Cox's request. Arguing the committee's position before Sirica, Dash relied heavily on a position that Cox himself had taken while solicitor general. The law overwhelmingly supported the rejection decision that Sirica rendered. Cox did not appeal but set to work.

Cox posed a long-range threat to Nixon, but the clash between the CIA and the president's former closest aides, Haldeman and Ehrlichman, served to erode public confidence. On May 21, while the former CIA director Richard Helms appeared before the Senate Foreign Relations Committee, the agency's deputy director Vernon A. Walters testified before the House Armed Services Intelligence Subcommittee. Walters told of his and Helms's June 23, 1972, meeting, at Haldeman and Ehrlichman's initiative, during which the White House aides had asked the CIA to block FBI investigation of Watergate. Walters's notes of the meeting recorded Haldeman as stating "it is the President's wish." The Senate Foreign Relations Committee had heard Walters testify a week earlier and asked Helms if he remembered Haldeman's exact words. Helms did not but said that at the time he assumed Haldeman spoke for the president. Both Helms and Walters swore that Haldeman and Ehrlichman both knew the CIA had no involvement in the Watergate break-in before they requested the June 23 meeting.

On May 30 and 31 the two former aides testified before the Senate Appropriations Subcommittee about the role of the CIA in the Watergate affair. Directly contradicting the two top CIA administrators, Haldeman and Ehrlichman insisted that the White House had not attempted to obtain CIA assistance in blocking the FBI's investigation. Walters and Helms seemed credible; Haldeman's and Ehrlichman's denials did not. The damage to Nixon was obvious.

During the exchange of contradictory testimonies, the *New York Times* reported that in 1969 and again in 1970 the CIA had investigated but had found "no substantial evidence to support the Nixon administration's view that foreign governments were supplying undercover agents and funds to radicals and Black Panther groups."[5] This finding undercut Nixon's more recent statement that "some of the disruptive activities were receiving foreign support," a factor that he used as partial explanation for the drafting of the Huston Plan. Two weeks later the *New York Times* published a text of the plan. Several accompanying documents identified its proposed operations as "clearly illegal."

The last week of May a minor incident regarding Nixon's San Clemente house eroded a bit more of the president's credibility. On May 25, in response to a charge that Nixon had used campaign funds to buy the house, his office issued a statement detailing how the president had financed the purchase of the house and surrounding land and how he later sold some of the acreage. The next day the deputy press secretary Gerald L. Warren advised reporters that the government had spent $39,525 on the property to improve security, most of it for a protective screen and fence. Two days later, however, the Associated Press reported that it had checked the building permits that were public record and learned that the government really had spent more than $100,000 on property improvements, not all of them related to security. Within the next month, the General Services Administration, which has charge of such work, three times revised its original figure of $39,525 that Warren originally had released. The final account totaled $703,365 and included the installation of a swimming pool heater and $4,834 for den furniture.

On June 5 the Ervin Committee resumed hearings following the Memorial Day recess. Of the first six witnesses who testified between that date and June 14, five left no doubt that Nixon's closest aides were implicated in the Watergate break-in and cover-up. On the first day Sally J. Harmony, a former secretary to Liddy, told of typing summaries of wiretapped telephone conversations and using stationery with a Gemstone letterhead (the code name for Liddy's intelligence operation). Harmony also recalled viewing photographs of documents from the Democratic National Committee headquarters and shredding files after the break-in.

The next witness, twenty-six-year-old Robert Reisner, an administrative assistant to Magruder, remembered sending Gemstone documents to Mitchell. Reisner also recalled that copies of all memos that went to Mitchell also went to Haldeman. Reisner said that Magruder, the afternoon following the break-in, telephoned from California and directed the office manager, Robert Odle, to take home the Gemstone folder.

Hugh W. Sloan Jr., the former treasurer of CREEP, provided the committee an account of how Magruder and Frederick C. LaRue, one of Mitchell's assistants, had pressured him to commit perjury regarding Liddy's budget. Sloan also disclosed that Dean had requested that he take the Fifth Amendment. Unwilling to follow either suggestion, the thirty-two-year-old Sloan resigned from CREEP. On June 7 Nixon's 1972 director of scheduling, Herbert L. Porter, during his testimony admitted that with Magruder's encouragement he had perjured himself at the Watergate burglary trial.

Maurice H. Stans, the chairman of the Finance Committee of CREEP, on the other hand, declared himself free of blame and of any knowledge of the Segretti dirty tricks program, the break-in, and the cover-up. He emphasized that his committee only raised money and paid bills. During heated questioning by Senator Ervin, Stans insisted that there was no connection between the break-in and his destruction six days later of the records of campaign contributions made before April 7, 1972. He said he destroyed them to protect the anonymity of contributors and because no law required keeping them.

Magruder took the stand on June 14 for what became a five-hour session. He began by reading a brief prepared statement admitting "errors in judgment" and pointing out that as far as he knew "at no point during this entire period from the time of planning of the Watergate to the time of trying to keep it from public view did the President have any knowledge of our errors in this matter." The cooperative Magruder added that in his desire to "give you the facts" he would "name others who participated with me in the Watergate affair."[6]

The "others" were those who worked closest to the president. Magruder claimed that Mitchell had authorized Liddy's espionage activities, that Colson had pressured the men to get them under way, and that Haldeman's chief aide, Gordon Strachan, had read summaries of taped telephone conversations from the Democratic National Committee and knew of the Watergate plans in advance. Contradicting Stans, Magruder recounted meeting with him and Mitchell on June 24, 1972, to discuss the break-in. Magruder also described the involvement of Mitchell, Haldeman, Dean, and others in the cover-up. During his testimony, Magruder admitted to having repeatedly perjured himself and to having persuaded Porter to do the same before the grand jury and at the Watergate trial. Despite the incriminating nature of Magruder's testimony, the former CREEP director was only a preliminary episode in the proceedings, because his confessions and charges stopped at the door of the Oval Office. The main event would be John Dean, who, as everyone who followed Watergate knew, would incriminate the president.

Between Magruder's and Dean's testimonies, the hearings recessed for a week in deference to the Brezhnev-Nixon meetings in Washington. Tension mounted during the wait because of disclosures published in the *New York Times,* the *Washington Post,* and *Time.* At the beginning of the hiatus on June 16, Dean met for five hours in executive session with Dash, Baker, and their staff members, and what he told them was soon leaked to members of the press. They reported that when the hearings resumed, Dean would charge Nixon with participation in the cover-up and with an attempt to stop tax audits of friends; he would describe Hunt's demand for money in return for his silence and Mitchell's acquiescence in Hunt's demand. Press reports also asserted that Dean would claim that Haldeman had ordered the telephone tap on the chair of the Democratic National Committee and that Colson had prior knowledge of the taps.

Another press story described the April 15, 1973, meeting of Assistant Attorney General Henry Petersen, the president, and then Attorney General Richard Kleindienst, at which Petersen had urged the president to suspend Haldeman and Ehrlichman because of their integral involvement in the cover-up. The story reminded readers that on April 30, when the president publicly announced the resignations of his two assistants, he had emphasized that the resignations were not "evidence of any wrong doing by either one. Such an assumption would be unfair and unfounded."

The press also reported Dean's story that he had custody of $15,200 in leftover 1972 campaign funds and that he borrowed $4,850 of the money, leaving his personal check as a record, to finance his marriage and honeymoon. Dean repaid the money and deposited the entire amount in a special account when he left the White House on April 30, 1973. Hugh Scott, the Republican leader in the Senate, at his daily news briefing, used this information in an attempt to discredit Dean. Scott concluded that "a man who can embezzle can easily tell lies." The next day Scott added that the story had "considerably shaken" Dean's credibility. Because of the leaks to the press from the June 16 executive session, Ervin canceled the scheduled additional executive sessions.

In the midst of the Ervin Committee revelations, the federal district court in Washington, D.C., found the Finance Committee of CREEP guilty of concealing the $200,000 cash contribution from financier Robert L. Vesco. The court ordered the maximum possible penalty, a $3,000 fine. Five months earlier the Finance Committee had pled no contest for its failure to report cash payments to Liddy.

On June 25 Dean finally took the stand as the person the Watergate Committee assumed would be its most important witness. For six weeks during May and June, Dash had questioned Dean; only Ervin knew of the meetings. The Dash-Dean sessions gave Dash background information and helped Dean jog his memory and organize his recollections. Because of these sessions, Dean came to the hearings well prepared. The first day he read, for more than five hours, a 245-page statement describing the mood of the White House staff as well as the events themselves.

He opened with his conclusion that "the Watergate matter was an inevitable outgrowth of a climate of excessive concern over the political impact of demonstrators, excessive concern over leaks, an insatiable appetite for political intelligence, all coupled with a do-it-yourself White House staff, regardless of the law." Dean then told, among other things, of the political intelligence work of Jack Caulfield and Anthony Ulasewicz, the meetings regarding Liddy's plan, and the details of the cover-up. Almost immediately after the break-in, Dean maintained, "a pattern had developed where I was carrying messages from Mitchell, Stans, and Mardian to Ehrlichman and Haldeman — and vice versa — about how each quarter was handling the cover-up." Dean related Nixon's involvement in the cover-up and his instructions to Dean "to keep a good list of the press people giving us trouble, because we will make life difficult for them after the elections." According to Dean, the president wanted to have the Internal Revenue Service harass his "enemies."

In a solemn, unemotional voice Dean recounted his first meeting with Nixon on September 15, 1972. Dean left "with the impression that the President was well aware of what had been going on regarding the success of keeping the White House out of the Watergate scandal." He later described his March 21, 1973, meeting with the president, a meeting during which Dean likened the cover-up to "a cancer growing on the Presidency and that if the cancer was not removed that the President himself would be killed by it." Dean claimed to have told Nixon that the cover-up could not continue and had further recommended that the president "get out in front of this matter." To Dean's disappointment, he realized later that day that Nixon planned to continue the cover-up.[7]

For the next four days the committee and its staff questioned Dean; one side emphasized events to establish complicity and the other side to discredit his testimony. At stake was Nixon's presidency. Dean, who had challenged the president and accused him of criminal activities, proved an unshakable witness to Nixon's defenders. Years later Dash called Dean the most impressive witness he had ever observed.

During his initial questioning of Dean, the Republican vice chair of the Watergate Committee framed what became the central question in the entire investigation: "What did the President know and when did he know it?"[8] By posing this question, Senator Baker intended to protect Nixon, in essence, by forcing investigators to produce specific evidence tying Nixon to the break-in or the cover-up. In reality, Baker's clear question accentuated the Nixon-Dean polarization. Nixon and his supporters, however, believed that in such a polarization the public would side with the president, without evidence to the contrary.

Although newspaper editorials cautioned readers that Dean's charges were uncorroborated, the *Dallas Times Herald* observed that the testimony had "set off shock waves" and had driven Nixon "into a grave defensive position that now demands credible refutation." The *Nashville Tennessean* believed that Dean's charges could "be answered only in the same open way — and by the President himself." Dean bore the onus of an administration turncoat and a lawyer who in the past had lied, but much of what he described concurred with the testimonies of Magruder, Walters, Helms, and McCord. Dean's testimony also conformed to the numerous newspaper stories based on leaks from grand jury and Justice Department investigations.

When Dean completed his testimony on Friday, June 29, the Ervin Committee recessed the hearings until July 10. During this break Watergate stories continued to attract national attention. On June 28, just before Dean finished, Hunt testified before the House Armed Services Subcommittee on Intelligence that he had used CIA equipment in his investigations. The next day Colson admitted that he had sent Hunt to find scandalous information about Senator Ted Kennedy. Colson also admitted to having allowed a reporter to read classified State Department cables. The same day Ehrlichman appeared on a CBS–TV interview and repeated his claim that he had played no part in the Watergate break-in or cover-up.

On July 4, CBS–TV presented a "status report" on the Watergate investigation conducted by Justice Department prosecutors Seymour Glanzer, Earl Silbert, and Donald Campbell. This report, sent to Special Prosecutor Cox, recommended the indictment of Mitchell, Dean, Ehrlichman, and Haldeman. In addition, it recommended reduced charges in exchange for guilty pleas by Magruder, Gray, and Strachan.

Two days later the chairman of American Airlines, George A. Spater, released a statement admitting that his airline illegally contributed $55,000 to Nixon's campaign. Federal laws prohibited political contributions from corporations. Spater explained that Herbert W. Kalmbach, Nixon's personal attorney, had solicited the money.

On July 7, Senator Ervin released to the press, with the prior consent of Nixon, a copy of the letter the president had sent advising that "I shall not testify before the Committee or permit access to Presidential papers." Nixon explained as his reason the "constitutional obligation to preserve intact the powers and prerogatives of the Presidency." Elaborating on his position, Nixon cited President Harry S. Truman as a precedent; in 1953 the former president had refused to honor a House Committee subpoena for documents.[9] The day after Nixon's refusal, two committee members, Democrat Herman Talmadge and Republican Edward J. Gurney, appeared on ABC–TV's *Issues and Answers* and criticized Nixon's position, although they agreed that their committee lacked the authority to subpoena the president.

On July 9, Tom Charles Huston, a former White House assistant, testified about the 1970 intelligence-gathering plan that bore his name and that he had helped draft. He told the House Armed Services Intelligence Subcommittee that Nixon never formally canceled the plan as he had claimed in his speech to the nation on May 22, 1973. Also on July 9, the *New York Times* reported that during the 1972 campaign, White House officials operated two programs to sabotage Democratic presidential candidates. The public learned that two of Haldeman's assistants, Dwight Chapin and Gordon Strachan, conceived of one program and, after Haldeman's approval, hired Donald Segretti to implement the dirty tricks operation. Magruder managed the second sabotage program, with help from Colson. Unreported campaign contributions financed both programs.

The Ervin Committee reconvened, with John Mitchell as its first witness. Mitchell, appearing under a subpoena, offered no opening statement and during his two and a half days of questioning volunteered little information in his generally terse answers. Repeatedly, he contradicted the testimonies of Dean and Magruder and insisted that the president had no prior knowledge of the break-in and was unaware of the cover-up. Mitchell acknowledged that he knew of the cover-up payments to the burglars and of perjured testimonies but never told Nixon that Haldeman, Ehrlichman, and others had committed these crimes. When Senator Talmadge asked Mitchell why he withheld this information, the former attorney general replied, "The reelection of Richard Nixon, compared to what was available on the other side, was so much more important."

Mitchell further explained that he learned of what he labeled "the White House Horrors" only after the Watergate break-in. These included the proposed bombing of the Brookings Institute, the forging of State Department cables to implicate President Kennedy in the assassination of South Vietnamese president Ngo Dinh Diem, the unauthorized wiretapping, the burglary of the office of Daniel Ellsberg's psychiatrist, and the secret investigations of Senator Ted Kennedy's Chappaquiddick accident, among other activities. Mitchell believed that had the president known of these horrors he would have "lowered the boom" and enforced the law in these areas and, by doing so, would have endangered his reelection.

During the second day of questioning, in response to Senator Daniel Inouye, Mitchell explained again that "my reasons — my motives — had to do with an entirely different subject matter and that had to do with the White House horror stories, not the Watergate." To Senator Baker, Mitchell repeated his rationale "that the most important thing to this country was the reelection of Richard Nixon. And I was not about to countenance anything that would stand in the way of that reelection."[10] Mitchell remained defiant to the end, although to believe him meant to disbelieve Magruder, Dean, Reisner, McCord, Stans, and Sloan. The public rated Mitchell accordingly. Indeed, both the Gallup and Harris Polls found that the public viewed Dean more favorably than Mitchell, Ehrlichman, or Haldeman.[11]

Richard A. Moore, the special public relations counsel to Nixon, testified after Mitchell. The fifty-eight-year-old Moore contradicted Dean's testimony several times, although he said Dean reported accurately the substance of their private conversations. Dash considered Moore "a White House apologist and genteel hatchet man against John Dean." On occasion, Dean had mentioned that he confided in Moore, but beyond that Moore's name rarely surfaced during the hearings.

While the committee questioned Moore, in another room two majority staff members, Scott Armstrong and Gordon Eugene Boyce, and one minority counsel, Donald G. Sanders, questioned Alexander Butterfield in routine preparation for his appearance before the committee. At the time, Butterfield headed the Federal Aviation Administration, but from January 1969 to March 1973 the former career air force officer had served as Haldeman's immediate deputy. As a friend of Haldeman since college, Butterfield enjoyed his confidence and after January 1970 assumed many of Haldeman's administrative duties. Butterfield's office door was next to the Oval Office. He traveled with the president whenever Haldeman stayed in Washington. In spring 1971, when Nixon decided he wanted a White House taping system installed to preserve a record of conversations, Haldeman gave the assignment to Butterfield, who made the arrangements with the Secret Service. Only Butterfield, his secretary, two or perhaps three Secret Service officers, Nixon, Haldeman, and Haldeman's aide, Lawrence Higby, knew of the system, which taped approximately 4,000 hours of telephone conversations and meetings in the Oval Office, the presidential office in the Old Executive Office Building, Camp David, the Cabinet Room, and the Lincoln Sitting Room.

During the questioning of Butterfield, Armstrong asked him how the White House kept records of conversations between the president and his aides. As he posed the question, he handed Butterfield a copy of the notes from the president's Watergate attorney, J. Fred Buzhardt, summarizing the subjects Dean and Nixon had discussed in twenty-three conversations. Butterfield only partially answered the question. Later in the session, Sanders commented that Dean once expressed a suspicion that Nixon had taped one of their conversations and asked Butterfield if Dean had reason for his suspicion. Butterfield could not evade such a direct question without lying, and he was too honest to do that. Although Butterfield thought that perhaps Higby or Haldeman already had revealed the existence of the taping system, he learned later that they had not and that his answer to Sanders had given the committee the single most explosive bit of information it would receive during its investigation.

Butterfield was immediately called to testify publicly at 2:00 P.M. on Monday, July 16. Because Sanders, who had asked Butterfield the key question, worked for the minority side of the committee, Baker requested that Dash permit Fred Thompson, the minority counsel, to start the questioning. Asking routine questions about the deputy's White House responsibilities, Thompson inquired, "Mr. Butterfield, are you aware of the installation of any listening devices in the Oval Office of the President?" Butterfield replied, "I was aware of listening devices; yes, sir." After thirty minutes, Ervin thanked Butterfield and dismissed him. He then announced that he had just received a letter, dated that day, from Buzhardt, Nixon's counsel. The letter confirmed Butterfield's testimony "that the President's meetings and conversations in the White House have been recorded since the spring of 1971." Actually, the taping system first began operating on February 16 that year.[12]

With Butterfield's announcement, the tapes immediately became the focal point of the Watergate affair. Dean had told the country that the president was deeply involved, but neither he nor anyone else could offer documentary evidence to corroborate the charge. The tapes held the truth. Without the documentary evidence that the tapes supplied, Nixon might have prevailed in his struggle to remain in office. Even after the court subpoena, Nixon might well have avoided impeachment had he shredded or burned the tapes, repeated the importance of presidential confidentiality, and left the courts and Congress to take whatever actions they wished.

The day the public learned about the taping system, Nixon was in the hospital with viral pneumonia, but apparently he had made a decision about the tapes earlier. In his memoirs, he wrote that he first listened to some of the tapes on June 3 and concluded that although embarrassing and ambiguous, "they indisputably disproved Dean's basic charge that I had conspired with him in an obstruction of justice over an eight-month period." Nixon also agreed with the premise "that destruction of the tapes would create an indelible impression of guilt."[13] Moreover, he believed in July 1973 that the courts would sustain the concept of executive privilege, based on the separation of powers between the legislative, judicial, and executive branches. Originally, Nixon wanted the tapes so that he could draw from them when writing his memoirs and so that future historians would have a detailed record of his administration. Ever distrustful, he also thought that some of the persons with whom he had held discussions might later distort his or their position or advice. The tapes would offer the truth. Nixon knew, furthermore, that Presidents Kennedy and Johnson had taped conversations and that their presidential libraries housed those tapes. Nixon planned to leave similar material. Future generations of scholars, he believed, removed from the passions of an anti-Nixon generation, would evaluate him more favorably and would downplay the importance of Watergate. Nixon believed that in the history of his administration the Watergate cover-up should be a footnote, compared to his brilliant orchestration of withdrawal of troops from Vietnam, of Soviet détente, and of relations with the People's Republic of China. Nixon's mistaken judgment in this instance cost him his presidency. The demand for release of the tapes came from Republicans as well as Democrats, from conservatives as well as liberals, and from Nixon's supporters as well as his critics.

Watergate Complex in 1973 (Copyright Bettmann/CORBIS)

Washington Post *reporters Carl Bernstein and Bob Woodward in 1973 (AP/Wide World Photos)*

The president with John Ehrlichman, presidential assistant (National Archives)

H. R. Haldeman, chief of staff (National Archives)

"Heee's makin' a list, checkin' it twice! Gonna find out who's naughty or nice . . ." *Charles Colson, presidential assistant, and the enemies list, 1973* (Doonesbury, *copyright G. B. Trudeau. Reprinted with permission of Universal Press Syndicate. All rights reserved.*)

Judge John J. Sirica (Washington Star)

Senate Watergate Committee hearing room (Washington Star)

Howard Baker and Sam Ervin (U.S. Senate Historical Office)

Howard Baker, Sam Ervin, and Samuel Dash (Washington Star)

John Mitchell on his way to testify (Washington Star)

Presidential Press Conference, October 26, 1973 (National Archives)

John Dean testifying (U.S. Senate Historical Office)

John Ehrlichman testifying (U.S. Senate Historical Office)

Nixon announces to the nation that he is releasing transcripts of the tapes, April 29, 1974 (National Archives)

Peter Rodino (Democrat, New Jersey), Jerome Zeifman (committee counsel), and Larry Hogan (Republican, Maryland) of the House Judiciary Committee (Washington Star)

Hugh Scott (Republican, Pennsylvania), Barry Goldwater (Republican, Arizona), and John Rhodes (Republican, Arizona) outside the White House after meeting with the president, August 7, 1974 (National Archives)

President Nixon, with a clean desk, meeting with Vice President Ford, August 9, 1974. (National Archives)

President Nixon, with family, saying goodbye to staff, August 9, 1974 (National Archives)

The Fords and the Nixons exchange goodbyes, August 9, 1974 (National Archives)

President Nixon waves farewell, August 9, 1974 (National Archives)

The Struggle for the Tapes

From Disclosure to the Saturday Night Massacre

We have repeatedly stressed our deep disturbance at the President's refusal to release the Oval Office tapes.
— Wall Street Journal *editorial, August 9, 1973*

President Nixon is impeaching himself in the minds and hearts of his countrymen.
— Dallas Times Herald *editorial, October 22, 1973*

In view of our years of support for the man and for many of his policies, it is with regret that we now find it necessary, for the good of the country, to call upon Richard M. Nixon to resign.
— Salt Lake Tribune *editorial, October 22, 1973*

The tapes held out the promise of a quick ending to the Watergate affair, at least as far as resolving the question of presidential involvement. From the beginning, the public overwhelmingly favored release of the tapes. The more the president resisted, the more his popularity declined and the more his supporters crossed over and became opponents. Nixon believed he could weather the storm of protests because he knew other presidents had refused to release documents to congressional committees. In such instances Congress's only recourse was impeachment, a procedure it had used only once, and that was in the immediate aftermath of the Civil War. To fend off the various demands for the tapes, Nixon resorted to more and more detailed, contorted explanations. Increasingly, public opinion found such explanations unsatisfactory. By late October the struggle for the tapes erupted into a crisis.

The day after Alexander Butterfield's testimony, the Ervin Committee unanimously requested the president to "provide the Committee with all relevant documents and tapes . . . that relate to the matters the Select Committee is authorized to investigate."[1] Nixon refused on the constitutional principle of separation of powers but added that "the tapes would not finally settle the central issues before your Committee." He explained that he had listened to some of the tapes and that they were "entirely consistent with what I know to be the truth and what I have stated to be the truth." But "they contain comments that persons with different perspectives and motivations would inevitably interpret in different ways." Ervin commented to the committee that the president claimed that the tapes "sustain his position. But he says he's not going to let anyone else hear them for fear they might draw a different conclusion."[2]

In response, the committee voted, again unanimously, to issue two subpoenas to Nixon to turn over specific tapes and documents. This vote placed Nixon with Thomas Jefferson as the only presidents ever to be subpoenaed. In 1807 Jefferson had released the letter requested by the subpoena but refused to travel to Richmond, Virginia, to testify at a trial, stating that he would have testified if the trial were being held in Washington.

The same day that the Ervin Committee issued its subpoenas, Judge Sirica also issued Nixon a subpoena for certain tapes and documents on behalf of Special Prosecutor Cox. Three days later, on July 26, Ervin and Sirica received letters from the president with similar rejections. To Ervin, Nixon cited executive privilege. To Sirica, he claimed he followed the example of his predecessors, "who have consistently adhered to the position that the President is not subject to compulsory process from the courts."[3]

Howard Baker, vice chair of the Ervin Committee, observed that "the issue was joined" and hoped for a compromise. He suggested that the president and the committee agree on "an informal panel of distinguished Americans not now holding a position in Government" to review the tapes and decide what was and was not relevant to the investigation.[4] An editorial in the conservative *National Review* echoed Baker's proposal: "It would be easy to devise a method of getting only the relevant data without invading either personal privacies or national security."[5] Nixon would not compromise.

Both the Ervin Committee and Cox turned to the U.S. District Court to seek enforcement of their subpoenas. Judge Sirica started with the Cox subpoena. To argue his claim of executive privilege, the president obtained the services of Professor Charles Alan Wright of the University of Texas Law School, a specialist in constitutional law. Wright submitted a brief of thirty-four legal-sized pages. Cox's reply brief totaled sixty-seven legal-size pages plus an eighty-five-page appendix. Sirica then heard Wright and Cox present oral arguments, after which he announced he would render a decision within a week.

While the court, the special prosecutor, the Ervin Committee, and the president concerned themselves with the subpoenas, politicians, newspapers, and polls voiced their opinions about the tapes and Nixon's refusals to release them. James L. Buckley, the only member of the Senate elected on a Conservative Party ballot, declared that Nixon "has painted himself into a very tight corner, unnecessarily and foolishly. I think clearly in the instant case the consensus of the American people will be that the President, while he has the right to exercise the privilege, ought not to be exercising it."[6] Senator Barry M. Goldwater, the 1964 Republican nominee for president and the author of the best-seller *The Conscience of a Conservative,* called Nixon's separation of powers claim "a smoke screen." Goldwater went further: "I think the President must release these tapes and he must come before the Senate Watergate Committee and the television cameras and tell the truth."[7] Nixon, of course, had his defenders. Senator Jesse A. Helms of North Carolina concluded, "The people think it's much to do about nothing, that it's a political vendetta."[8]

The assessments in newspaper editorials varied. In Vermont the *Burlington Free Press* called "the entire Watergate affair . . . nothing but one big political stunt,"[9] while the *Fort Worth Star–Telegram* called Nixon's response to the subpoenas "proper and appropriate."[10] The *Wichita Beacon* recommended destruction of the tapes "forthwith."[11] In Mississippi the *Biloxi Daily Herald,* on the other hand, termed Nixon's response "a disappointment,"[12] and the *Washington Evening Star* believed that "for everybody's sake, we urge the President to settle out of court."[13] In three editorials, the *Wall Street Journal* counseled compromise, pointing out that "we have repeatedly stressed our deep disturbance at the President's refusal to release the Oval Office tapes."[14]

Among Republican conservatives, Buckley and Goldwater commanded more respect than any other senators. In the esteem of corporate America no newspaper rivaled the *Wall Street Journal.* On August 3, the voice of intellectual conservatism, the *National Review,* joined the honored conservative chorus calling for Nixon to release the tapes. Watergate, the editorial declared, "has drained his political sinew, his moral authority, and his credibility."[15]

Public opinion polls paralleled the views of Goldwater and the *National Review* rather than those of Helms and the *Burlington Free Press.* In its August 1973 poll, the Harris Survey found that only 32 percent of Americans awarded Nixon a "positive" overall job rating. The Gallup Poll conducted the first week in August registered a 31 percent overall approval rate and a 67 percent disapproval of his decision to keep the tapes. The fall in the president's popularity from January to August was the sharpest decline ever recorded for a president.

The decline in Nixon's support did not stem entirely from Watergate. The same day the public learned of the White House taping system from Butterfield, Secretary of Defense James R. Schlesinger admitted that the United States had secretly bombed Cambodia during 1969 and 1970 and that senior civilian and military officials had falsified reports, thereby withholding information from Congress to prevent public disclosure. During the next ten days Americans learned that the president had personally authorized the raids, totaling more than 3,600 flights; that the United States had secretly bombed neutral Cambodia; and that Secretary of State William P. Rogers had repeatedly lied about the bombing in classified testimony before the Senate Foreign Relations Committee. Nixon had told the nation on April 30, 1970, that since 1954 U.S. policy "has been to scrupulously respect the neutrality of the Cambodian people."[16]

Disclosure of the secret bombing precipitated a flurry of bills to limit presidential powers to order military forces into combat without congressional approval. On July 18, the House passed its bill by a 244 to 170 vote. Two days later the Senate voted 71 to 18 for a bill similar in intent but different in detail. Nixon warned Congress that he would veto any bill that incorporated the essence of the House and Senate proposals.

During late July and early August, witnesses continued to testify before the Ervin Committee. After Butterfield, Herbert Kalmbach explained how he had raised and distributed $220,000 to the seven men arrested in the Watergate break-in. He maintained that Ehrlichman approved the operation and stressed the need for secrecy while Dean issued specific instructions. The former White House secret agent Anthony T. Ulasewicz told how he transferred the money to burglars and their lawyers. Gordon C. Strachan reported that his boss, Haldeman, knew about G. Gordon Liddy's intelligence-gathering project two months before the break-in and that after the break-in Haldeman wanted Strachan to destroy Liddy's files.

Ehrlichman took the witness chair on July 24. In his prepared statement, the former chief domestic adviser to the president said he welcomed "this opportunity to lay out the facts" as he already had done before three grand juries, other House and Senate committees, and FBI investigations. He praised Nixon's ability and policies, accused Dean of repeated "falsehoods," and explained that Nixon "made a very deliberate effort to detach himself from the day-to-day strategic and tactical problems" of the 1972 campaign. Concluding his statement, Ehrlichman stressed, "I did not cover up anything to do with Watergate."[17]

During the five days of questioning that followed, Ehrlichman remained confident and disputed the testimonies of Dean, Patrick Gray, and Mitchell. Chief counsel Sam Dash later wrote that Ehrlichman "used the witness chair as a platform to challenge the committee and to justify his conduct and that of Richard Nixon and Bob Haldeman."[18] Most of the spectators reacted negatively to Ehrlichman's arrogance and testimony, which the minority counsel Fred Thompson later noted contained "glaring weaknesses."[19] Thompson also found the "moans and groans from the audience, hisses, applause, sustained applause on some occasions and other demonstrations" regrettable, embarrassing, and unfair.[20] When Senator Inouye finished questioning Ehrlichman, he muttered, "What a liar," an opinion he had not intended the microphone to pick up and broadcast. Ehrlichman proved to be a difficult witness for the committee.

Haldeman followed Ehrlichman in the witness chair and, with a cooperative, respectful manner, offered a striking contrast to his pugnacious predecessor. In a long, prepared opening statement, Haldeman asserted that "President Nixon had no knowledge of or involvement in either the Watergate affair itself or the subsequent efforts of a cover-up." The former chief of staff to the president also claimed complete innocence and reported that the atmosphere in the White House during Nixon's first term was "not one of fear or repression, but one of excitement, extremely hard work, dedication, and accomplishment." Like Ehrlichman, Haldeman accused Dean of masterminding the cover-up because he was "sort of the Watergate project officer in the White House." Haldeman added that Dean "apparently did not keep us fully posted." At one point Haldeman exclaimed, "I don't know now whom to believe. I may add that until the recent period both John Mitchell and Jeb Magruder denied any Watergate involvement."[21] Dash later wrote that during Haldeman's three days before the committee, he "appeared as an absent-minded witness who could not recall any details of practically anything that had happened during the relevant periods about which he was questioned. The Haldeman testimony was very much like a replay of Mitchell's testimony, but without the pipe."[22]

The most startling information to surface during Haldeman's appearance came when he said he had listened to the tapes of the Nixon-Dean conversations of September 15, 1972, and March 21, 1973. At the time Haldeman listened, he no longer worked at the White House. Senator Talmadge asked, "Why would a private citizen be more entitled to listen to those tapes than a Senate committee of the Congress of the United States?"[23]

The nastiest comment regarding Haldeman's testimony came during a recess on the third day when a reporter asked Haldeman's lawyer, John J. Wilson, if he thought Senator Weicker had questioned Haldeman fairly. Wilson replied that he didn't mind Weicker, "What I mind is that little Jap." The reference to Senator Inouye, a native-born American of Japanese ancestry, troubled Ervin, who pointed out that Inouye had lost an arm fighting bravely for the country in World War II and had won the Distinguished Service Cross for heroism. Baker added, "I have a great affection for him as well as a great admiration for him."[24] Subsequently, Wilson sent Inouye a letter of apology.

Six witnesses testified in the next four days of hearings. Their testimonies further damaged Nixon's credibility and undermined his cover-up story. The former FBI director Patrick Gray, the former attorney general Richard Kleindienst, and Assistant Attorney General Henry Petersen swore that between March 21 and April 15, 1973, the president never asked them anything about the Watergate investigations taking place. Yet on April 30, 1973, Nixon had informed Americans that "on March 21, I personally assumed the responsibility for coordinating intensive new inquiries into the matter and I personally ordered those conducting the investigations to get all the facts and report them directly to me, right here in this office."[25]

The next three witnesses continued to contradict Nixon's public statements and the testimonies of Haldeman and Ehrlichman. The former CIA director Richard Helms and Deputy Director Vernon Walters told of being pressured by the White House to use the CIA to block the FBI investigation of Watergate. Walters said that Dean had asked the CIA to post bail for the burglars and to put them on the CIA payroll so they would have incomes. The former deputy director Robert E. Cushman Jr. reinforced the statements of Helms and Walters.

Damning as these testimonies were, and dramatic as the Ehrlichman and Haldeman testimonies had been, the hearings proved anticlimactic after Butterfield's revelation about the taping system. On August 7, therefore, when the committee declared a month's recess, most of those who followed the affair breathed a sigh of relief. Thirty-three witnesses had filled thirty-seven days of hearings and 3,573 pages of testimony.

The hearings, however, had a monumental impact. They caught and sustained the nation's interest. Dean's testimony focused attention on Nixon's role in the cover-up, and a sufficient number of the president's aides had detailed their involvement to convince the majority of Americans, 73 percent according to the Gallup Poll, that Nixon was involved. Senator Baker had reduced Watergate to eleven words: "What did the President know and when did he know it?" Initially, the question pleased Nixon's supporters because few persons believed that his active role in the cover-up could be documented; the question stopped the Watergate affair at the door to the Oval Office. Once the nation learned of the tapes, this perception changed. Nixon's refusal to release tapes underscored the centrality of Baker's question and increased Dean's believability. The public began to consider whether Nixon had something to hide, and the Congress, the special prosecutor, and the courts demanded the tapes to learn the answer. At stake was Nixon's presidency.

On the evening of August 15, 1973, with the hearings in recess, the president addressed the nation "to speak out about the charges made and to provide a perspective on the issue for the American people." He repeated his statement of May 22 that he "had no prior knowledge of the Watergate break-in," that he "neither took part in nor knew about any of the subsequent cover-up activities," and that he "neither authorized nor encouraged . . . illegal or improper campaign tactics." Nixon reminded his audience that Dean had failed to corroborate his accusations. The president emphasized that because he "trusted the agencies conducting the investigations," he "did not believe the newspaper accounts that suggested a cover-up." He again explained why "the principle of confidentiality of Presidential conversations " prevented his release of the tapes to the court. Finally, he warned of "a continued, backward-looking obsession with Watergate" and of "those who would exploit Watergate in order to keep us from doing what we were elected to do."[26]

Two incidents during the following week document the toll of Watergate on Nixon's patience. Five days after his national address, as the president was entering the convention hall in New Orleans to address the annual national convention of the Veterans of Foreign Wars, he turned abruptly, grabbed his press secretary Ron Ziegler by the shoulders, and shoved him toward the White House press corps that followed the president, saying, "I don't want any press with me. You take care of it."

The second incident occurred two days later, this time in San Clemente at the president's first news conference in five months. The CBS reporter Dan Rather prefaced his question with "Mr. President, I want to state this question with due respect to your office, but also as direct as possible." Nixon retorted, "That would be unusual." Rather responded, "I would like to think not, sir. It concerns —." The president interrupted, "You are always respectful, Mr. Rather. You know that."[27]

The questions at the press conference exemplified how Watergate dominated the news in August 1973. Of the twenty questions reporters asked, seventeen dealt with subjects that touched the Watergate investigations. Two questions concerned Vice President Agnew, then under federal investigation on charges of extortion, tax fraud, and bribery. On August 6 the *Wall Street Journal* published the first major story about the Agnew investigation. An inquiry about Cambodia was the only other question not tied to Watergate. All the questions put the president on the defensive. The Associated Press reporter Frances Lewine, for example, asked, "If disclosure carries such a risk, why did you make the tapes in the first place?" Peter Lisagor of the *Chicago Daily News* stated, "Mr. President, you have said repeatedly that you tried to get all the facts. . . . Yet former Attorney General John Mitchell said that if you had ever asked him at any time about the Watergate matter, he would have told you the whole story, chapter and verse." Lisagor followed with his question, "Was Mr. Mitchell not speaking the truth when he said that before the Committee?" Clark R. Mollenhoff of the *Des Moines Register and Tribune* and a former Nixon aide, asked, "Where is the check on authoritarianism by the executive if the President is to be the sole judge of what the executive branch makes available and suppresses?" Even the question about Cambodia carried a barb. After reminding Nixon of his April 30 statement that the United States had respected Cambodian neutrality, a reporter inquired, "If you in light of what we now know, that there were fifteen months of bombing Cambodia previous to your statement, whether you owe an apology to the American people?"

Nixon's replies added nothing to the positions and explanations he had offered in the past. He reiterated that he had always supported a thorough investigation, that he could not breach the principle of presidential confidentiality, that the court would exonerate Haldeman and Ehrlichman, and that "people who did not accept the mandate of '72" exploited Watergate "in order to keep the President from doing his job."[28]

The next issue of *Time* revealed the inadequacy of Nixon's explanations and the seriousness of the problem he faced. In its cover story, the mainstream news weekly concluded that the president "made no real effort to answer the damaging charges and questions that have emerged from three months of testimony before the Ervin Committee," including

- why he did not respond to acting FBI director L. Patrick Gray's astonishing assertion to him on July 6, 1972, that certain White House aides were trying to "mortally wound" the president by interfering with the FBI and CIA;
- why he did not know about "the illegal disbursement of huge sums by his aides to the original seven Watergate defendants";
- why, when he launched his own investigation last March 21, he did not immediately solicit the aid of the FBI or the CIA;
- how he and his administration could have been misled for nine months by only one man, Dean.

The article also reported that "the Scripps-Howard papers, which customarily support Nixon, dismissed the President's speech as 'regrettable, not to say disappointing,' branded his policy on the tapes 'a grave mistake,' and added that 'people with nothing to hide do not hide things.'" Moreover, the article described the results of the Oliver Quayle Poll, which found "that if the 1972 election were to be repeated today, Senator George McGovern (who received only 38 percent of the popular vote) would win with 51 percent."[29] The poll confirmed John Mitchell's belief that if the voters knew about the background of the Watergate break-in and "the White House Horrors," they would have rejected Nixon and elected McGovern. For Nixon, more bad news followed.

On August 29, Sirica ordered the president to turn over the tapes and documents to the judge himself for first inspection. Sirica believed he had taken a middle course between his belief that "no privilege existed for matters of a criminal nature" and Nixon's legitimate concern for protection of confidentiality. After examining the tapes, Sirica planned to give the relevant, unprivileged portions to Cox. Nixon immediately announced that he would not comply with the court order. The following day, after conferring with his lawyers, the president reported that he would appeal the ruling to the court of appeals. Cox also appealed the ruling because he opposed judicial censorship and wanted the president to give the tapes directly to the grand jury.

The next week the president held another news conference, his second in the space of two weeks. By way of contrast, he had held thirty-one news conferences during his first fifty-five months in office, considerably fewer than once a month. Six of the fourteen questions concerned Watergate; a seventh dealt with governmental expenditures at the two Nixon houses; and an eighth inquired about Agnew. Once again Nixon revealed hostility toward the press when he replied to a question about "rebuilding confidence" in his leadership. He admitted that it was "a problem, it is true." He continued: "But for four months to have the President of the United States by innuendo, by leak, by, frankly, leers and sneers of commentators, which is their perfect right, attacked in every way" led to a wearing away of public confidence.

Nixon's two news conferences soon after his August 15 speech indicated his strategy, as *Time* emphasized, to avoid a response to any specific charge, to discredit reporters who kept asking questions, and to tie up the tapes in an endless legal contest. He hoped that the public would eventually tire of Watergate and as interest diminished that reporters and politicians would turn to other subjects and issues. Nixon had no other choice — except to tell the truth, ask forgiveness, and hope to escape impeachment.

September brought little relief for the embattled president. On September 4 a Los Angeles grand jury indicted Ehrlichman, Liddy, Egil Krogh Jr., and David R. Young Jr. for the 1971 burglary of the office of Lewis Fielding, Daniel Ellsberg's psychiatrist. The defendants, except for Ehrlichman, were members of the Plumbers and had operated from an office in the White House; Ehrlichman had organized the group. Four days later the Harris Poll reported that 66 percent of Americans agreed with the statement, "If it had not been for the press exposés, the whole Watergate mess would never have been found out." On September 10 the House of Representatives voted 334 to 11 to cite Liddy for contempt of Congress because he refused to testify before the House Armed Services Special Subcommittee on Intelligence, which was investigating possible CIA participation in the Watergate affair. Three days after the House vote, the seven judges who constituted the U.S. Court of Appeals for the District of Columbia issued a unanimous statement urging Special Prosecutor Cox and President Nixon to settle out of court their disagreement over the tapes.

In September two prominent politicians also made news by speaking about Watergate. At a reception for members of the Republican National Committee, former Texas governor John B. Connally told reporters, "There are times when the President of the United States would be right in not obeying a decision of the Supreme Court." In a speech on the Senate floor, Democratic senator Ted Kennedy countered, "If President Nixon defied a Supreme Court order to turn over the tapes, a responsible Congress would be left with no recourse but to exercise its power of impeachment."[30]

On September 14, four of the seven Watergate burglars requested Judge Sirica to allow them to change their pleas to not guilty and to grant them a new trial on the grounds that Hunt and "high officials of the executive branch" had pressured them into pleading guilty to protect national security. They told the judge they had taken part in the break-in on the understanding that it was an authorized government operation. Three days later Hunt petitioned Sirica to permit him to withdraw his guilty plea; he also asked Sirica to dismiss the charges against him on the grounds that the prosecution had not observed due process. Sirica denied the requests.

The same day that Hunt petitioned Sirica, Donald H. Segretti pleaded guilty to four counts of campaign law violations. Appearing before a U.S. magistrate in Washington, Segretti agreed to cooperate with the special prosecutor. He also arranged to testify before the Ervin Committee under an immunity grant. The former White House special counsel Charles W. Colson then made news by invoking the Fifth Amendment and refusing to testify on the grounds that his answers might incriminate him.

On September 20, Nixon's attorney Charles A. Wright and Special Prosecutor Cox both advised the court of appeals that they had failed to reach a compromise on the tapes. Wright repeatedly maintained that no court could order the president to release private presidential papers against his will. Whichever way the appeals court ruled, the other party intended to appeal to the Supreme Court. A constitutional crisis loomed.

A Harris Survey released the tabulations of the answers to its questions, "If you had to do it over again, who would you vote for for President in 1972 — McGovern or Nixon?" As in the Oliver Quayle Poll, McGovern won the hypothetical election. The initial phase of the cover-up, therefore, had fulfilled its primary objective of impeding investigation and withholding information regarding the illegal activities that Nixon's aides had taken to ensure his reelection. The Harris Survey also found that 60 percent of Americans believed Nixon "knew about the cover-up," 24 percent believed he "did not know," and 16 percent were "not sure."[31] The Gallup Poll of early September 1973 recorded that only 35 percent of Americans approved of the president's handling of his job.

After a seven-week recess the Ervin Committee resumed its hearings on September 24, with E. Howard Hunt as its first witness. The previous March, when Sirica provisionally sentenced Hunt to more than thirty years in prison, he told the convicted conspirator that he might reduce the final sentence if Hunt cooperated with the grand jury and Senate investigations. With little likelihood of a presidential pardon, with no hope of financial support from secret Republican funds, and with the cover-up story exposed, Hunt decided that cooperation best served his self-interest.

Hunt testified that Colson knew about Liddy's espionage operation in January 1972, that Colson urged him to falsify diplomatic cables to implicate President Kennedy in the assassination of South Vietnam's president, and that Colson sent him to burglarize the apartment of Arthur Bremer immediately after Bremer shot Alabama's governor George C. Wallace during the 1972 primary campaign. Hunt also told of White House aides destroying materials relating to espionage activities. At the end of his prepared opening statement, he emphasized that he considered his various assignments "as a duty to my country."[32]

A combative Patrick J. Buchanan followed Hunt. The presidential speechwriter criticized the committee for failure to extend to him "elementary courtesy" regarding notification of his appearance and accused the committee staff of "character assassination." He dismissed as "utter fraud" and "altogether untrue" the assertion that the clandestine activities of Liddy, McCord, Hunt, Ulasewicz, Segretti, and others contributed to the failure of Muskie to win the Democratic presidential nomination. In his answers to questions, Buchanan followed the traditional maxim that the best defense is a good offense. He admitted no wrongdoing and left an image of a confident, articulate, defender of Nixon.[33]

A repentant Segretti followed the sparring Buchanan and described the dirty tricks he had conducted to deny Muskie the nomination. The thirty-two-year-old lawyer admitted, among many other things, that he stole Muskie's stationery and wrote and mailed spurious letters on which he forged Muskie's signature. Segretti also told how he disrupted political meetings by placing stink bombs and by paying persons to act in "an unruly manner." He considered such actions "similar to college pranks" and "nothing improper or illegal." According to Segretti, Dwight L. Chapin, Nixon's press secretary, hired him, and Nixon's personal attorney Herbert Kalmbach paid him. The committee canceled Chapin's appearance when he said he would plead the Fifth Amendment rather than answer questions.

The Hunt, Buchanan, and Segretti testimonies, as well as those of Martin D. Kelly and Robert M. Benz, who worked for Segretti, generated little interest. Nixon's culpability, which the tapes presumably would reveal, remained the focus of attention. The public, moreover, already knew the contours and much of the detail of campaign sabotage and campaign contributions. Hence, American Airlines, Minnesota Mining and Manufacturing Company, Braniff, Phillips Petroleum, and Goodyear Tire and Rubber Company also generated only a modest shock when they pleaded guilty to making illegal contributions to Nixon's 1972 campaign. Suddenly, however, news about Vice President Spiro Agnew jolted the country.

Throughout August, September, and early October, the disclosures of Agnew's graft slowly unfolded in public and provided a front-page diversion from the Watergate story. A year earlier the Internal Revenue Service, following up anonymous tips, started an investigation into the relationship of Baltimore County officials and the army of contractors, real estate agents, architects, consultants, and engineers who helped build Baltimore's suburban sprawl. The IRS uncovered substantial evidence of regular kickbacks of fees to public officials in exchange for contracts, and then called U.S. attorney George Beall. A member of a prominent Republican family, Beall was the younger brother of Maryland's U.S. senator J. Glenn Beall Jr. In December 1972, a Baltimore grand jury was convened to investigate these activities. A month later, one contractor told of payoffs to Agnew going back a decade, when he had served as Baltimore County Executive, but continuing after he became vice president. Agnew quickly retained a lawyer. By summer 1973 the grand jury had gathered what it believed was irrefutable evidence to convict Agnew of bribery, extortion, and tax evasion.

During June and July Beall kept Attorney General Elliot Richardson informed of the Agnew case. On August 6 Richardson told Nixon. Later that day Agnew met the president to proclaim his innocence. At a news conference two days later, Agnew denounced the charges against him as "damned lies, false and scurrilous and malicious." He also promised full cooperation because he had nothing to hide.

Nixon faced a dilemma. The previous spring he had considered Agnew as insurance for his presidency because Nixon believed Congress would hesitate to impeach him if it meant moving Agnew to the White House.

Fully briefed by the Justice Department, however, Nixon knew Agnew was guilty and consequently wanted the vice president to resign. Conservatives, on the other hand, considered Agnew their champion. Needing their support in his Watergate battles, Nixon did not want to antagonize them by failing to stand by Agnew. On August 22, 1973, when a reporter asked, "What is the state of your confidence in your Vice President at this point in time?" Nixon replied that his "confidence in his integrity has not been shaken." Two weeks later Nixon again expressed his "confidence in the Vice President's integrity."[34]

On September 13 Agnew's lawyers and Justice Department officials started plea bargaining in earnest. Agnew wanted to resign with honor and avoid prison. The prosecutors who had worked long and hard to build a case wanted to go to trial. Attorney General Richardson feared that Nixon's position was tenuous; believing Agnew unfit to assume the presidency should anything happen to Nixon, he wanted Agnew gone, the quicker the better. Richardson nursed presidential ambitions himself. On September 15 the prosecutors offered their final proposal. They would accept Agnew's resignation, combined with a plea of no contest to the charges. In return, Agnew would avoid prison. Agnew told his lawyers to break off negotiations.

Agnew attempted to save himself by asking the House of Representatives to investigate the charges against him because only that body could initiate impeachment proceedings and because impeachment was the only method to remove a vice president from office. After the House leadership rejected Agnew's request and the Baltimore grand jury called its first witness, the vice president filed a motion in federal district court to prohibit the Justice Department from giving additional evidence to the grand jury. Agnew contended that no criminal court could indict or convict a vice president. Implicitly, Agnew raised the question whether a court could indict a president. On September 29, before the National Federation of Republican Women, Agnew delivered a polemical defense of himself, criticized officials within the Justice Department, and announced, "I will not resign if indicted."[35]

Nixon countered. He sent word to Agnew that if he again attacked the Justice Department, Nixon would block any plea bargain. The Justice Department then published its legal judgment that although a criminal court could not indict a president, it could indict a vice president. On October 7 Agnew capitulated and agreed to resume negotiations. He accepted the essence of the deal he had rejected when terminating the earlier bargaining.

At 2:05 P.M. on October 10 a messenger delivered Agnew's resignation to Secretary of State Henry Kissinger. A few minutes later the former vice president appeared in Baltimore District Court and pleaded no contest to a single charge of federal income tax evasion. The judge fined Agnew $10,000 and sentenced him to three years of unsupervised probation. Two days later Nixon nominated the Republican leader of the House of Representatives Gerald Ford as vice president. Senate Republicans and the Republican National Committee had favored New York's governor Nelson Rockefeller, and the conservative wing of the party had supported California's governor Ronald Reagan. Nixon rejected both as having personalities too strong. His first choice was John Connally, but Nixon believed the Senate would refuse to confirm him. Nixon did not view Ford as presidential, but he knew both houses of Congress would confirm him; he also thought Ford's nonpresidential bearing might cause Congress to pause before moving to impeach Nixon himself. In his speech nominating Ford, Nixon never mentioned Agnew's name or the reason for the vacancy.

The Agnew case raised angry voices across the country. In its first issue after the vice president's resignation, *Time* pointed out that the Justice Department's leniency "was no shining example of equality under law" and characterized Agnew as "a man morally and intellectually unfit for national leadership."[36] The *Charleston (W. Va.) Gazette* called the Agnew story "a sorry chronicle of immorality, deceit, and hypocrisy" and repeated the obvious — that "the nation's best known critic of 'soft' judges gratefully accepted a token sentence from a lenient court."[37] Agnew never acknowledged wrongdoing. The court and the nation viewed his plea as an admission of guilt, but the former vice president interpreted his plea as an unselfish act in the national interest to spare the country a trial.

The Agnew scandal clearly damaged Nixon. The *Miami News* remarked that "George McGovern was rightly responsible for his poor judgment in choosing Tom Eagleton as a running mate. Likewise, Nixon must accept responsibility for creating this unprecedented national disgrace." The *Wall Street Journal* hoped that "Agnew's turnabout would be an inspiration for others in government. . . . Our fondest hope is that President Nixon would set aside his own confrontation-prone constitutional battle and agree to release key Watergate tape recordings."[38]

The steady erosion of public confidence may have been personally unpleasant for Nixon, but the real threat to his presidency remained the possibility that the court might order him to turn over the tapes. Two days after Agnew resigned, the U.S. Court of Appeals for the District of Columbia, by a five to two vote, upheld Judge Sirica's August 29 ruling that the president give him the tapes for inspection before transfer to the special prosecutor.

The appeals court allowed the president a week to file an appeal to the Supreme Court.

Four days later, Melvin R. Laird, Nixon's chief domestic affairs adviser and secretary of defense during Nixon's first term, became the first high-ranking White House official to discuss with reporters the possibility that the House of Representatives might start impeachment proceedings if the president defied a Supreme Court ruling. The next day Judge Sirica ruled that he lacked jurisdiction to force the president to release the tapes to the Ervin Committee. Sirica's ruling had no impact because Nixon already faced a court-ordered deadline related to the special prosecutor's original subpoena. Tensions mounted.

On Friday evening, October 19, Nixon announced his "decisive actions . . . that would avoid the necessity of Supreme Court review." Rather than transfer the tapes to Sirica, as the court ordered, Nixon planned to submit "a statement prepared by me personally from the subpoenaed tapes." To authenticate the accuracy of the summaries, he would permit Senator John Stennis (D-Miss.) "unlimited access to the tapes." The president said he was breaching the principle of confidentiality "with the greatest reluctance," but by giving a senator, rather than a judge, access he avoided the establishment of "a precedent that would be available to four hundred district judges." In return for the concession, Nixon wanted an end to "the constitutional tensions of Watergate"; he wanted the special prosecutor never again to subpoena tapes or papers. The president announced further that both Chairman Ervin and Vice Chairman Baker of the Senate committee had agreed to the proposal, as did Senator Stennis. Cox, however, rejected the plan. Accordingly, Nixon directed the special prosecutor, "as an employee of the executive branch, to make no further attempts by judicial process to obtain tapes, notes, or memoranda of Presidential conversations." Nixon also made it clear that in the future he would give nothing to the special prosecutor. This position, combined with Sirica's ruling that he could not compel the president to give material to the Ervin Committee, meant that Nixon intended to keep his files locked. More important, the announcement meant that he would not obey the court and would not appeal the court's ruling. Nixon's strategy would fail, however, without Cox's acquiescence.

Behind the scenes that Friday evening and all day Saturday, Nixon's chief of staff, Alexander Haig, and other White House aides negotiated with Attorney General Richardson and other Justice Department officials to overcome Cox's strenuous objection. Twice, Cox argued, courts upheld his subpoenas, and he would accept nothing less than compliance. He reminded Haig and Richardson that when he accepted appointment, he did so with the promise of complete independence.

Nixon broke the impasse by ordering Richardson to fire Cox. Richardson refused and resigned, with regret. When nominating Richardson as attorney general on April 30, Nixon had stated, "I have given him absolute authority to make all decisions bearing upon the prosecution of the Watergate case and related matters." In his resignation letter, Richardson reminded Nixon that at the time of his confirmation as attorney general he had pledged publicly that he would "not countermand or interfere with the Special Prosecutor's decisions or actions." At the time Richardson gave that pledge, Nixon declared that Richardson had his "full support." When Richardson personally submitted his resignation, Nixon asked him to place national interest above his personal pledge and remain on the job. Richardson replied that he thought honoring his pledge was in the national interest.

Shortly thereafter, Haig telephoned Deputy Attorney General William D. Ruckelshaus and told him the president ordered him to fire Cox. Ruckelshaus refused and also resigned. Haig next telephoned Solicitor General Robert H. Bork, who agreed to come to the White House. There the former Yale professor, as designated acting attorney general, drafted a letter of dismissal and sent it to Cox by messenger. In 1987, when President Reagan nominated Bork for a seat on the Supreme Court, the opposition of those who viewed him as an accomplice in this chain of events successfully blocked the appointment.

At 8:25 P.M. that Saturday evening, Press Secretary Ron Ziegler announced that the president had accepted the resignations of Richardson and Ruckelshaus, had fired Cox, had abolished the Office of the Watergate Special Prosecutor Force, and had returned the Watergate case to the Department of Justice. Forty minutes later FBI agents arrived at Cox's office and placed it under guard. The agents refused to let staff members remove anything, even pictures of their wives and children. The press immediately labeled this series of events the Saturday Night Massacre.

Nixon had seriously misjudged the national mood. The *Salt Lake Tribune,* which had endorsed him for president in 1960, 1968, and 1972, observed that Nixon "considered himself above the rule of law" and concluded that "in view of our years of support for the man and for many of his policies, it is with regret that we now find it necessary, for the good of the country, to call upon Richard M. Nixon to resign." If he failed to do so, the editorial continued, "Congress should move with alacrity to impeach him."[39] The *Honolulu Star– Bulletin* reminded its readers that it twice had endorsed Nixon for president but now believed he "should resign." The *New Orleans States–Item* accused the president of "acting in open defiance of Congress and the Courts" and of having "gone back on his word to Mr. Cox, Mr. Richardson, Congress, and the American people. . . . We have reached a point where we no longer can believe our President." In Florida, the *St. Petersburg Times* called for Nixon's resignation. The *Dallas Times Herald* judged Nixon's actions since "last spring" as an "arrogant disregard for the courts and the Congress" and concluded that "President Nixon is impeaching himself in the minds and hearts of his countrymen." The *Louisville Courier–Journal* agreed: "Here is a President who says he wants no stone left unturned in discovering the whole truth about the Watergate scandals, but refuses to obey court orders for production of his tapes."[40]

Nixon was criticized in other quarters as well. The Monday following the Saturday Night Massacre, delegates to the AFL–CIO biennial convention approved a resolution calling for Nixon to resign. A year earlier, by contrast, during the presidential campaign, the AFL–CIO endorsed no candidate but supported Nixon's Vietnam policy. Also on Monday, the Speaker of the House of Representatives, Carl Albert, met with party leaders to begin a preliminary study on the possible impeachment of the president. The next morning Republican leaders in Congress warned Nixon's emissaries that the House would vote for impeachment unless the president surrendered the tapes. Judge Sirica, meanwhile, contemplated whether or not to hold Nixon in contempt of court for refusing to comply with the court order.

The fire storm of criticism forced Nixon to retreat, regarding both the tapes and the special prosecutor. On October 23 he sent the White House attorney Charles Alan Wright to Sirica with the news that the president would obey the court and turn over the subpoenaed documents and tapes. At a news conference three days later, the president promised "total cooperation from the executive branch." By the time Nixon made this promise, fifty-three senators had cosponsored a resolution authorizing Sirica to appoint a special prosecutor independent of the executive branch of government.

The president's answers to questions at his next news conference indicated the severe limits of his conception of "total cooperation." He stated that in the future he would "not provide Presidential documents to a Special Prosecutor" but would provide "information that is needed from such documents." Repeatedly, Nixon explained he had "a constitutional responsibility to defend the Office of the Presidency from any encroachment on confidentiality."

Once again Watergate dominated a presidential news conference. Of the seventeen questions reporters asked, fourteen dealt with Watergate, despite the announcement the day before that Nixon had placed U.S. armed forces on worldwide alert because of Soviet threats in the Middle East. Indeed, when Secretary of State Kissinger made this announcement at a press conference, distrust of Nixon immediately surfaced. Reporters questioned whether the president had alerted the military to rally support following the negative reaction to the Saturday Night Massacre. Nixon returned the media's distrust with antagonism. He opened his news conference with a statement about the situation in the Middle East, explaining the procedure by which the United States had helped to produce a cease-fire in the sixteen-day Arab-Israeli Yom Kippur War. He considered the potential Soviet intervention as a Cold War crisis second only to the Cuban Missile Crisis. Ironically, during this crisis Nixon, occupied by Watergate, did not participate in any of the White House deliberations. Then the president said, "Turning now to the subject of our attempts to get a cease-fire on the home front, that is a bit more difficult." At one point during the news conference, Nixon commented on recent news coverage of his actions. He maintained that he had "never heard or seen such outrageous, vicious, distorted reporting in twenty-seven years of public life." Another time he accused newspapers and television networks of reporting information, "knowing it was untrue." When asked what specific coverage had "so aroused [his] anger," Nixon replied he was not angry. "You see," he continued, "one can only be angry with those he respects."[41]

Once again a Nixon news conference did little to stop the negative slide of his presidency. The *Wall Street Journal* characterized the president as "a pitiful, helpless giant" at the mercy of his critics. The editorial reminded its readers that for his plight, Nixon "has no one to blame but himself." The same day, October 29, *Time* ran its cover story, "Richard Nixon Stumbles to the Brink," and concluded that the Saturday Night Massacre left Nixon's "survival in the Oval Office in grave doubt." *Time* described the situation as one of the nation's "gravest constitutional crises."

On October 30, the *New York Times* reported yet another story that gave Americans reason for distrusting the Nixon administration. Richard Kleindienst admitted that in 1971, while he was serving as an assistant attorney general, he had been ordered by President Nixon to halt Justice Department action against the International Telephone and Telegraph Corporation (ITT). Yet at his confirmation hearings for attorney general, Kleindienst testified under oath that the White House had made no attempt to influence the case. (Subsequently, on November 4 Kleindienst confessed to committing perjury during his confirmation hearings.)

Also on October 30, the House Armed Services Subcommittee on Intelligence issued its report on CIA involvement in Watergate. Top White House officials, the report concluded, had attempted to use the CIA to block the FBI investigation of the June 1972 break-in. The story, of course, was familiar, but the report certified its credibility.

The next day brought still more negative Watergate news. The White House attorney J. Fred Buzhardt Jr. notified Judge Sirica that two of the nine tapes the court had ordered did not exist. Buzhardt explained that one four-minute conversation on June 20, 1972, had taken place on a White House family telephone that was not part of the taping system. The special prosecutor wanted this particular segment because it recorded the first conversation between Nixon and Mitchell following the burglary. As for the second one, the machine had run out of tape; it would have covered the fifty-five-minute conversation between Nixon and Dean on April 15, 1973. According to Dean, Nixon commented during their meeting that he never should have discussed with Colson the possibility of clemency for Howard Hunt. Dean also claimed that he and Nixon discussed hush money for the defendants and that he told the president that he had briefed Ehrlichman and Haldeman on every detail of Watergate. Buzhardt never explained why the White House waited so long to notify the court that these two crucial conversations were never taped.

As reaction set in to the announcement about the nonexistent tapes, the president nominated William B. Saxbe as attorney general. The respected Republican senator from Ohio had criticized the president for his December 1972 bombing in southeast Asia and for his handling of Watergate. Robert H. Bork thereupon named Leon Jaworski special prosecutor. A conservative "Democrat for Nixon" from Texas and a former president of the American Bar Association, Jaworski had served in the Justice Department under Attorney General Robert F. Kennedy and had sat on four presidential commissions during the Johnson administration. Jaworski also had amassed a small fortune as a corporate lawyer in Houston. Before accepting the position, the Texan received guarantees that he would have total independence and that the president could not discharge him without the consent of the Democratic and Republican leaders of the House, the Senate, the House Judiciary Committee, and the Senate Judiciary Committee. Jaworski made it clear that he would bring the president to court, if necessary. Initially, Cox's staff of young lawyers viewed with suspicion the law-and-order but soft-spoken Jaworski. Saxbe and Jaworski were solid appointees, but respectability could not offset the impact of the Saturday Night Massacre and the belated news that two of the nine subpoenaed tapes did not exist. Still, Nixon, at least, had taken a noticeable positive step.

The events of autumn continued to erode support for Nixon. In September the Harris Survey found that 31 percent of Americans believed Nixon should resign; by November the figure had jumped to 43 percent. The survey also revealed that between September and November the percentage of

Americans who disapproved of the president's handling of the Watergate tapes had increased from 71 percent to 83 percent.[42]

Equally graphic and threatening to the Nixon presidency was the steady increase among Nixon supporters who no longer found him credible. Their criticism was specific and expressed a common sense difficult to refute. From Kansas, the *Emporia Gazette* asked, "How much more does the President expect his supporters to endure? . . . Many of us out in the far-flung parts of the nation have had enough. If he is innocent, he should reverse his course and cooperate wholeheartedly with all the people who are investigating the Watergate mess — the Senate Committee, the Special Prosecutor, the grand jury — everybody."[43] From Columbia, South Carolina, the *State* asked, "Will the incredible series of events involving the President and the Watergate affair never end? We devoutly want to believe in the President and in what he says and does. But at every turn, after yielding to him the benefit of doubt, a subsequent event surfaces to wring out his credibility again."[44] The *Wall Street Journal* commented that "in general, though, the press coverage of Watergate has been repeatedly and massively vindicated by events. The press did not invent the burglary, nor did it imagine the cover-up."[45]

Nixon's refusal to release the tapes placed him in defiance of the positions of a growing number of Republican newspapers and politicians, the majority of Americans, and the unanimous membership of the Senate Watergate Committee. The country already had heard Republican calls for impeachment, were Nixon to defy a court order to release the tapes. The president could delay the court order with various stratagems, but the reaction to the Saturday Night Massacre demonstrated beyond any doubt that he eventually would have to obey the court and relinquish the tapes.

CHAPTER SEVEN

From the Saturday Night Massacre to the Tape Transcripts

November 1973 to May 1974

The President Should Resign.
— Time *editorial, November 12, 1973*

Does anyone believe anything any more?
— Kansas City Times *editorial, November 28, 1973*

There can no longer be a charge that he was railroaded out of office by vengeful Democrats or a hostile press.
— Chicago Tribune *editorial, May 9, 1974*

On November 12, 1973, *Time*, a symbol of Richard Nixon's middle America, published the first editorial of its fifty-year history, "The President Should Resign." It opened with the assertion that Nixon "has irredeemably lost his moral authority, the confidence of most of the country, and therefore his ability to govern effectively." Because *Time* had "endorsed Nixon for President three times," its editors had reached their conclusions "with deep reluctance."

The editorial summarized the pattern of corruption that included the resignation of the vice president, the indictment of two former cabinet members, and the indictment, convictions, or confessions of seven close presidential aides. It then cataloged Nixon's involvement in the Huston Plan, the Plumbers, the misuse of the FBI and the CIA, the job offer to the presiding judge at the Ellsberg trial, and the withholding of wiretap information from that judge. Finally, "as a staggering climax to all that went before," the editorial recounted Nixon's initial refusal to obey the court and release the White House tapes, his firing of Special Prosecutor Archibald Cox, and his "sudden claim that two crucial tapes do not exist."[1] The editorial ended by stating that the president's resignation "would show the true power of popular government."

Time's editorial confirms that Nixon had lost mainstream Republican support, and it gave legitimacy to calls for the president to resign. Nixon launched a public relations campaign to counter the pressure. The pressure, however, continued, fueled in part by a steady stream of news stories of actions that further damaged the president's credibility. Special Prosecutor Leon Jaworski and Judge John Sirica demanded that Nixon honor the court order to release the tapes while the House Judiciary Committee took initial steps on the road to impeachment. Media attention to these events, in turn, contributed to an atmosphere of tension, revelations, and animosities.

In May the president desperately attempted to blunt the demand for the tapes. Instead of releasing them, he published an edited transcript of them. The coarse language and content of the transcripts appalled most Americans and failed to lessen the demand for the tapes themselves. Rather than resolving the problem, Nixon's ploy produced a crisis equal to the Saturday Night Massacre.

On the political spectrum, William F. Buckley's conservative *National Review* represented the right, just as *Time* stood in the political mainstream. In its reaction to the Saturday Night Massacre, the *National Review* stopped short of calling for the president's resignation, but it maintained that Nixon had been "in direct defiance of the courts" and concluded that "if Mr. Nixon becomes convinced . . . that he has irretrievably lost the support and trust of a solid majority of the people, it will then be his duty to resign." Because all the polls indicated that Nixon had lost the "support and trust of a solid majority," the only question was whether the loss was retrievable. The *National Review* believed the answer would be evident within "a few more months at most."[2]

An increasing number of Republican politicians echoed the *National Review* and *Time*. Senator James L. Buckley (C-N.Y.) maintained that the missing tapes "dramatically shifted the burden of the proof" to Nixon. On ABC's *Issues and Answers,* Senator Edward W. Brooke (R-Mass.) stated that the president had lost the country's confidence and should resign. On CBS's *Face the Nation,* Senator Charles McC. Mathias, Jr. (R-Md.) called for Nixon to release everything Cox had requested. Senator Peter H. Dominick (R-Colo.) pronounced, "There can be no more deals and no more technical arguments about evidence." Instead, he argued that Nixon "should permit complete access to all tapes, papers, files, documents, and memoranda" that Cox and the Senate Watergate Committee requested. Senator Barry Goldwater repeated his August 1973 advice that the president "show up some morning at the Ervin Committee and say, 'Here I am, Sam. What do you want to know?'" Robert Ray, the Republican governor of Iowa, agreed: "Perhaps the only alternative left is an appearance by the president before the Senate Watergate Committee." Ray's

Massachusetts counterpart, Francis W. Sargent, voiced even less optimism: "I don't see how Mr. Nixon could recover." Nixon's former attorney general Elliot L. Richardson observed, "Behind the layers of secrecy successively peeled back by persistent investigations, we caught an ugly glimpse of the abuse of power. It has been a frightening glimpse."[3]

The editorials, the evaluations and suggestions of Republican politicians, and the laments of newspapers in places as varied as Charleston, South Carolina, and Emporia, Kansas, combined to undermine the charge that criticism of the president stemmed from partisanship. Criminal convictions, moreover, made news on a regular basis and proved that the charges rested on fact, not on wishful partisanship. Early in November, for example, Donald Segretti received a prison sentence for his participation in the dirty tricks against the candidates in the 1972 Democratic Party primaries. Four days later Judge Sirica sentenced six of the Watergate burglars to prison terms. At the sentencing, James W. McCord offered no excuses: "My participation in Watergate was in error and wrong." He then added, "I believed then as I believe now" that the president had authorized the burglary.[4] The next day an editorial in the *Nashville Tennessean* declared, "The crisis is very real. It has not been manufactured by the media, or the opposition Democrats, or the 'Nixon haters.' It is the product of men in government he selected and trusted."[5]

The willingness to corrupt democratic processes involved more than Nixon's assistants, cabinet members, and vice president. Three days after Sirica sentenced McCord and the others, Orin E. Atkins, chairman of the board of Ashland Oil, and Claude C. Wild Jr., vice president of Gulf Oil, pleaded guilty to having made illegal campaign contributions, using corporate funds, to Nixon's reelection campaign. They joined the long list of corporations guilty of similar crimes.

In the midst of this torrent of evidence of illegal activity, increasing criticism from former supporters, and calls for resignation, Nixon launched what he and the press called "Operation Candor." He intended to explain his actions and policies to the public and to Republicans. The appointments of Leon Jaworski and William Saxbe, Nixon hoped, had signaled a departure from previous positions. Then, on November 7, the president closed an address to the nation about energy shortages "with a personal note," in which he called Watergate "deplorable" but declared he had "no intention whatever of walking away from the job I was elected to do." He promised to do everything possible to remove "any doubts as to the integrity of the man who occupies the highest office in this land." Five days later he released a detailed statement concerning the two conversations the taping system had missed. To help the court determine the subjects on his mind on the days of those conversations,

Nixon announced he would voluntarily submit portions of tapes and diary notes he had made for postpresidential use in writing his memoirs. On November 15, at the conclusion of a speech before the annual convention of the National Association of Realtors, Nixon again closed with a reference to Watergate. He acknowledged "overzealous" persons had made mistakes, "mistakes that I would never have tolerated." But he insisted again, "I am not going to walk away" from "the job I was elected to do."[6]

Another part of Operation Candor consisted of a series of six meetings with the 234 Republicans in Congress to provide them the opportunity to question the president about Watergate. After one meeting with fifteen senators, which lasted more than two hours, the minority leader Hugh Scott stated that "everyone in the room — everyone — agreed on the need for full disclosure." Howard Baker urged Nixon to testify before the Ervin Committee. Tennessee's other senator, William E. Brock, later remarked, "It was more comments than questions."[7] The meetings with House Republicans proved equally lacking in results. Nixon actually held eight, rather than the planned six, meetings, all within a week, and forty-six Democrats were included among those who were invited.

On November 17, while on a five-day southern trip with stops in Florida, Georgia, and Tennessee, Nixon held a press conference in Orlando at the annual convention of the Associated Press Managing Editors Association. Watergate dominated once again, and once again the president reiterated that he had no intention of resigning. He explained the two missing tapes by saying that his setup was "no Apollo system," that President Johnson had "much better equipment." When asked if it were true that he had paid $792 in federal income tax in 1970 and $878 in 1971, he replied yes, because he had benefited from a large tax deduction when he donated his vice presidential papers to the government. He had made the transaction, he added, on the advice of Johnson early in 1969. A few minutes later, Nixon postponed a question and volunteered additional information about his personal finances. He said he welcomed "this kind of examination, because people have got to know whether or not their President is a crook. Well, I am not a crook."

In answering a question regarding executive privilege, Nixon recognized that privilege had limits and reminded his audience that he had waived the "privilege with regard to all members of my staff who have any knowledge of or who have had any charges made against them in the Watergate matter." Nixon added that he also had "voluntarily waived privilege with regard to turning over the tapes." Above all, he wanted "to avoid a precedent that might destroy the principle of confidentiality for future Presidents." He identified "the Jefferson rule" as his guide, because in that case, according to Nixon,

Chief Justice John Marshall ruled for Thomas Jefferson when that president turned over a summary of correspondence to the Court rather than the letters themselves. Nixon said he had followed Jefferson's precedent to guarantee a "very free flow of conversation, and that means confidentiality — I have a responsibility to protect the Presidency."[8] During the other three stops on his southern trip, Nixon avoided in his speeches any mention of Watergate. A few days after his return to Washington, a Library of Congress study cited errors of interpretation and fact in Nixon's version of the Jefferson case.

What little credibility Nixon may have gained by mid-November with his Operation Candor quickly dissipated when the White House counsel, J. Fred Buzhardt Jr., informed Judge Sirica that an eighteen-and-a-half-minute segment of the subpoenaed June 20, 1972, tape carried a buzz tone but no conversation. The tape recorded a conversation between the president and Haldeman the day after Nixon's return to Washington from Florida, where he had been at the time of the break-in on June 17. Before the two men met, Haldeman had spent ninety minutes with Ehrlichman, Mitchell, Dean, and Kleindienst.

On November 26, a troubled Sirica conducted a hearing at which the president's personal secretary, Rose Mary Woods, testified to having apparently erased five minutes of the tape when she interrupted transcribing it to answer the telephone. The *National Review* commented: "Believers in the accidental theory could gather for lunch in a phone booth."[9] No one on the president's staff offered an explanation to account for the remaining thirteen and a half minutes. Sirica demanded an answer and appointed a six-person panel of electronic experts, jointly selected by Jaworski and the White House, to examine "the authenticity and integrity" of the tapes. Two days later Buzhardt testified that each of the subpoenaed tapes contained blank gaps lasting several minutes.

Similar editorials in the *New York Times,* symbol of the liberal northeastern establishment that Nixon and his staff so disliked, and the *Akron Beacon Journal,* a representative of middle America, quickly revealed the broad consensus against the president. On November 29 the *New York Times* argued that "since Mr. Nixon refuses either to resign or to clarify his own role in Watergate, the only alternative, it seems to us, is impeachment itself." Three days later the *Beacon Journal* lamented that "the Richard Nixon we endorsed and the Richard Nixon most Americans voted for, is not the Richard Nixon we now know." In recommending impeachment, the editorial maintained that "the continuing scandal is at least as divisive as an impeachment proceeding would be, and impeachment would have an end in sight." Like its New York counterpart, the

Ohio newspaper reminded its readers that an impeachment was "not a conviction"; impeachment, however, would force Nixon "to submit evidence that he would not, for whatever reason, submit voluntarily." Impeachment, moreover, "is a process approved by our founding fathers in the Constitution." The disclosure of the erased eighteen minutes had shaken most interested Americans. The *Kansas City Times* ended its editorial on the subject with the question, "Does anyone believe anything any more?"[10]

Events not directly associated with Watergate, meanwhile, continued to tarnish the administration and to reflect poorly on Nixon's judgment. On November 30, Egil Krogh, an Ehrlichman assistant but since the previous February the undersecretary of the Department of Transportation, pleaded guilty in federal district court to the violation of the civil rights of Dr. Lewis Fielding, Daniel Ellsberg's former psychiatrist. Describing his role in the burglary of Fielding's office, Krogh stated that Nixon personally told him to have the Plumbers learn all they could about Ellsberg's motives and those of his associates and that the assignment involved national security. Krogh then declared that his conscience no longer permitted him to "assert national security as a defense" for the burglary.[11]

The next week Gerald R. Ford took the oath of office as vice president. The sixty-year-old Grand Rapids, Michigan, resident, a congressman since 1948, enjoyed widespread support as the nation's first vice president to assume office under the Twenty-Fifth Amendment of the Constitution. Although Ford was a staunch partisan, Democrats and Republicans respected him for his candor, honesty, and decency. The confirmation vote in the Senate (92 to 3) and in the House (387 to 35) indicated the noncontroversial character of Nixon's choice. Politicians and the public, on the other hand, remained keenly aware that the necessity for a new vice president stemmed from Nixon's unfortunate selection of Spiro Agnew as his running mate.

Two days after Ford took office, the president released the most comprehensive record of "assets and liabilities, expenses and income" in presidential history. He did so "to remove doubts that have been raised, and to correct misinformation that currently exists about what I have earned and what I own." Furthermore, he asked the Joint Congressional Committee on Internal Revenue Taxation to examine the record and to determine whether "my tax returns should have shown different results." Finally, he announced his intentions to give his San Clemente house "to the people of the United States."[12] Some of the records Nixon released revealed a 1970 income of $262,942 and a tax payment of $792, a 1971 income of $262,384 and a tax payment of $878, and a 1972 income of $268,777 and a tax payment of $4,298.

Once again, newspapers that previously supported the president voiced strong criticism. The *Cincinnati Post* scolded Nixon for not "setting a good example" and pointed out that "in the past four and a half years, his net worth rose from $307,000 to close to a million, yet his tax payments have tended to go down instead of up."[13] Editorially, the *Wall Street Journal* commented that Nixon's "marginal deductions" were "a mistake in judgment and an insensitivity to the standards a President ought to follow."[14]

Two days later the first tapes that Nixon surrendered arrived at the special prosecutor's office. Six persons crowded into the office and listened to the March 21, 1973, tape. Silent, they heard the president coaching Haldeman about the need to offer evasive answers: "If you're asked, you just say, 'I don't remember, I can't recall. I can't give an answer to that that I can recall.'" Two of the listeners, Assistant Special Prosecutors Richard Ben-Veniste and George Frampton Jr., later wrote that "we knew that we had turned the corner of Watergate." Nixon had obstructed justice, and the tape proved it. Jaworski listened to the tape and advised the president's chief of staff, Alexander Haig, to hire "the finest criminal lawyer you can find . . . and let him study the tapes."[15] From that day, the special prosecutor and his key assistants were convinced of the president's guilt and hypocrisy. For Nixon, the future held impeachment or resignation and a possible prison sentence.

In an end-of-the year interview, the news commentator Walter Cronkite placed Nixon's problems in perspective, self-inflicted and otherwise. "Watergate just happened to come," Cronkite observed, "at the same time as the demand for honesty in relations between the sexes, in advertising, in ecology, in almost everything. . . . That's what is forcing the President's hand right now."[16]

By January 1974, 25 percent of Republican voters and 40 percent of independent voters believed the country probably would benefit if the president resigned. The Harris Survey also found that the majority of Republicans and 75 percent of all Americans believed it was wrong that a person with an annual income of $8,000 paid more taxes than Nixon had paid. Only 26 percent of Americans believed the president had told the truth about the financing of his two houses.

Still, Nixon retained a seemingly irreducible core of support that offered a simple explanation for the president's problems. The *Portland Oregonian* insisted, "The Democratic Congress, without a formal declaration of war, has launched a full-scale attack of unmitigated ferocity on the executive branch and its Republican head, Richard M. Nixon."[17] The *Arizona Republic* in Phoenix maintained that "the liberal Democratic bloc, with the full support of the Eastern seaboard mass media, has determined the President must resign."[18]

Relentlessly, week after week, investigations, indictments, confessions, trials, charges, and countercharges were reported, whether by the print media or by radio and television. The legal processes in a democracy are complex and time-consuming, and with the president involved, the public had a right to know about each procedural step. And the public seemed interested. Early in the new year, for example, the IRS announced that it would reexamine the president's tax returns because of questions voiced by the press. E. Howard Hunt won release from prison, pending consideration of his appeal. Attorney General William Saxbe condemned the Ervin Committee for issuing subpoenas for more than 500 White House documents and tapes. The White House announced that the Boston attorney James D. St. Clair would replace Fred Buzhardt as the head of the president's Watergate legal team, with Buzhardt remaining as counsel to Nixon.

In a broad sense Nixon kept Watergate in the news by refusing to release the tapes and by employing every stratagem possible to delay the investigation. In his fight, moreover, he courted public opinion by cloaking his actions as being in the interest of the office of the presidency. On January 8, 1974, for instance, Nixon released two "white papers," one of seventeen and one of eight pages, detailing his involvement in two 1971 decisions concerning an increase in the federal subsidy for milk and an antitrust suit against ITT. Neither case, of course, related to Watergate, but both reflected on the Nixon administration. These two white papers concluded Operation Candor, which had started in November with the series of meetings with members of Congress and continued with his press conference, with his five-day southern trip, and with his release of his financial records. Both the milk subsidy increase and the ITT case were controversial and had been in the news off and on for almost two years. The ITT case first broke in February 1972 during the Senate's confirmation hearings on Richard Kleindienst for attorney general.

The president's two white papers rebutted the charges that in exchange for campaign contributions he had ordered an increase in the subsidy for milk and that the Justice Department drop its case against ITT. In Iowa, the *Des Moines Register* concluded that the white papers provided "more background than had been told before, but they add up to reiteration of the Presidents's previous statements that at no time was he influenced by political campaign contributions." The editorial pointed out that the white papers included no documents and tapes bearing on the case. The *Lincoln (Nebr.) Star* agreed: "Without the evidence, the white papers represent nothing more than a holding action." The *Albuquerque Journal* observed, "Like many of President

Nixon's recent public addresses, the white papers . . . are adequate for those who need not be convinced, but they served no useful purpose for those who do." Even some of the newspapers that believed Nixon found little to celebrate. The *Salt Lake City Desert News* pointed out, "The President's plea that he could not veto the price increase because it would alienate dairy farmers, makes one wonder why he wasn't more concerned about alienating milk consumers who foot the bill." In both the milk and the ITT cases, the editorial continued, "the government took what seems to have been the path of least resistance. Brave and bold the administration's decisions weren't." From Phoenix, the *Arizona Republic* lamented that Operation Candor had been "something less than a success." The *Chicago Sun–Times* decided that "Mr. Nixon by and large deserves good marks for his statements. . . . But he cannot expect now to have undocumented narratives accepted on faith."[19]

On January 15 yet another Watergate story filled most newspapers' front pages. The panel of experts appointed by Judge Sirica to examine the eighteen-minute gap on the June 20, 1972, tape submitted its unanimous findings. At least five and possibly as many as nine separate hand-manipulations of the Uher 5000 recorder produced the erasure. Rose Mary Woods's claim that she erased five minutes of the tape when she accidentally pressed the wrong button lost credibility. Between October 1 and November 21, only five persons had access to both the tape and the Uher 5000 machine: Woods; Nixon; Stephen Bull, the presidential assistant who had storage responsibility for the tapes; Fred Buzhardt; and Major General John C. Bennett, deputy to Chief of Staff Haig. Sirica held several days of hearings and recommended a grand jury investigation into the possibility that one or more persons intentionally destroyed evidence.

Newspaper editorials across the country reacted to the report. In West Virginia, the *Charleston Gazette* concluded that "no one in his right mind could be made to believe that a person could push the record and erase buttons five to nine times by hand accidentally. It had to be deliberate." The *Toledo Blade* declared, "The only logical inference any reasonable person could draw is that it was done because the evidence recorded would have been extremely damaging to the President's case." The *Detroit News* asked, "How much is the public supposed to swallow without getting completely sick to its stomach?" The *Dallas Times Herald* maintained, "It is beyond belief that an 'accident' could have been repeated in one segment of a tape five times in a row" and called the report "a damaging blow to President Nixon." In South Carolina the *Greenville News* was more cautious but ended its editorial commenting that "even the President's strongest and most faithful supporters cannot stand another year of multiple controversies without more positive aid from the White House." The *Arizona Republic,* perhaps Nixon's most loyal supporter, admitted "the damage to President Nixon's image is immense."[20]

The Republican Party's two most visible officials, aside from the president, quickly tried to counter this latest criticism. On January 20, Senate Republican leader Hugh Scott appeared on CBS's *Face the Nation* and revealed he had the "information available . . . which would indicate that on specific items the President would be exculpated entirely."[21] Scott refused to describe what he meant by information. He commented, however, that he did not believe the campaign to impeach the president was a political movement. At a press conference two days later Vice President Ford disclosed that the day before he had spent an hour and a half with Nixon and that the president had volunteered to show material relating to Watergate. Ford asserted that this "information will exonerate the President. It will totally undercut the testimony of John Dean." But Ford added, "I haven't had time to read the information" and because "this information has been turned over to Jaworski, it would be improper for the White House to release it now."[22] Ford and Scott did not advance Nixon's credibility because they offered no evidence that would exonerate him. An Associated Press story soon reported that Jaworski had uncovered no evidence that contradicted Dean's testimony. The *Chicago Tribune,* which had endorsed Nixon in 1972, called Ford's explanation that he lacked time to read the material "lame" and dismissed equally "as lame" his claim that the White House could not release the information. The editorial reasoned that "the only conceivable justification for withholding proof that Mr. Nixon is innocent would be that it pins the blame on somebody else who, presumably, is under investigation." If this were true, the "informed source in the prosecutor's office is lying and every moment's delay in making the information public amounts to a national disgrace."[23]

The same week Barry Goldwater offered a grim assessment; he predicted "that Watergate would cost every Republican candidate a 'disastrous' ten percent of the total vote this year." He added, "I can sense a strong feeling right here on the Hill . . . that many Republican members of Congress would like to run this year without Mr. Nixon."[24]

The last week in January 1974 brought three more front-page stories. First, Egil Krogh Jr., once the head of the White House Plumbers, received a prison sentence for his role in the office burglary of Dr. Lewis J. Fielding. Nixon's supporters, however, found encouragement in that Krogh never implicated the president in the burglary. Second, the Ervin Committee announced that it would postpone indefinitely the last two items on its schedule: the dairy industry contributions to Nixon's 1972 campaign and the $100,000 that the industrialist Howard R. Hughes had transferred to Bebe Rebozo, Nixon's close personal friend. The third important story appeared when California state judge Gordon Ringer reported he would summon the president as a defense witness in the trial of John D. Ehrlichman, G. Gordon Liddy, and David R. Young Jr., three more of Nixon's aides charged with the Fielding burglary. The next day the president announced he would not appear as a witness, citing constitutional grounds.

Nixon devoted the last part of his State of the Union message on January 30, about one-ninth of the total length, to "the so-called Watergate affair." He told the nation he had given the special prosecutor "all the material that he needs to conclude his investigations. . . . The time has come to bring that investigation and the other investigations of this matter to an end." The president promised to cooperate with the House Judiciary Committee in its investigation but warned he would never do "anything that weakens the Office of the President of the United States or impairs the ability of the Presidents of the future to make the great decisions." Finally, Nixon reaffirmed that he had "no intention whatever of ever walking away from the job that the people elected me to do."[25]

Nothing had changed. Once again Nixon courted public support by expressing his willingness to cooperate, subject only to limitations he would determine. He wanted to end the affair, and he would not resign. Unless he reversed his position on the tapes, however, the Watergate affair would continue until the Supreme Court rendered a decision. Not certain how the Court would rule, Nixon would use every means possible to impede the progress of the case. He still hoped that the public would tire of the issue, that the Court would rule in his favor, and, if it ruled against him, that the House would fail to impeach him.

By the time Nixon gave his State of the Union message, Leon Jaworski had been special prosecutor for three months. On his second day on the job, he sent his first request to the president for files concerning the ITT case. Other requests quickly followed. Within two weeks Jaworski met with Chief of Staff Alexander Haig and Nixon's lawyer, Fred Buzhardt, and wanted to know why the materials had not arrived. Six days later Jaworski sent a letter listing all the tapes and documents he and his predecessor had requested and the president had not sent. On December 6 Jaworski informed Nixon that if certain tapes and documents did not arrive within a few days, he would subpoena them. The president had fired Cox for similar action. Jaworski demanded a timetable of when to expect the materials. By this time his actions had convinced his initially suspicious staff that he had every intention of directing the investigation independently, wherever it led.[26]

On December 12 Jaworski received from Judge Sirica seven of the nine tapes that Cox had subpoenaed. Sirica had reviewed the tapes and ruled, case by case, on the president's claims that portions were unrelated to Watergate and, therefore, outside the jurisdiction of the special prosecutor. Six of Jaworski's closest assistants listened first to the tape of the March 21, 1973, meeting between Nixon and Dean. Since April 1973 Nixon had insisted that he first learned from Dean about the cover-up on March 21. Dean, however, had dated Nixon's knowledge as months earlier. The tape corroborated Dean's testimony, and more. By the time Jaworski listened to all the tapes, he "believed the President to be criminally involved in the Watergate cover-up." By January 7 Jaworski's office had prepared a 128-page document "outlining Nixon's apparent complicity."[27] Two days later Jaworski requested more tapes.

Haig replied to Jaworski that the president probably would not turn over any additional tapes, stating that "it's a calculated risk he's prepared to take."[28] A week later Jaworski played the first tape for the grand jury. Nixon's new Watergate lawyer, James St. Clair, informed Jaworski that he had all the tapes he needed. Through St. Clair the president achieved delay but also avoided an unequivocal refusal; Nixon did not want Jaworski to report to Congress that the president had stopped cooperating. From Jaworski, Nixon faced a threat that could end his presidency.

The House Judiciary Committee posed an equally formidable threat to the president. Immediately following the Saturday Night Massacre, Democratic House leaders agreed to have that committee start an inquiry into whether these actions were sufficient grounds for impeachment. Just before Christmas, committee chairman Peter Rodino appointed John M. Doar as majority counsel for the inquiry. A native of Wisconsin, the fifty-two-year-old Doar had earned his law degree from the University of California at Berkeley. After practicing law for ten years with his father in New Richmond, Wisconsin, Doar spent eight years in the Civil Rights Division of the Justice Department before moving in 1968 to a private practice in New York City. Later that year he won election as president of the New York City Board of Education. As majority counsel for the Judiciary Committee, he managed to avoid publicity and partisanship, for he was a Republican. The Republican members of the committee named Albert E. Jenner Jr., a widely respected Chicago trial lawyer, as chief minority counsel.

Doar and Rodino proceeded deliberately. Doar built his case essentially from documents rather than from witnesses. Some Democrats criticized him for moving too cautiously. Many Republicans also found the pace too slow because they wanted an impeachment vote as soon as possible, to distance it from the November elections.

Rodino, a native of Newark, New Jersey, had represented that district in Congress since 1948. Critics could not stereotype him. Although an ardent supporter of civil rights legislation, he opposed government aid for abortions and once voted in favor of a "no-knock" provision in a District of Columbia crime bill. Until President Nixon ordered the invasion of Cambodia in spring 1970, Rodino, a World War II veteran, supported the Vietnam War. Above all, Rodino, himself an attorney, intended to lay the procedural groundwork for impeachment without a trace of partisanship. The Doar-Rodino approach eventually won overwhelming endorsement. On February 6, the House, by a vote of 410 to 4, authorized the Judiciary Committee to subpoena anything and any person, the president included, in its investigation. Doar soon asked St. Clair for a long list of tapes and documents, especially those covering the period between February 20 and April 18, 1973.

Doar and his staff, quickly numbering over 100 and including a recent Yale Law School graduate named Hillary Rodham, spent much of January and February on the question of the definition of an impeachable offense. The constitutional provision covering impeachment offered little guidance: "The President, Vice President, and all Civil Officers of the United States, shall be removed from Office on Impeachment for, and conviction of, Treason, Bribery, or other high Crimes and Misdemeanors." Charges against Nixon obviously fell under this last, vague category. On February 21, Doar presented to Rodino a report, "Constitutional Grounds for Presidential Impeachment."

The Doar report concluded that "impeachment is a constitutional remedy addressed to serious offenses against the system of government." These offenses, the report stated, need not be traditionally criminal because the original intent of those who wrote the Constitution "quite clearly" included "some ultimate check on the conduct of the executive." The punishment stipulated "removal from office and possible disqualification from future office," implied that "high crimes" referred not to statutory abuses but to offenses "that subvert the structure of government, or undermine the integrity of office and even the Constitution itself." After reviewing the British practice of impeachment, as well as several cases of American impeachment, the report pointed out that in those, "the criminality issue was not raised at all." Although stressing that the abuse of power, not criminality, justified impeachment, the report concluded that "not all presidential misconduct is sufficient to constitute grounds for impeachment. There is a further requirement — substantiality." Finally, the Doar report argued that scrutiny of a president "must be considered as a whole in the context of the office, not in terms of separate or isolated events."[29]

Not all Republicans, including many of those serving as members of the Judiciary Committee, accepted Doar's systematic reasoning. Nixon's lawyers issued their own interpretation that the impeachment process must demonstrate criminality. Then, on February 25, at his first news conference in four months, Nixon declared, "You don't have to be a constitutional lawyer to know that the Constitution is very precise in defining what is an impeachable offense. . . . That a criminal offense on the part of the President is the requirement for impeachment." In response to the fourth question regarding impeachment, the president replied, "I do not expect to be impeached."[30] To defend himself from impeachment, Nixon employed a staff that included twelve full-time and four part-time attorneys. He then requested from Congress an additional $1.5 million appropriation to hire another twenty attorneys.

The *Wall Street Journal* offered its interpretation. The newspaper agreed with Doar "that an impeachment need not be based on a violation of criminal law" but added that such a conclusion "is a point without much relevance to the current proceedings." The editors reasoned that the grounds on which the House might impeach the president were also criminal violations. Moderates, who hold the decisive votes, the editorial continued, would want solid evidence. In closing, the editors suggested that "the Judiciary Committee would be wise to concentrate on the alleged criminal offense. . . . In this case, if there were no criminal offenses there are no high political grounds."[31]

The seriousness with which the *Wall Street Journal* approached the impeachment issue reflected a widespread public belief that the Watergate investigation might well lead to the nation's first presidential impeachment conviction. Increasingly, Republicans realized that this possible outcome threatened their own political careers. The result of a special election in Michigan's Fifth Congressional District on February 19 strongly suggested that voters had turned against Republicans. In the election to fill the seat Gerald Ford vacated when he became vice president, a Democrat won for the first time in sixty-four years. Ford personally had campaigned for the Republican candidate, Robert VanderLaan, a politician who had never lost an election and who served as majority leader in the Michigan State Senate. The Democrat who won, Richard VanderVeen, by contrast, had never won a previous election, despite several attempts. VanderVeen had labeled his campaign "a referendum on President Nixon" and had called for Nixon's resignation. The *Saginaw News* believed the election outcome lent "credence to the harpings of Senator Barry Goldwater who has been saying all along that the Republican party was going to pay a heavy price at the polls this year because of Watergate and the President's failure to clear himself of its ugly shadows." The *Nashville Tennessean* concluded the election could not help but bring "qualms of fear to Republicans in other parts of the nation — such as Tennessee." The editorial conjectured that the Republican Party "could be facing one of the most disastrous off-year election defeats in its history if Mr. Nixon is still in the White House in November."[32]

For the Nixon administration, the negative news seemed endless. On February 25, the day the president expressed his interpretation of grounds for impeachment, Herbert Kalmbach pleaded guilty to a charge of accepting on behalf of the president's reelection campaign a $100,000 contribution in exchange for a promise of an ambassadorship. The former associate chairman of the Finance Committee to Re-elect the President also pleaded guilty to raising secret campaign funds for congressional campaigns. Nixon's assertion "that ambassadorships have not been for sale, to my knowledge," provoked the *Louisville Courier–Journal* to comment that "like so many of the stands the White House has taken during the Watergate scandals, the latest presidential statements . . . again prompt the question: If the President really didn't know, who was running the things at the White House?"[33] Kalmbach's promise may have been crude and direct, but the political practice of rewarding financial supporters with ambassadorships was nothing new. Kalmbach's guilty plea, however, when added to guilty pleas by other Nixon staff — Dean, Magruder, Segretti, LaRue, Krogh, and Porter — indicated a pattern of criminality that crowded, at least, at the door of the Oval Office.

Four days after Kalmbach pleaded guilty, the federal grand jury investigating the Watergate cover-up submitted its indictment to Judge Sirica. The jury indicted seven former Nixon assistants, including the four with whom Nixon had worked most closely: Mitchell, Haldeman, Ehrlichman, and Colson. No previous president had ever had his four closest advisers indicted. Those indicted also included Mitchell's former assistant attorney general, Robert C. Mardian; Haldeman's chief assistant, Gordon C. Strachan; and the chief attorney for CREEP, Kenneth W. Parkinson. All but Haldeman were lawyers. The charges against the seven were conspiracy, false declaration, obstruction of justice, and perjury. Subsequently, Mardian had his conviction overturned and Parkinson won acquittal. Before releasing the seven defendants on their own recognizance, the court first photographed and fingerprinted them.

The grand jury in addition submitted a sealed report to Sirica that contained information about Nixon's involvement in the cover-up, supported by reference to specific testimony of witnesses and tapes. The released report did not contain any analysis of or comments about the material. The jury requested that Sirica transmit the sealed report to the House Judiciary Committee. Jaworski left immediately for a weekend at his Texas home while his staff planned a few days of rest after nine months of investigations and two months of drafting the final two reports. Almost at once, editors from *Newsweek* and the *Washington Post* telephoned the special prosecutors's office to confirm whether the grand jury had wanted to indict the president along with the other seven. The special prosecutor's staff could not contain the rumors. Within a few days, the news routinely included the story, based on unnamed sources, that in a straw vote the grand jury had voted unanimously to indict Nixon.

During the discussions between the grand jury and the staff in the Office of the Special Prosecutor, Jaworski had argued against indicting the president. The second week in March, to answer the steady stream of inquiries that flooded his office, Jaworski drafted and released a formal statement regarding presidential indictment. He explained that in a situation of "legal doubt," he opposed an indictment even if the evidence might justify one. Moreover, he pointed out that "in the first instance," the House Judiciary Committee was a more "appropriate body" to evaluate evidence regarding possible criminal activity of a president. The special prosecutor's inclusion of the phrase "in the first instance" highlighted the grand jury's point in the preamble to its indictment report, that should Congress, "in the first instance" not act, the grand jury reserved the right to consider, in the second instance, indictment at a later time.[34]

Nixon did not challenge the special prosecutor's request for Sirica to deliver the sealed report of evidence to the House Judiciary Committee, but Haldeman and Strachan filed a writ of mandamus against transmission. Sirica ruled against the two former Nixon aides, who then appealed. The U.S. Court of Appeals denied the appeal, and subsequently, on March 25 the committee received the sealed report.

On March 5, just after the submission of the grand jury report, voters in Ohio's First Congressional District elected only the fourth Democrat in the twentieth century. The three previous Democratic victories had been in years of Republican disasters: 1912, when the Republican Party split into two parties; 1936, when Franklin D. Roosevelt won by his greatest margin; and 1964, when Goldwater led his party to a resounding defeat. In 1972 the Republican House candidate had won 70 percent of the vote in the Cincinnati district; in the March 1974 election, the Republican candidate's percentage dropped to 48 percent. Ohio voters, when combined with those in Vice President Ford's former Michigan congressional district, indicated that the longer Watergate continued, the more voters would vent their scorn on all Republican politicians.

The day after the Ohio special election, the president held his second press conference within ten days. Of the eighteen questions asked by reporters, fourteen related to Watergate. Three journalists inquired about the tape of the March 21, 1973, meeting with Haldeman and Dean. Nixon replied that on that date Dean had told him for the first time "that payments had been made to defendants for the purpose of keeping them quiet, not simply for their defense." The president also maintained that "when individuals read the entire transcript of the twenty-first meeting, or hear the entire tape, where we discussed all these options, they may reach different interpretations, but I know what I meant, and I know also what I did." Nixon responded to a question about impeachment, saying that "the crime of obstruction of justice is a serious crime and would be an impeachable offense" but added he did not expect the House Judiciary Committee to find him guilty of such a crime. He emphasized again his desire for a speedy conclusion to the Watergate investigation, reaffirmed his policy of "full disclosure," and reiterated that he would "do nothing to weaken the Office of the Presidency." Finally, he twice said that he would answer written questions from the House Judiciary Committee and was willing to meet with its two ranking members.[35]

The president's statement at this March 6, 1974, press conference of having first learned on March 21, 1973, that his staff had paid hush money to the Watergate burglars contradicted his public statement of August 15, 1973. On that date Nixon claimed to have learned on March 21, 1973, that "the money had been used for attorneys' fees and family support, not that it had been paid to procure silence from the recipients." Nixon's new statement brought his public position into agreement with the tapes but revealed a disregard for the law. The payment of money to induce silence of indicted persons constituted an obstruction of justice. Title 18, section 1510 of the U.S. Code, moreover, further criminalized the delay of reporting information about an obstruction of justice.

Nixon's press conference remarks predictably drew negative and positive editorial reactions. Some editorials observed the president "moving toward a greater openness and accessibility."[36] Yet these editorials held that Nixon still had stopped short of candor. The Los Angeles Times summarized this broad perspective: "From the very beginning of the Watergate scandal, he has fought to limit the scope of every inquiry into his own possible involvement." The editorial reminded its readers that the president had not honored "his pledge of full cooperation with Archibald Cox," had not honored "his pledge of full cooperation with Leon Jaworski," had fought the Senate Watergate

Committee "every step of the way for evidence material," and had indicated that he "may pursue the same contentious tactics in his relations with the House Judiciary Committee."[37] Nixon believed he had no other option than resistance, evasion, and delay. He continued to hope the public would become so annoyed with the slow process of the investigation that the House Judiciary Committee and the special prosecutor would be forced to complete their work as quickly as possible, without obtaining all the material they had subpoenaed. Such public displeasure certainly existed. The *Seattle Times* remarked, "People are weary of the everlasting Watergate controversy" and have little interest "in the details of the daily jousting between Capitol Hill and White House lawyers." America wanted, the editorial concluded, the truth about Watergate, but they did not "want it to be the center of government attention for month after month after month." The *Wall Street Journal* similarly observed that "the last thing we need is another round in the historic but ultimately petty battle about the prerogatives of the branches of government."[38] Whatever the frustrations, however, the investigatory process continued at its slow pace.

Hardly a day passed without a Watergate story. The same day as Nixon's press conference, the president's lawyer, St. Clair, told the House Judiciary Committee that Nixon would refuse any future requests for materials relating to Watergate; the documents the Watergate grand jury turned over to the House committee were "more than sufficient." March 7, the day after Nixon's press conference, a second Watergate grand jury indicted six men involved in the September 1971 burglary of the office of Dr. Lewis J. Fielding. In addition to Ehrlichman and Colson, the jury indicted three who already were sentenced to prison terms for their roles in the Watergate break-in: G. Gordon Liddy, Bernard Barker, and Eugenio Martinez. Attorney General William Saxbe made news when he stated that a president had the same responsibility as other citizens to report to law-enforcing officials any information regarding a crime. And then Nixon created more news.

On March 15 the president traveled to Chicago for public appearances in hopes of reducing the overwhelmingly negative image of Watergate. Before that city's Executives Club, Nixon skipped the traditional speech and immediately opened the floor to a fifty-minute question and answer session. The friendly audience focused only five of their fifteen questions on Watergate and asked a sixth about his personal taxes. Once again Nixon repeated his familiar positions. He wanted "the full story out," he wanted "a prompt and just conclusion," and he promised to "cooperate as fully as I possibly can." But he again vowed to "do nothing to weaken the Office of the Presidency" and reiterated "the necessity of protecting the confidentiality of the Presidential conversations." The charges against him Nixon dismissed as "all totally false." He declared that "from a personal standpoint, resignation is an easy cop-out," but it would "lead to weak and unstable Presidencies in the future," and, therefore, he would not take the easy course. Then he declared that "while I leave the podium, I don't expect to leave the Presidency until January 20, 1977."[39] Nixon's explanations and positions, so often stated, pitted the word of the president against the charges that politicians, media representatives, and investigators levied. Conscientious followers of the Watergate investigations realized that circumstantial evidence totally supported those aligned against the president. The struggle would continue until the investigations produced what observers called "a smoking gun" in the president's hands.

The day after his Chicago appearance, Nixon gave a short speech when he arrived at the Nashville Metropolitan Airport. Later that evening he offered some informal comments before a friendly audience at the opening of the new home of the Grand Ole Opry House. In honor of his wife's birthday, he played "Happy Birthday" on the piano, followed by "My Wild Irish Rose." He then lauded country music because "it comes from the heart of America, because this is the heart of America," because "it talks about family, it talks about religion," and because it "radiates a love of this Nation, patriotism." He capped his appearance by playing "God Bless America."[40]

Three days later Senator James L. Buckley (C-N.Y.) pointed to "the widespread conviction that Watergate and all that it has brought in its wake has done unique and perhaps irrevocable damage to our entire system of government." To resolve the crisis, he declared, "Richard Nixon must resign as President."[41] The war of words continued; a few hours after Buckley issued his ominous call, Nixon answered questions in Houston before the annual convention of the National Association of Broadcasters.

Despite the president's opening statement, reporting his decisions about oil-producing countries lifting the oil embargo they had placed against the United States as a result of its support of Israel in the Yom Kippur War, ten of the eighteen questions reporters asked him pertained to Watergate, presidential accessibility, and media coverage. The first question concerned Buckley's recommendation. Nixon replied, "It would be bad statesmanship" for a president to resign if the charges against him were false, regardless of polls. Paul McGonigle from KOY Radio in Phoenix commented favorably on the president's accessibility of late. Nixon responded that "the press conference is a very useful medium through which a President can convey his views to the American people." Because he stood before broadcasters, several questions focused on the press. Once Nixon paraphrased his "friend," Jack Horner, who served for many years as senior White House correspondent for the *Washington Star:* "There is always an adversary relationship between the President and the press. That is healthy, that is good." Nixon continued, "The President should treat the press just as fairly as the press treats him." He also said he realized "that bad news is news, and good news is not news. . . . I am not obsessed by how the press reports me. . . . I am not going to be diverted by any criticism from the press."

Yet the media's questions regarding Watergate rankled the president. Like a stuck tape, Nixon repeated before the broadcasters all his previous positions. He defended "the confidentiality of Presidential conversations and communications," explained that the House Judiciary Committee had sufficient information to complete its investigation, and insisted he wanted to bring Watergate "to a conclusion as quickly as we can." The break-in, he believed, "should not have been covered up, and I have done the very best that I can over the past year to see that it is uncovered. I have cooperated completely with not only the grand jury but also with other investigative agencies." The problem developed, he reiterated, because "I frankly paid too little attention to the campaign." Both Dan Rather of CBS News and Tom Brokaw of NBC News challenged Nixon on his claim of complete cooperation. In response, the president refined his position to mean cooperation that did not violate the principle of confidentiality. He closed the press conference by saying, "I will not participate in the destruction of the Office of the Presidency of the United States while I am in this office."[42]

The bad news for the president did not stop with the delivery that March of the sealed grand jury report to the Judiciary Committee. On April 3 the Internal Revenue Service announced that its audit revealed Nixon owed $432,787 in back taxes, plus $33,000 in interest penalties. The assessment rested primarily on the finding that Nixon had donated his prepresidential records to the National Archives after the date the law permitted such tax-deductible contributions. Although unrelated to Watergate, the tax affair further diminished the public's perception of Nixon's personal conduct.

Two days after the tax report, the president flew to Paris to attend a memorial service for the French president Georges Pompidou. That same day a jury found Dwight Chapin guilty on two counts of perjury. While he served as Nixon's appointments secretary, Chapin also helped instruct Donald Segretti in his dirty tricks campaign. A few days later a judge sentenced Herbert L. Porter for perjury before the grand jury. As Magruder's deputy at CREEP, Porter had helped devise the cover-up by testifying that Liddy alone had planned and approved the break-in. Neither the Chapin nor the Porter case directly touched Nixon, except to contribute to a general impression of an administration lacking morality.

More threatening to Nixon than the convictions of his former aides was the second tape crisis, then nearing a climax. Both Doar and Jaworski were determined to obtain the tapes, and Nixon had less public support than he had had during the first crisis the previous October. For a month the House Judiciary Committee and St. Clair remained deadlocked over Nixon's refusal to submit additional tapes. On April 11 the committee voted thirty-three to three to subpoena forty-two tapes it originally had requested late in February. The subpoena, the first a House committee ever issued to a president, called for Nixon to comply by April 25. At St. Clair's request, the committee extended the deadline to April 30.

Jaworski confronted the president in much the same manner. Throughout the winter, Nixon, through St. Clair, had parried Jaworski's requests. Twice St. Clair informed Jaworski that Nixon would consider requests for materials on a case-to-case basis. On April 16 a frustrated Jaworski applied to Judge Sirica for a subpoena to obtain tapes to use in preparation for the trials of Mitchell, Haldeman, Ehrlichman, and four other Nixon aides whom the grand jury had indicted. Among the tapes Jaworski sought was the June 23, 1972, tape of the conversation between Haldeman and Nixon. The president now faced two subpoenas and a crisis.

In a national television and radio address on April 30 Nixon explained his response to the Judiciary Committee's subpoena. Rather than send the subpoenaed tapes, the president announced that he would send the committee transcripts of the tapes plus transcripts of other conversations not subpoenaed but that dealt with Watergate. Nixon pointed to a pile of notebooks, "more than 1,200 pages," and proclaimed "everything that is relevant is included — the rough as well as the smooth." Nixon invited the Democratic chairman and the most senior Republican member of the House Judiciary Committee to listen to the tapes and evaluate the authenticity and completeness of the transcripts. Once again, Nixon repeated that "the President has nothing to hide in this matter." He also explained that parts of the transcript "will seem to be contradictory with one another, and parts will be in conflict with some of the testimony given in the Senate Watergate Committee hearings." He recognized the tapes contained "ambiguities" and that "different people with different perspectives might interpret [them] in drastically different ways." But he insisted the transcripts would show that "I had no knowledge of the cover-up until I was informed of it by John Dean on March 21."[43]

Although the immediate reaction among the Republican members of the committee was favorable, the Judiciary Committee voted the next day to send the president a letter informing him that he had not complied with its April 11 subpoena. Only one Republican, William S. Cohen of Maine, joined the Democrats in the vote. The released transcripts fascinated the public as they were published by nearly fifty newspapers, some with weekend supplements and others with daily installments. National Public Radio read the transcript over its 164 stations. CBS Television compared passages with clips of previous, contradictory testimonies. Dell and Bantam Publishers rushed the transcripts into paperback editions; within a week some 3 million copies were in print.

As an attempt to win public support, Nixon's release of the transcripts proved an unqualified disaster. The negative impact rivaled that following the Saturday Night Massacre. The Senate Republican leader, Hugh Scott, characterized the transcripts as "deplorable, disgusting, shabby, immoral." Senator Robert W. Packwood (R-Oreg.) characterized Nixon's concept of government as "rather frightening." Emmet Hughes, speechwriter for President Eisenhower, argued that his former boss never would have tolerated such conversations as the transcript revealed: "Anybody who would have engaged in even a sixty-second exchange like those would have been thrown out." The House Republican leader, John J. Rhodes, suggested that Nixon reconsider resignation.[44] William Randolph Hearst Jr., editor in chief of the Hearst newspaper chain, concluded in his editorial that "President Richard M. Nixon has made it impossible for me to continue believing what he claims about himself in the Watergate mess." Regarding the tapes, Hearst wrote, "I have never heard anything as ruthless, deplorable and ethically indefensible as the talk on those White House tapes."[45]

The transcripts convinced many newspapers to withdraw their support of the president and to join the campaign to remove him from office. From Montana, the editors of the *Billings Gazette* declared that they had changed their position and wanted to add their "voice to those calling for President Nixon to resign." Reminding their readers that they had endorsed Nixon for president and had "credentials as being a newspaper which could in no sense be labeled anti-Nixon," the *Fort Worth Star–Telegram* concluded that "there are now reasons for the House to vote a bill of impeachment." The *Topeka Daily Capital* observed, "It's time to hand President Nixon his hat. Having voted twice for the President we confess to a certain heart sickness when we read [the transcripts]." The *Omaha World–Herald* opened its long editorial: "The *World–Herald* three times endorsed Richard Nixon as a candidate for the presidency"; the editors ended with: "The President should resign."

One of the nation's most important conservative newspapers also changed its position. The editors of the *Chicago Tribune* wrote, "We are appalled." They then pointed out that "two roads are open. One is resignation. The other is impeachment. Both are legitimate." Equally significant to the recommendation was their conclusion that "there can no longer be a charge that he was railroaded out of office by vengeful Democrats or a hostile press." One of the few newspapers that remained supportive of the president, the *Manchester Union Leader,* asserted that "in its back-stabbing of Nixon, the *Tribune,* along with a number of other papers, forfeits any pretext to speak for conservatives."[46]

The only prominent Republican to offer a favorable interpretation of the transcript was Vice President Ford, who claimed that they "without a qualification, in my judgment — [prove] the President innocent and [exonerate] him" of complicity in the break-in and cover-up. Ford called Dean "an admitted felon" and insisted that in conversation with him Nixon always spoke as "devil's advocate." Two days later, after the avalanche of negative reaction to the transcripts, Ford tempered his assessment and admitted he was "a little disappointed" by them and that "some of the language was pretty harsh."[47] Given that Ford would benefit most from Nixon's possible premature departure from office, the public would have understood if he had maintained a discreet silence.

The reasons for such a damning critique of the transcripts went beyond Nixon's foul language. In its editorial, the *Chicago Tribune* concluded that "he is preoccupied with appearance rather than substance. . . . He displays dismaying gaps in knowledge." The *Roanoke Times* pointed out that the "transcripts show the President of the United States involved in obstruction of justice." William Randolph Hearst Jr. wrote that the transcripts portrayed "a gang whose main concern is the maintenance of personal power — at any cost." The *Fort Worth Star–Telegram* expressed its concern as a question: "If the law enforcement agencies of this country can be used to punish political enemies, how can we then hold ourselves superior to lands where mere political opposition is a crime?" The *Topeka Daily Capital* accused Nixon of displaying "contempt for law." These assessments appeared in newspapers that had endorsed Nixon for reelection in 1972 and had stayed with him as late as the transcript crisis; they indicated again the extent to which Nixon continued to lose his political base.

Nixon's substitution of the transcripts for the tapes themselves won little support. The *Los Angeles Times* observed, "This raises, inevitably, the suspicion that the evidence he is withholding may be even more incriminating than the evidence he has been willing to release."[48] Hearst commented further that

Nixon "released them only because he had to, finally, and because he some-how thought the censored versions would do him some good with the pub-lic. God knows what the unexpurgated tapes would show."[49] The Gallup Poll found Americans favored release of the tapes, rather than the transcripts, by 62 to 24 percent.

Closer analyses of the transcripts damaged Nixon even more. Honey-combed throughout them were at least 1,787 passages marked "unintelligible" and "inaudible." Careful scrutiny revealed a curious pattern. During one nine-minute conversation with Ehrlichman and Haldeman, for example, the tran-script contained 54 inaudibles, 29 of them by Nixon. Immediately following that meeting, Nixon spent forty minutes with Dean and asked for his resig-nation. The transcript of that meeting contained only 5 Nixon inaudibles.

In addition to the unintelligible and inaudible spots, the transcripts con-tained thirty-five sections labeled "material unrelated to Presidential action." Suspicious about the validity of the transcripts, the House Judiciary Com-mittee checked them against the actual tapes of eight conversations Nixon had previously submitted. Discrepancies existed, and in most instances the transcripts presented a version less damaging to Nixon than the original tapes. The committee also found that the transcripts omitted segments of the tapes without identifying where the gaps occurred or offering reasons for the omis-sions. From the taped conversation of March 22, 1973, for example, the tran-script skipped a 2,500-word section that included a passage in which Nixon said, "I don't give a shit what happens. I want you to stonewall it, let them plead the Fifth Amendment, cover-up, or anything else, if it'll save it — save the plan." Jaworski and his staff compared copies of their eight tapes with the transcripts and concluded the submitted transcripts were unreliable.

Time observed, "The transcripts showed a President creating an environ-ment of deceit and dishonesty, of evasion and cover-up." Newspapers and news magazines highlighted excerpts from Nixon's comments, including "March 13, 1973, 'Is it too late to go the hang out road?'; March 21, 1973, 'The problem that you have are these mine fields down the road'; and April 14, 1973, 'I thank you both for arranging it that way and it does show the isolation of the President.'" Interspersed throughout the transcripts were numerous notations of "expletive deleted" that replaced "hell," "damn," and stronger profanities. Cartoonists, comedians, and talk-show hosts and participants made great fun of the term and the number of times it appeared.

Nixon's transcript gamble failed completely. Because of the transcripts, former supporters in the press, especially the *Chicago Tribune,* joined the ever lengthening list of newspapers that called for his resignation or impeachment.

The gaps and discrepancies reinforced the determination of the House Judiciary Committee and the special prosecutor to require Nixon to honor their subpoenas. In mid-May the Roper Poll found the number of Americans who favored impeachment had climbed to 58 percent, compared to 53 percent before Nixon released the transcripts. This release was simply a version of his October offer of transcripts of subpoenaed tapes that Senator John Stennis could verify as accurate. In response to Cox's rejection of that offer, Nixon launched what became known as the Saturday Night Massacre, after which public opinion forced him to retreat, to appoint a new special prosecutor to replace Cox, and to release some actual tapes. On April 30, 1974, Nixon faced another court deadline to turn over more tapes. This time he took a harder line, stating he would not retreat. His action meant that the Supreme Court would have to resolve the impasse.

CHAPTER EIGHT

The Consensus and the Resignation

Portions of the tapes of these June 23 conversations are at variance with certain of my previous statements.
— Richard M. Nixon, August 5, 1974

What he sought in his oblique manner was a vote of confidence from his Cabinet, some expression of sympathy for his plight. . . . But all he encountered was an embarrassed silence.
— Henry Kissinger, Years of Upheaval, *1982*

Despite his plea that we put Watergate behind us, it has been his own delaying tactics that have made it impossible for the nation to end this ordeal.
— Houston News *editorial, August 7, 1974*

By early May the president faced a united, broad-based opposition that included the courts, the House of Representatives, the special prosecutor, and the press. All demanded that he release the tapes. These forces inexorably pushed Nixon toward impeachment or resignation. Opinion polls a year earlier indicated he already had lost public support; that loss increased steadily month by month throughout the ensuing year. During Nixon's final three months in office fewer and fewer Republicans remained who believed his explanations. On August 9, 1974, as Nixon left the presidency, Americans demonstrated a consensus of opinion regarding a vital public issue that was unprecedented in the nation's peacetime history. They understood the issue, knew its complexities and its importance; they had discussed, read, and heard about Watergate for the past two years.

The transcripts constituted only one part of the president's strategy to resolve his crisis without releasing the tapes. On May 1, 1974, Nixon introduced his other strategy when, through his attorney James St. Clair, he announced he would reject any House Judiciary Committee request for additional tapes and documents. The same day, St. Clair petitioned Judge Sirica to quash Jaworski's subpoena for tapes on the grounds of executive privilege. Nixon's chief of staff Alexander Haig also announced the president would release no more tapes.

On May 5 Jaworski met with Haig and St.Clair and attempted to reach an accord whereby Nixon would give the special prosecutor tapes of eighteen of the sixty-four conversations he had subpoenaed, in return for which Jaworski would withdraw the subpoena. Jaworski advised Haig and St.Clair that the grand jury had authorized him to name the president as an unindicted coconspirator and to date he had not made that information public because of the pending House impeachment proceedings. After Haig and St. Clair relayed Jaworski's compromise offer, Nixon listened to the eighteen tapes and concluded that rather than reveal the information on them he preferred to have the nation learn of his status as an unindicted coconspirator.

Nixon instructed St. Clair to tell Sirica that a member of the executive branch could not sue another member of the same branch. This move incensed Jaworski, who maintained that it violated the specific agreement Haig had arranged with him on Nixon's behalf. Jaworski also sent Nixon's legal adviser Fred Buzhardt a copy of Acting Attorney General Robert Bork's announcement when he named Jaworski special prosecutor. At the time, Bork stated that Jaworski had the right to take the president to court to obtain tapes and papers, if necessary. Jaworski also informed the Senate Judiciary Committee that Nixon was attempting to circumvent and restrict the powers of the special prosecutor. Although having no authority in the matter, the committee by a fourteen to one vote adopted a resolution that Jaworski had acted within the scope of his authority. Senator Kennedy cast the only dissenting vote on the grounds the resolution did not go far enough. On this issue Nixon won the support of virtually no one.

On May 9, while Sirica considered St. Clair's motion, Congressman Peter Rodino banged the gavel in Room 2141 of the Rayburn House Office Building to open the Judiciary Committee impeachment hearings. After the opening statement, the committee members voted thirty-one to six to conduct their inquiry behind closed doors. Of the committee's thirty-eight members, two were women and three were black; half were under the age of fifty and eleven were serving their first terms. For months the majority and minority counsels, John Doar and Albert Jenner, and their staffs had been compiling data from the Senate Watergate Committee, the Watergate grand jury, the Internal Revenue Service, and congressional fact-finding committees. Among these materials were nineteen White House tapes. Doar's staff had divided the materials into thirty-six topics, each with its own loose-leaf notebook. Topic by topic Doar led the members through the material. After negotiation, the committee permitted St. Clair to attend the sessions but not to participate in discussions.

To facilitate its work, the Judiciary Committee sought eleven tapes and specific diaries of Nixon's White House meetings. On May 15 the committee approved two subpoenas. A week later Nixon wrote to Rodino declining to comply, arguing that "the Committee has the full story of Watergate, in so far as it relates to Presidential knowledge and Presidential actions." Nixon also informed Rodino that he would reject any future subpoenas.[1]

In the interim Judge Sirica rejected St. Clair's argument that one member of the executive branch could not sue another and ordered Nixon to give Jaworski the sixty-four tapes he had subpoenaed on April 18. The president petitioned the court of appeals to overrule Sirica. Jaworski countered by petitioning the Supreme Court to bypass the court of appeals and to consider the case immediately because of "imperative public importance." Twice since World War II the Court had taken such action. To help St. Clair argue against Jaworski, Nixon hired Charles Alan Wright, a professor at the University of Texas Law School. On May 31 the Supreme Court ruled in favor of Jaworski and set a calendar: June 21 for filing of briefs and July 8 for beginning of oral arguments.

Nixon's potential confrontations with the Supreme Court and with the House Judiciary Committee occurred in a news media atmosphere that gave him scant comfort. Within the past two months judges had sentenced Liddy, Chapin, Kleindienst, Magruder, Colson, Kalmbach, and Ehrlichman for various crimes. The Watergate grand jury, by unanimous vote, had named Nixon an unindicted coconspirator. Judge Gerhard A. Gesell, the U.S. District Court judge presiding at the Plumbers trial, ruled that President Nixon had no constitutional authority to order a break-in on grounds of national security. The Internal Revenue Service reported that the president and his wife had not yet paid the $148,080 they owed on their 1969 taxes. The Senate Watergate Committee officially ended its existence and released its final 2,217-page report. Lowell Weicker, a Republican member of the committee, publicly charged that the Nixon administration had undermined, abused, and violated every major part of the Constitution. He also charged that the cover-up continued. The vice chairman of the Senate committee, the Republican Howard H. Baker, reported that the CIA had withheld information regarding the Watergate break-in. As in their responses to the publication of the transcripts, the *Chicago Tribune* and a host of other newspapers again withdrew their support of Nixon and called for either his resignation or impeachment. Watergate dominated the news, and almost all the stories reflected negatively on the president.

With so many persons involved and with so much at stake, opportunity abounded for spreading rumor, innuendo, and false information. Members of the press and government officials have long exchanged information in private. Presidents and their staffs have secretly passed information to favorite reporters to enhance their own image or to damage the image of their opponents. During the primary campaigns of 1972, for example, a CREEP official passed to the columnists Rowland Evans and Robert Novak copies of internal memos that the dirty tricks operators had stolen from Senator Muskie's office. Bill Gulley, director of the White House military office, later identified Melvin R. Laird, secretary of defense during Nixon's first term, as "one of the biggest leakers in the Administration"; Laird's aide, according to Gulley, made a "daily run" to Evans and Novak. Haldeman also considered Evans and Novak to be journalists who would release information to promote specific White House projects.[2] To discredit John Dean, someone in the White House had leaked information that he had borrowed $4,000 from campaign funds to finance his honeymoon. Pat Buchanan once instructed Press Secretary Ron Ziegler to "feed not only the *Star*, but other pro or neutral papers."[3] And although Deep Throat leaked no specific information, he leaked the knowledge that a big story lay behind the break-in. Reporters consistently coaxed information from secretaries, Senate and House staffers, and anyone else who might prove useful.

The relationship between a president and the press depends a great deal on the personality of the president. Since World War II presidents have viewed the press with varying degrees of hostility, at least at certain times. For example, President John F. Kennedy, whose good rapport with the press no successor has equaled, asked the *New York Times* to remove its journalist, David Halberstam, from his Vietnam assignment and canceled the White House subscription to the *New York Herald Tribune*. President Lyndon B. Johnson's false statements and distortions of fact led reporters to refer to his credibility gap. The mutual distrust between Johnson and reporters underlay the media's suspicions of his successor. Throughout the Watergate crisis, moreover, Nixon and his supporters purposefully attempted to discredit the press in order to undermine the credibility of its disclosures and then to reinforce the opposition of conservative independents and Republicans to the idea of impeachment. The magnitude of the Watergate affair, and Woodward and Bernstein's roles, merely intensified Nixon's relationship with the press, a relationship that all presidents had often found troubling. But hostility between Nixon and the press had its origins in the 1948 election campaign.

Nixon tried hard to keep the press, and therefore public opinion, with him, but the actions early in 1973 of Judge Sirica and of the acting director of the FBI Patrick Gray had led to the president's loss of control over the Watergate story. From summer 1973, Nixon's refusal to release the tapes, his firing of

Cox, his income tax problems, and his edited tape transcripts had turned almost the entire newspaper world against him. By the end of May 1974 President Nixon also had turned the House Judiciary Committee against him.

On May 30 the committee voted thirty-seven to one to issue a third subpoena for tapes of Watergate-related conversations and voted twenty-eight to ten to inform the president by letter that the committee would view his defiance of its May 15 subpoena as possible grounds for impeachment. On June 9 Nixon replied to the committee by reiterating his previous positions. He cited his desire to preserve the principle of separation of powers and maintained that the materials he already had given told "the full story of Watergate, in so far as it relates to Presidential knowledge and Presidential actions." Nixon ended his letter insisting that "the Executive must remain the final arbiter of demands on its confidentiality."[4] Thus the deadlock between the committee and the president continued.

The morning after Nixon sent the Judiciary Committee his letter, he left on a trip to the Middle East, with a two-night stopover in Salzburg, Austria. Then from June 12 to June 18 the president visited Egypt, Saudi Arabia, Syria, Israel, and Jordan. Before returning to the United States he stopped in the Azores Islands. The themes of the discussions he held with the heads of state were peace in the Middle East and cooperation with the United States.

Six days after his return, Nixon left on another overseas trip, this time to the Soviet Union, with a two-night stop en route in Brussels. He spent seven days in the Soviet Union and spoke to the Soviet people on radio and television. In Moscow the president attracted larger crowds than he did in New York City. At the end of his visit, he and the Soviet leader Leonid I. Brezhnev issued a joint communique expressing their two countries' mutual desire to strengthen cooperation and understanding and to promote world peace. Arriving home, Nixon told the nation that during his two trips he had traveled more than 25,000 miles, visited nine countries, and advanced the cause of peace.

The trips did take Nixon's mind away from Watergate, allowing him to exercise some of the power he had at his command and to enjoy the pomp and respect other nations accord the president of the United States. But with no specific crisis in U.S. relations with any of the countries the president visited and with the majority of Americans believing the House of Representatives should impeach him, Nixon's trips seemed hollow attempts to appear in the news as a world leader and thereby divert attention from Watergate. This brief respite was interrupted by the onset of House impeachment hearings.

On July 2, the day before the president left the Soviet Union, the House Judiciary Committee questioned the first of ten witnesses. The committee conducted this stage of its proceedings in closed sessions, the same policy it had pursued when spending six weeks examining more than 7,000 pages of documents and more than 600 statements. The political atmosphere was intense, fueled by the president's staunch defenders. His press secretary, Ron Ziegler, called the committee a kangaroo court. The committee, meanwhile, had worked to minimize partisanship and, to varying degrees, Republican members extended a measure of respect for Chairman Rodino's efforts. Rodino knew that the impeachment resolution needed support from Republicans on the committee if it were to command public credibility.

Typical of its willingness to compromise, the committee permitted St. Clair to suggest witnesses and to participate in their questioning. In one case, after resolving a dispute, the committee added all of St. Clair's suggestions to its own list. None of St. Clair's witnesses offered new evidence, and none helped Nixon's position. Alexander Butterfield stressed that Nixon "was highly interested in detail." Among Butterfield's many illustrations was his description of the president's directive "to log the comments made about each painting to see how popular it might be to guests who were awaiting appointments in the west lobby." Butterfield portrayed Haldeman as "entirely . . . an implementer. . . . The President was the decision maker. The President was 100 percent in charge."[5] John Mitchell's lawyer informed the committee that the former attorney general could not answer every question because of his own pending trial. Charles Colson suggested again that the CIA had undermined the president.

St. Clair summarized the president's defense on July 18. To justify impeachment, St. Clair argued, the evidence must document criminal action; investigators must produce a smoking gun. He pointed out that Nixon had dismissed his aides when he realized they might have committed crimes. Judge the president, St. Clair continued, on his conduct, not on his comments uttered in anger or frustration. St. Clair insisted that Dean, not Nixon, had orchestrated the cover-up. To support his contention that Nixon had not obstructed justice, St. Clair introduced an excerpt from a Nixon statement on the March 22, 1973, tape. Republicans and Democrats alike cried foul; Nixon had refused to release that tape to the committee. He and St. Clair, therefore, appeared to be withholding a tape that might embarrass the president yet using the same tape when it might help him. Doar's summary followed St. Clair's. The evidence, Doar concluded, justified impeachment. Doar proposed five impeachment charges: obstruction of justice, abuse of power, contempt of Congress and the courts, failure to enforce the laws, and denigration of the presidency.

The assessments and actions of the minority chief counsel, Albert Jenner, undermined Nixon's chances to block impeachment. From the time of his appointment the previous January, Jenner had avoided partisan concerns and cooperated closely with the majority's chief counsel, Doar. By July Jenner privately concluded that Nixon had lied and continued to lie. On July 19 Jenner joined Doar to urge the Judiciary Committee to recommend impeachment. For Republicans, even those who leaned toward impeachment, this was the last straw. Two days later they terminated Jenner's employment and selected Sam Garrison, Jenner's deputy, as their new minority chief counsel. The Republicans recommended that Rodino appoint Jenner as his associate counsel, which he did.

On July 22 the Judiciary Committee completed its information gathering and prepared for the final phase of its work, the discussion and vote on impeachment charges. By a 31 to 7 vote the committee concurred with the House of Representatives, which had voted 346 to 40 to permit live radio and television coverage of the forthcoming impeachment sessions. Only once before in the nation's history had the House held similar hearings.

While the Judiciary Committee progressed to its final phrase, the Supreme Court moved inexorably toward deciding whether the president could retain absolute control of the tapes. On July 8, eight justices on the Court heard contrasting arguments from St. Clair and Jaworski.[6] Since the previous July, when Butterfield disclosed the existence of Nixon's taping system, the question whether the president had absolute control over the tapes had been simple. The president claimed an absolute right to withhold information and defended his position. For a year, demands that he release the tapes had generated ever increasing public support. By July 1974 most Americans agreed with this position. While the Court weighed the constitutional issues, St. Clair intensified the suspense when he announced that the president might defy the Court's ruling, should it order him to release the tapes.

Nixon still nursed hopes of avoiding impeachment. In June, he recalled later, "it looked as if things were actually beginning to brighten." On June 7 the journalist Theodore White passed word to the president that he believed the House would not vote impeachment nor would the Senate convict. John Connally, the former Democratic governor of Texas and Nixon's secretary of the treasury from 1971 to 1972, agreed with this assessment, as did William E. Timmons, Nixon's director of congressional relations. Two weeks later Nixon telephoned Joe Waggoner, a Louisiana Democrat then in his seventh term in the House. Nixon considered Waggoner "totally realistic" and "a great source of strength to me throughout the whole Watergate period." The head of an informal group of congressmen, Waggoner told Nixon the House would not impeach unless, for some reason, the Supreme Court held him in contempt. On July 12, Vice President Ford conveyed his encouragement: "Don't worry, Mr. President, you've got this beat. We have a solid fifty-vote margin in the House." That afternoon the president and his family flew to San Clemente for a two-week vacation. In his memoirs, Nixon reflected on the weekend of July 20 and 21 as "the last time there was any real hope."[7]

On July 23 the Judiciary Committee member Lawrence Hogan (R-Md.) obliterated Nixon's cautious, thoroughly unrealistic optimism. At a press conference that morning, Hogan announced his belief, "beyond a reasonable doubt," that the president had committed impeachable offenses. He charged that Nixon had "lied repeatedly," had paid blackmail, had tried to misuse the CIA, and had praised those who he knew had committed perjury. As a conservative, a former FBI agent, and a candidate for his party's gubernatorial nomination, Hogan held a zero rating from the liberal pressure group, Americans for Democratic Action. His announcement stunned the political world.[8] Until then Republican members of the Judiciary Committee and the three conservative southern Democrats had kept their opinions to themselves regarding how they would vote on impeachment charges. Rodino, mindful of the need for Republican votes, expected William S. Cohen of Maine to favor impeachment and judged as likely the votes of Hamilton Fish Jr. of New York and Tom Railsback of Illinois. With luck, Rodino hoped to gain another two Republican votes from among New York's Henry P. Smith, Virginia's M. Caldwell Butler, and Illinois's Robert McClory. Hogan caught everyone off guard, and his announcement greatly increased the possibility of impeachment. Timmons soon telephoned San Clemente and told the president the three southern Democrats would vote impeachment. Nixon tried to enlist the support of Alabama's governor George Wallace to reverse the expected votes of the southern Democrats. Wallace politely refused. After Nixon hung up the telephone, he turned to Haig and declared, "Well, Al, there goes the presidency."[9]

The next day, July 24, the Supreme Court announced its decision, with an eight to zero vote, that President Nixon must turn over the sixty-four tapes the special prosecutor had subpoenaed. Three of the eight votes came from Nixon's appointees. Nixon had hoped for some "air," perhaps a six to three vote, in the ruling and thus hinted through his aides that he might defy the Court. With no air, Nixon accepted the inevitable and indicated he would comply. Only then did Nixon ask his chief legal adviser, Fred Buzhardt, to listen to the June 23, 1972, tape. Buzhardt did, telephoned St. Clair and Haig, and told them the tape was the smoking gun. Haig asked Buzhardt to listen a second time. He listened again and repeated his assessment.

The Court's ruling remained above criticism, owing to its unanimity and because five of the eight participating justices had been Republican appointees. Nixon himself had appointed three, including Chief Justice Warren E. Burger, who wrote the thirty-one-page opinion. Eisenhower had appointed the other two. In straightforward language, the opinion referred to the well-known 1803 case *Marbury vs. Madison,* and the justices reaffirmed the principle that the Court, and not the president, is the final arbiter of the Constitution. Coming the day after Hogan announced his support for impeachment, the Court's decision neutralized much of the remaining contention that partisanship motivated the impeachment procedure.

The yearlong struggle for the tapes ended, bringing to an abrupt end Nixon's holding action against subpoenas, first from the Senate Watergate Committee, then from the first special prosecutor, then from the second special prosecutor, and, finally, from the House Judiciary Committee. In his attempt to keep the tapes, the president had offered to permit Senator John Stennis to listen to the subpoenaed tapes and to verify a transcript of their content. When Special Prosecutor Archibald Cox rejected this proposal and insisted on the tapes, Nixon fired him. The strong negative reaction to Cox's firing forced Nixon to yield some tapes, including one with the unexplained eighteen-and-a-half-minute gap, but then he drew a line and declared he would release no more tapes. When the subpoenas kept coming, Nixon released transcripts and falsely maintained that he had released everything relevant. Throughout the struggle, Nixon employed every possible delaying tactic. His position, combined with his delaying tactics, cost him the support of the majority of Americans. From the beginning in July 1973, when Butterfield disclosed the existence of the Oval Office tapes, Nixon's claim of executive privilege seemed weak compared to Barry Goldwater's commonsense approach that Nixon should release the tapes to exonerate himself and bring the controversy to an end. The Supreme Court ruling, moreover, introduced a further issue when it affirmed that no president could place himself above the law and withhold materials that might prove his guilt in a crime.

The same day that the Supreme Court handed down its decision, the House Judiciary Committee started formal debate on articles of impeachment. At 7:45 P.M., July 24, 1974, with approximately 40 million Americans watching on television, Rodino solemnly opened the proceedings. That evening and the next day, every member of the committee, each of whom was a lawyer, had fifteen minutes to state a position. By the time each member had spoken, the outcome of the forthcoming impeachment vote appeared evident.

Southern Democrats favored impeachment, as did Republicans Lawrence Hogan, M. Caldwell Butler, and William Cohen, and Republicans Hamilton Fish and Thomas Railsback hinted that they also might.

On Saturday evening, July 27, after three days of debate, the Judiciary Committee approved article 1 of its impeachment proposals; the vote was twenty-seven to eleven. Six Republicans voted for impeachment, along with the twenty-one Democrats. Article 1 detailed the specific steps the president had taken to obstruct justice. It listed such unlawful activities as making false statements to investigative officers, making false public statements, condoning perjury, attempting to misuse the CIA, paying money to influence witnesses, and interfering with investigations by the Congress, the FBI, the Justice Department, and the Watergate special prosecutor. "Such conduct," the article concluded, "warrants impeachment and trial, and removal from office." Immediately after the vote, Rodino adjourned the committee until the following Monday. On Sunday, with the committee in recess, Nixon returned to Washington from his California vacation.

When the committee reconvened, it approved impeachment article 2 by a twenty-eight to ten vote. Robert McClory of Illinois became the seventh Republican to vote for impeachment. Article 2 listed specific abuses of power, including unlawful use of the IRS, the CIA, and the FBI, and concluded that Nixon had "acted in a manner contrary to his trust as President and subversive of constitutional government." Such conduct, the article stated, "warrants impeachment and trial, and removal from office." The next day, by a twenty-one to seventeen vote, the Judiciary Committee passed article 3 of impeachment. It reported that Nixon had failed to produce documents "as directed by duly authorized subpoenas issued by the Committee" on April 11, May 15, May 30, and June 24, all in 1974. Like the first two articles, this one called for impeachment, trial, and removal from office. Later that day the committee rejected, by a twenty-six to twelve vote, article 4, which charged the president with concealing information and providing false information regarding the U.S. bombing of Cambodia; by an identical vote it rejected article 5, which charged the president with income tax evasion.[10]

While the Judiciary Committee was considering articles 3, 4, and 5, St. Clair returned to work following a long weekend on Cape Cod. Then for the first time, he listened to the June 23, 1972, tape. Shaken, he told the president the tape contradicted what he, on behalf of the president, had argued before the Judiciary Committee. St. Clair reasoned, therefore, that he would be party to an obstruction of justice charge unless Nixon made the tape public.

The next day, Wednesday, July 31, Nixon asked Haig to read the transcript of the June 23, 1972, tape. Haig did and informed the president that he agreed with St. Clair and Buzhardt; the tape was the smoking gun. That afternoon Nixon asked Ron Ziegler to listen to the tape. Two days later, Nixon had Haig arrange for Charles E. Wiggins of California, a staunch defender of the president on the Judiciary Committee, to read the transcript. After reading it, Wiggins concluded that House impeachment and Senate conviction were inevitable. Nixon must report the information on the transcript, Wiggins added, or those persons who had read the transcript or had listened to the tape would become accomplices in the obstruction of justice. Other than from his immediate family, his close friend Bebe Rebozo, and his longtime personal secretary, Rose Mary Woods, Nixon found almost no support to continue the fight against impeachment. Still, he opted for one last chance. On Monday he intended to release to the public the June 23, 1972, tape and hoped, "by some miracle," the reaction would be less damning than he and his advisers expected.[11]

That Friday, August 2, while Wiggins recommended disclosure and Nixon agonized over his situation, the Louis Harris Associates conducted one of its public opinion polls, revealing that by 66 to 27 percent Americans favored impeachment. Typifying that sentiment and the reasoning behind it, an editorial that day from the *News and Courier* in Charleston, South Carolina, declared: "One after another, new developments have unfolded to shake our confidence and cause us to reconsider a long-standing position as a Nixon admirer and advocate." The movement to force the president from office, the editorial continued, "no longer can be identified as the sole possession of those who might be cataloged as Mr. Nixon's enemies, anxious to do him harm." Enlistments in the movement "of such respected people as our Sunday columnist James Jackson Kilpatrick and U.S. Rep. James D. Mann of South Carolina . . . have added depth and respectability." The paper concluded by calling for Nixon to resign, and should he refuse, for the Congress "to press ahead as quickly and decisively as possible with impeachment." Also on August 2, Judge Sirica sentenced John Dean to one to four years in prison for his role in the cover-up of the Watergate break-in. Two days earlier, Judge Gesell had sentenced John Ehrlichman to a prison term of twenty months to five years for perjury and conspiracy in the Fielding break-in case.

The Supreme Court ruling and the House Judiciary Committee votes finally brought Watergate to a climax. Nixon faced the choice of resignation or an impeachment trial and removal from office. If he planned to resign, the decision he favored, he had only a few days left as president. The weekend of August 3 and 4 he spent at Camp David with his family. On Sunday, Pat Buchanan, St. Clair, Haig, Ziegler, and Raymond Price journeyed north to meet with Nixon and help prepare a statement to accompany the release of the smoking gun tape. Rumors of plans to fight impeachment coexisted with equally strong rumors of impending resignation. At 4:00 p.m. on Monday, August 5, after several postponements that heightened the rampant public speculation, aides distributed to reporters transcripts of the tape and Nixon's two-page commentary. The irrefutable evidence of guilt was this exchange only a week after the break-in:

> HALDEMAN: That the way to handle this now is for us to have Walters [CIA deputy director] call Pat Gray [acting director of the FBI] and just say, "Stay the hell out of this . . . we don't want you to go any further on it."
> PRESIDENT: How do you call him in, I mean you just, well, we protected Helms from one hell of a lot of things.[12]

In his statement Nixon confessed he had never told his staff and counsel about the June 23, 1972, tape. He acknowledged his defenders had argued his case "with information that was incomplete and in some respects erroneous." The tape revealed that at least as early as June 23, 1972, Nixon knew who was responsible for the break-in. The taped conversations confirmed his participation in obstruction of justice, misuse of federal power, and systematic public deception. In a remarkable understatement, Nixon admitted that "portions of the tapes of these June 23 conversations are at variance with certain of my previous statements." Yet, despite all the evidence to the contrary, he continued to claim that "when all the facts were brought to my attention, I insisted on a full investigation and prosecution of those guilty." He ended his statement asserting that "the record, in its entirety, does not justify the extreme step of impeachment and removal of a President."[13] Nixon had admitted obstruction of justice, an impeachable and criminal offense by his own definition, yet declared that his record did not justify impeachment.

Reaction to Nixon's statement and to the content of the tape exploded in newspaper editorials across the country with an intensity and a unanimity rarely equaled in the nation's history. The *Albuquerque Journal* concluded correctly that it was "one of the few American dailies which has not, thus far, called for the impeachment, resignation or removal of the President." The *Milwaukee Journal* observed, "If there is a consensus about anything in America today it is that Richard Nixon must go — one way or another." The *Arkansas Democrat* agreed: "From all sides have come cries for him to resign." The editorial added, "We are disposed to judge the President most harshly for his arrogant contempt toward the great masses of the American people." The *Washington Star–News* concluded, "It is now virtually inconceivable that Nixon can last out his term. He has betrayed and affronted those loyalists who have bet their political lives on his veracity." It reminded its readers, "This newspaper has supported Richard Nixon in all his national campaigns." Newspapers in all regions of the country that once supported Nixon published similar laments. Because it had endorsed his presidential campaigns in 1960, 1968, and 1972, the *State*, in Columbia, South Carolina, took "no pleasure in reaching the conclusion that Mr. Nixon's resignation is in order." The *Orlando Sentinel Star* called for Nixon's prompt resignation: "He had lied to the country and even to his own lawyer, and he betrayed the faith of millions of Americans who believed him." The *Tulsa Daily World*, which had "supported Mr. Nixon through many adversities," called for his resignation because it saw no alternative. The *Dallas Times–Herald* reminded its readers of its endorsement of Nixon's election and reelection and then urged the president "to remove himself from office." The *Los Angeles Times* likewise favored resignation and expressed a feeling of betrayal because it had supported Nixon throughout his career, starting with his 1946 campaign for the House of Representatives.[14]

For all practical purposes, the nation's newspapers were unanimous that Nixon must leave office. The only disagreement concerned the method whereby he would leave. On August 5, when the president released the transcript of the June 23, 1972, tape, he closed his accompanying statement by saying that "as the constitutional process goes forward," it would find his record too strong for removal from office. In two editorials the *Greenville (S.C.) News* presented with clarity the issues involved regarding Nixon and impeachment. On Monday afternoon, August 5, the editors prepared an editorial for Tuesday's publication "reemphasizing the point that the President had not been proved guilty." About 6:00 P.M., however, they read Nixon's statement accompanying his release of the smoking gun tape. Troubled by the new revelations, the editors killed the unpublished editorials, having concluded that the president's statement and the transcript changed "the whole picture." Nixon's disclosures "appalled" the editors: "This situation is tragic for the nation. It is heartbreaking for those who have supported the President." Despite the reversal of its assessment of Nixon's culpability, the *Greenville News* did not join the clamor for his resignation. Instead, the next day the paper insisted that "to force President Nixon from office while he still maintains innocence . . . would be wrong constitutionally and politically." Once started, the impeachment process should determine Nixon's guilt or exoneration. "Any other course subverts the rule of law upon which American liberty and the American system of government rest."[15]

Nixon refused to admit guilt, and due process concerned other newspapers as well as the *Greenville News*. The *Charlotte Observer* maintained, "As long as Mr. Nixon insists that he is innocent of an impeachable offense, he should be given every opportunity to answer the charges against him." The *Philadelphia Inquirer* opposed resignation for the same reason. From the Midwest, the *Des Moines Register* observed, "Our view, like that of the *Wall Street Journal* printed on this page, is that the constitutional process of impeachment, trial, and removal from office if found guilty is the proper procedure." The *Wichita Eagle,* once a firm Nixon supporter, explained that "should President Nixon resign at any point before the conclusion of his trial a considerable body of Americans will remain convinced of his innocence." It also expressed concern that through resignation "a dangerous precedent will be set for the harrying out of office of future presidents guilty of nothing but personal unpopularity." The *Roanoke Times* favored impeachment for a different reason, because it would stand as an "enduring warning to future Presidents not to abuse powers in the ways charged against Mr. Nixon." A host of other newspapers voiced concern over due process or precedent, or about Nixon's profession of innocence, and thus supported impeachment rather than resignation. These included the *Columbus (Ohio) Dispatch,* the *San Diego Union,* the *Chicago Daily News,* the *Fort Worth Star–Telegram,* the *Detroit Free Press,* the *Daily Oklahoman,* the *Ann Arbor News,* the *St. Louis Post–Dispatch,* the *Dayton Daily News,* the *Milwaukee Journal,* the *Arkansas Democrat,* and the *St. Louis Globe–Democrat.* The majority of newspapers, however, just wanted Nixon to resign.

The nation's newspapers detailed the concrete reasons for their position, whether they counseled impeachment or resignation. The *Washington Star–News,* for example, explained that "the President has been forced to hand over the smoking pistol demanded by those of us who have insisted he be given the benefit of every doubt." The *Orlando Sentinel Star* agreed: "For those of us who demanded evidence before joining the crowd determined to drive a President from office, we now have it — in spades." Repeating the same point, The *Syracuse Herald–Journal* observed, "This newspaper consistently has called for any evidence to show he committed a serious offense. That evidence now is known to the American people by his own admission." The *Topeka Daily Capital* stated, "The tape transcript reveals incontrovertibly that . . . he was perfectly willing to participate in the cover-up — hiding the facts from the voters." The *Dallas Times–Herald* called Nixon's statement a "stunning confession of cover-up activities," and the *Chicago Tribune* wrote about "Nixon's own confessions." The *Salt Lake Tribune* concluded, "Mr. Nixon has, for all practical purposes, confessed his guilt to the Judiciary committee's first impeachment article." The *Biloxi Daily Herald* believed the tapes proved that Nixon "did indeed obstruct justice." The fact that all of these papers had supported the election and reelection of Nixon illustrates the widespread belief in the impeachable guilt of the president.

Several newspapers, which had earlier supported Nixon, observed that the impetus to drive the president from office transcended partisan politics. The day after Nixon released the tape and statement, for example, the *Birmingham News* wrote, "There is no longer any question of his being forced to resign for strictly political reasons." The *Kansas City Star* pointed out that "nobody is 'driving' him from office. He has done that himself." The *Pittsburgh Post–Gazette* graphically stated that with his release of the tape, "the President fit the noose more securely around his own neck." Until Nixon did that fitting, the *Post Gazette* had opposed resignation. The *Roanoke Times* believed the tape's release made it impossible for the president "to continue and nurture a Nixon myth, the fable of how an able and lonely President was driven from office by evil powers. President Nixon did himself in with his own tapes." The *Indianapolis News* asserted, "A President cannot be 'brought down' by communications media or by opposition politicians, but he can be destroyed — and was — by unprincipled advisors."[16]

The newspaper that made the most dramatic reversal of position, because it originally had taken the most pugnacious stance, was William Loeb's *Manchester Union Leader*. On July 30, 1974, after watching the House Judiciary Committee proceedings, Loeb concluded that "the 'liberals,' both Republican and Democratic . . . give the impression that they see a golden opportunity to reverse the terrible licking their hero, George McGovern, received in the Fall of 1972." The impeachment process, Loeb continued, was simply "a partisan attempt to overturn the decision of the voters two years ago." He called the committee members who voted against Nixon "vultures" and maintained they had received aid from "the left-dominated communications media." A week later, after Nixon's release of the smoking gun tape, Loeb opened his editorial: "And now President Nixon has impeached himself." Loeb wrote that "what the President condoned was use of the CIA to head off an FBI investigation. That amounts in our view to undermining national security by suborning one of its most vital arms for purely political purposes." After discussing impeachment and resignation, Loeb concluded that "either way, what this nation now needs is a change at the top. And soon."[17] The symbol of far-right political journalism had joined an anti-Nixon mainstream that pulled in virtually every newspaper in the country.

Just as the smoking gun tape drained the last of the president's newspaper support, so too did it all but eliminate his political support. Within twenty-four hours after the release of the tape's transcript, every member of the House

Judiciary Committee, seventeen of them Republicans, publicly announced their intent to vote for impeachment. For ten of these Republicans this meant an about-face; ten days earlier they had voted against article 1 of impeachment, which charged the president with obstruction of justice. The Republican leader in the House, John J. Rhodes, announced that he too would vote for impeachment. Robert P. Griffin, the Senate Republican whip, concurred and called for Nixon's resignation: "It's not just his enemies who feel that way. Many of his friends, and I count myself one of them, believe now that this would be the most appropriate course."[18]

At 11:00 A.M. on Tuesday, August 6, the day when almost every daily newspaper in the country carried an editorial about the smoking gun tape that Nixon had released the day before, the president convened a cabinet meeting. He began with comments about inflation and then shifted to Watergate. He acknowledged the difficulty of the situation but announced he would not resign. In the interest of the presidency and the nation, he would instead follow the procedure outlined in the Constitution. Secretary of State Henry Kissinger believed that what Nixon "sought in his oblique manner was a vote of confidence from his Cabinet. . . . But all he encountered was an embarrassed silence."[19] Vice President Ford broke the silence with a short statement about "the difficult position I'm in." After expressing "personal sympathy" for Nixon, Ford continued, "I wish to emphasize that had I known what has been disclosed in reference to Watergate in the last twenty-four hours, I would not have made a number of the statements I made either as Minority Leader or as Vice President."[20] George Bush, chair of the Republican National Committee, reported on the disaster that he believed the Republican Party would face in the forthcoming congressional elections. He wanted, therefore, a quick end to Watergate. Obviously, the only quick end meant a Nixon resignation. Kissinger recalled, "It was cruel. And it was necessary. For Nixon's own appointees to turn on him was not the best way to end a Presidency. Yet he had left them no other choice."[21] Word of Nixon's intent to face an impeachment trial rather than resign soon leaked to the media.

Less than an hour after the cabinet meeting, Kissinger went unannounced to the Oval Office. The purpose of his visit was to suggest that the president resign because a lengthy impeachment trial would be too demeaning and too damaging to the country. Nixon thanked Kissinger but remained noncommittal. The president thereupon talked with his director of congressional relations, William E. Timmons, who gave the disheartening news that eighty Senators favored impeachment.

Ford, meanwhile, had gone to Capitol Hill to brief those present at the Senate Republican Policy luncheon about the cabinet meeting. He encountered a growing anger over the content of the tape. When told that the president believed himself innocent of impeachable action, they became increasingly agitated. Barry Goldwater blurted out that Nixon should resign immediately. The essence of this meeting, including Goldwater's recommendation, quickly reached reporters. Later that afternoon Republican leaders in the Senate decided that Goldwater should go to the White House and describe to the president the certainty of impeachment. When asked if he would meet with Goldwater, Nixon agreed but suggested that he be accompanied by House leader John Rhodes and Senate leader Hugh Scott.

Wednesday morning, August 7, Nixon returned a telephone call to H. R. Haldeman in California. Haldeman urged Nixon, if he planned to resign, to consider "a blanket pardon for all the Watergate defendants." The pardon, Haldeman reasoned, would spare the country years of trials and lawsuits. Moreover, to deflect criticism of the pardons, he recommended that the president grant amnesty to the Vietnam draft dodgers. Nixon listened but gave no specific answer.[22] At noon that day Goldwater had lunch at the home of Dean Burch, a presidential counselor to Nixon and former chair of the Federal Communications Commission. Haig had arranged the meeting in order to caution Goldwater about the state of Nixon's mental health. Nixon's chief of staff characterized the president as someone capable of going off in any of several directions. He needed to realize, Haig advised, that he had no options left.

At 5:00 P.M. Haig intercepted Goldwater, Scott, and Rhodes on their way to the Oval Office and warned them not to suggest resignation explicitly. Then the four Republican politicians had an awkward, painful exchange. At the climax, Nixon asked Goldwater how many votes he had. Goldwater replied, "Ten at most, maybe less. Some aren't firm." Nixon turned to Scott, who said he agreed with the count. "It's my decision," Nixon snapped as he ended the meeting. Following this, Goldwater, Scott, and Rhodes told reporters they had not discussed a resignation decision. When Goldwater returned to his Senate office, he telephoned Katharine Graham, owner of the *Washington Post*. He recounted the scene in the Oval Office and said, "Nixon was wobbling" and was capable of irrational action. Goldwater then asked her, the owner of a paper that he and Nixon most disliked, to refrain for a day from emphasizing that Nixon's presidency was over. Let him resign without further pressure, Goldwater advised. In his memoirs, he recounted that the next day, "the *Post* was as circumspect as it could be." He praised it for placing the country's interest above its own: "I will never forget their recognition of responsibility as long as I live."[23] That same afternoon Rodino passed word to Timmons that if Nixon resigned, Rodino would not pursue impeachment charges against him. Speaker of the House Carl Albert agreed with Rodino's position.

Goldwater, Haig, and the others had sound reasons for their cautious dealing with Nixon. Pressures to resign had placed enormous stress on him, owing both to the historical significance and the fact that resignation ran counter to his basic instincts. For a week the president alternated between resisting and accepting resignation. Throughout this week, however, Nixon consistently emphasized that he would be the one to make the decision, and no member of the cabinet, Republican senator, or member of Congress would push him into a humiliating situation. Those who talked with the president that week worried about his stability.

In his memoirs, Nixon reported that on August 1 he told Haig he "had decided to resign." That evening Haig told speechwriter Ray Price to draft a resignation speech. The next day Nixon had second thoughts and ordered Price to stop drafting the speech and to begin work on a statement to release with the smoking gun tape. During the August 3 and 4 weekend, at Camp David, Nixon placed the possibility of resignation in abeyance until after he had evaluated the public's reaction to the tape. This position reflected the president's belief that he had committed no crime serious enough to merit impeachment as well as his acceptance of Pat Buchanan's argument that Nixon must be certain he no longer enjoyed sufficient support for staying in office. On Monday evening, a few hours following the release of the smoking gun tape and after the Senate Republican whip Robert Griffin had called for the president's resignation, Haig told Kissinger that "Nixon was still hesitating."[24] At 11:00 A.M. the next day Nixon informed his cabinet that he would face the Senate trial. As late as the afternoon of Wednesday, August 7, Haig told Goldwater, Scott, Rhodes, and Kissinger that although Nixon leaned toward resignation he still might change his mind. About 6:00 P.M. Nixon telephoned Kissinger, asked him to come to the Oval Office, and told him he would resign.

At 9:00 P.M. Nixon again telephoned Kissinger and asked him to come to the Lincoln Sitting Room in the White House. In his memoirs Nixon described an hour's meeting during which the two men discussed foreign policy and reminisced about their five and a half years shaping and conducting U.S. foreign relations. In his memoirs Kissinger remembered that "the meeting lasted nearly three hours." He recalled the president as in control of his emotions but "not calm," "shattered," and "deeply distraught."[25] Raymond Price reported in his memoir that while Nixon and Kissinger met, he worked on the president's resignation speech scheduled for the next evening. Price remembered Nixon telephoning him at 10:35, 10:38, and 11:07 P.M. to discuss the content of the speech. Kissinger did not mention these interruptions. At 4:15 A.M., 4:30 A.M., and 5:07 A.M. Nixon again telephoned Price about the speech.

Nixon began his last full day as president having had little sleep and with the incredible stress that because of his conduct in office he would become the first president in the nation's history to resign. Shortly after 11:00 A.M. Nixon spent seventy minutes with Vice President Ford, beginning by announcing his decision to resign the next day. At 12:23 P.M. Ziegler told reporters, who crowded into the White House press room, that the president would address the nation at 9:00 P.M. Although Ziegler did not reveal the subject of the speech, his tearful eyes left little doubt about the accuracy of the speculation over the impending resignation, which dominated the city and the national news. After the departure of Haldeman and Ehrlichman on April 30, 1973, Ziegler had become one of Nixon's closest intimates. At 7:30 P.M. Nixon met in the Executive Office Building with congressional leaders of both parties and officially told them of his decision. He then moved to the cabinet room and spoke almost half an hour to forty-six members of Congress. Nixon and many of those in attendance shed tears. At 9:00 P.M., however, a composed president sat before the television cameras.

In his resignation speech Nixon declared, "I no longer have a strong enough political base in the Congress to remain in office." He personally wanted "to continue to fight through the months ahead for my personal vindication." Such a fight, he reasoned, would absorb too much attention and time from Congress and himself, to the detriment of the country. Nixon never indicated he had obstructed justice and systematically lied to the country for more than two years, confessing only to faulty judgment: "I would say only that if some of my judgments were wrong — and some were wrong — they were made in what I believed at the time to be the best interests of the Nation."[26] Nixon also reviewed his foreign policy achievements and praised Vice President Ford. After some time with his family, Nixon went to the Lincoln Sitting Room and until 1:30 A.M. telephoned staff, supporters, and friends, expressing his appreciation for their support. With seemingly nothing politically to gain, he continued his career-long practice of telephoning.

At 9:30 A.M., Friday, August 9, the president spoke in the East Room to the White House staff, cabinet members, and a few friends. Surrounded by his family, and televised nationally, he spoke in maudlin tones of his parents, of the White House, and of the White House staff and referred to himself with self-depreciation. He repeated the admission in his resignation speech that "we have done some things wrong in this Administration. . . . Mistakes, yes. But for personal gain, never."[27] After Nixon spoke, he and his wife flew by helicopter to Andrews Air Force Base in the suburbs of Washington and there boarded the presidential plane "The Spirit of '76" for their trip to California. At 12:03 P.M., with Nixon airborne, Chief Justice Warren E. Burger administered to Gerald Ford the oath of office as president. One of Nixon's legacies to the nation was a president who was the first person never to have won a vote as candidate for either vice president or president. In his first remarks as president, Gerald Ford declared, "My fellow Americans, our long national nightmare is over."

Most Americans agreed. On the question whether Nixon should leave office, the country stood unusually united on an issue of such supreme importance. Democrats and their supporters and allies among voters, the media, and special interest groups had never liked or respected the president. What gave respectability and credibility to the two-year struggle to uncover the cover-up was the indispensable role of Republicans and conservatives.

The smoking gun tape removed the last remaining doubts about Nixon's culpability. A unanimous Supreme Court ordered the president to release the tapes. After the revelation of the June 23, 1972, tape, the seventeen Republican members of the House Judiciary Committee supported impeachment. The Republican leadership in both houses of Congress and the 1964 presidential nominee Barry Goldwater urged resignation. Senate Republican leaders had concluded that ninety of the one hundred members would vote to convict the president. Even the senior cabinet member, Secretary of State Kissinger, recommended resignation. The overwhelming majority of newspaper editorials advocated resignation or impeachment, including such ardent conservative newspapers as the *Chicago Tribune* and the *Manchester Union Leader*. A public opinion poll by Louis Harris Associates found that 66 percent of Americans favored impeachment, a higher percentage than the percentage of popular vote any presidential candidate ever has received in an election. This rare national consensus had forced the president from office.

CHAPTER NINE

Ends and Means

Watergate and the Cold War

If some of my judgments were wrong — and some were wrong — they were made in what I believed at the time to be the best interests of the Nation."
— *Richard M. Nixon, August 8, 1974*

It is always easy for politicians and above all Presidents to believe that the best interests of the nation lie in their own re-election.
— Wall Street Journal, *August 12, 1974*

He was the most dishonest individual I ever met in my life. President Nixon lied to his wife, his family, his friends, long- time colleagues in the U.S. Congress, lifetime members of his own political party, the American people, and the world.
— *Barry Goldwater,* Goldwater, *1988*

When President Nixon resigned the presidency on August 9, 1974, Americans stood with uncommon unanimity on a crucial political issue that initially had divided them. In the end, a unified country demanded that the president leave office because he had obstructed justice, abused presidential power, and repeatedly lied to the American public. Most Americans, along with political commentators, believed the American system worked, that the country was a government of laws, not of individuals. Nixon's political career and its ignominious end, however, reflected negatively on the politics and values of the Cold War as well as on himself. The historian Melvin Small, in his authoritative study of the Nixon administration, has concluded that "one can easily make a case that Watergate was emblematic of Nixon's behavior throughout his career." With equal validity he ends his book with the assessment that "the period from the end of World War II to the end of the cold war was in good measure an age of Nixon."[1]

The four presidents who preceded Nixon shared with him important broad patterns of behavior. In public and political discourse they often used exaggerated rhetoric, crisis analysis, and oversimplification.[2] In government operations, their record included a large degree of unnecessary secrecy. Senator Daniel Patrick Moynihan chaired the bipartisan Commission on Protecting and Reducing Government Secrecy, which held hearings and programs from January 1995 to December 1996. In the book he wrote following that investigation, he concluded that during the Cold War a "culture of secrecy" grew in Washington and kept information and records from public scrutiny. Philosophically, the premise of presidents regarding this culture of secrecy has been that the ends justify the means.

Many historians would ascribe to President Franklin D. Roosevelt these presidential modes of behavior. In his exhaustive study, *Roosevelt and the Isolationists, 1932–1945,* Wayne S. Cole documents this record. Patrick J. Maney, in his perceptive analysis, *The Roosevelt Presence: A Biography of Franklin Delano Roosevelt,* agrees: "It was a short step from Roosevelt's treatment of noninterventionists to the abuses of presidential power that occurred in the name of national security during the Johnson and Nixon presidencies."[3] The Roosevelt abuses included the misuse of the FBI and the Internal Revenue Bureau.

During times of national and international emergencies, the balance of power in the U.S. government shifts toward the president at the expense of Congress. The system of checks and balances loses some of its force and effectiveness. In the title and organizing concept of his best-selling book, *The Imperial Presidency,* the prize-winning historian Arthur M. Schlesinger Jr. describes this phenomenon. No doubt the imperial presidency explains much of the behavior that historians find in the administrations of Roosevelt and the post–World War II presidents. Still, as Small correctly maintains about Nixon: "No president before or after ordered or participated in so many serious illegal and extralegal acts that violated constitutional principles."[4] Nixon did more than step over a political and constitutional line; he jumped.

Scholars and presidents agree that domestic conditions and foreign policy are inseparably intertwined. In the book John F. Kennedy wrote to advance his 1960 presidential campaign, for example, he expressed this truism when he wrote that the "line dividing domestic and foreign affairs has become as indistinct as a line drawn in water. All that happens . . . at home has a direct and intimate bearing on what we can and must do abroad. All that happens to us abroad," he continued, "has a direct and intimate bearing on what we can and must do at home."[5] More than four decades later, President William Jefferson Clinton in his inaugural address reiterated the same theme: "There is no longer a clear division between what is foreign and what is domestic."

In 1989 the historian Walter LaFeber, in *The American Age,* his major synthesis of U.S. foreign policy, explained to readers that he approached his study "in the belief that how Americans act at home reveals much about how they act abroad." The next year the political scientist Bruce Russett expressed the same premise on the opening pages of his influential book. Public opinion, he wrote, "operating in democratic political systems shapes and constrains national security policy." A few pages later he observes that "success or failure of international policy is in fact substantially driven by domestic political developments."[6] Professional historians have published an abundance of specialized studies that illustrate in detail the relationship between domestic and foreign affairs, including, among other areas, public opinion, economics, ethnic groups, media, and anticommunism. Indeed, most studies of foreign affairs contain some examination of domestic considerations.[7]

An event that lasted as long as Watergate and that had as profound an impact on government and the public, not surprisingly, is interlaced with foreign affairs. The timing of some public events illustrates this. The sixteen-day Yom Kippur War in October 1973 raged while Nixon struggled to retain control of the tapes, a struggle that erupted into the firing and resignations that occurred during the Saturday Night Massacre. During this period the president failed to attend a single formal White House meeting concerning the war; and when he announced his order of a worldwide military alert, critics wondered if he had done so to divert attention from the Saturday Night Massacre. On October 24, 1973, President Nixon vetoed a bill severely limiting presidential war powers. On November 7, Congress overrode the veto. Between these two dates the Saturday Night Massacre dominated the media's attention. The War Powers Act that passed stipulated that a president must notify Congress within forty-eight hours after troop deployment and must withdraw troops within sixty days unless they are authorized by Congress to stay longer. Another event that publicly tied Watergate to foreign affairs took place on the evening of November 7, when the president gave his speech, "An Address to the Nation about the Policies to Deal with the Energy Shortages." After explaining these policies, Nixon shifted attention from them when he took the opportunity "to close with a personal note" and then declared he had no intention of resigning from office.

In his memoirs, Secretary of State Henry Kissinger revealed that Nixon would have fired him had Watergate "not overwhelmed" the president.[8] He concluded further that "the debacle of Watergate . . . finally sealed the fate of South Vietnam by the erosion of Executive authority."[9] With that erosion of authority, Kissinger noticed that "Nixon's attention span for foreign policy was also declining."[10] Other officials, such as the FBI director Clarence Kelley and the presidential aide Leonard Garment, Nixon's former law partner, noted his brooding and feared a paralysis in his ability to function as president. The detailed annotations that Nixon once made on the daily news summaries almost disappeared.

In June and July 1974, with his authority and his presidency unraveling, Nixon made his last two trips abroad: to the Middle East from June 12 to 18 and to Moscow from June 27 to July 3. At the time he suffered from painful, life-threatening phlebitis, but he insisted on traveling and then disobeyed further his doctor's advice by remaining on his feet for long periods of time. Egypt gave him a tumultuous welcome, and the Soviet leader Leonid Brezhnev treated him sympathetically. Other than momentarily bolstering Nixon's bruised ego, the trips served little national purpose.

In specific ways, Watergate had its origins in Nixon's concern about foreign affairs. His reaction to the role of Daniel Ellsberg in the publication of the Pentagon Papers led to the creation of the Plumbers, who burglarized the office of Ellsberg's psychiatrist in September 1971, the Chilean embassy in May 1972, and the Democratic National Committee headquarters in June 1972.[11] Nixon's reaction to the leaks to newspapers of information on the U.S. bombing of Cambodia led to illegal wiretaps on some journalists and some members of the National Security Council. When he believed that the Brookings Institution, a liberal think tank in Washington, had a copy of the report on former President Johnson's bombing halt in Vietnam, Nixon wanted it immediately, by any means necessary.[12] The relationship between Watergate and foreign affairs is apparent. Less obvious is the degree to which Nixon absorbed his core values and model of presidential behavior from the currents so pronounced during the post–World War II era.

Following World War II, the United States faced world conditions that had changed dramatically from the prewar era. In response, President Harry S. Truman forged a foreign policy that departed from the main tenets of the nation's earlier policies. To explain his policies, and to win public support for them, Truman resorted to crisis analysis, oversimplification, and exaggerated rhetoric. On March 4, 1947, he expounded to Congress and to Americans the doctrine of containment, the concept that formed the foundation of U.S. foreign policy from that time until the collapse of the Soviet Union in 1989 and 1990. In perhaps the most important speech of his presidency, Truman pointed out, "At the present moment in world history nearly every nation must choose between alternative ways of life." American aid to Greece and Turkey, he explained, constituted "an investment in world freedom and world peace. . . . It must be the policy of the United States to support free people who are resisting attempted subjugation." When the House of Representatives voted on the appropriation of funds, the freshman member Richard Nixon supported "world freedom and world peace." Twenty-two months later in his inaugural address, Truman dedicated the nation to the principle that "all peoples" deserve the right "to govern themselves as they see fit."[13]

Truman's approach spawned a backlash that gained momentum after the communists won the Chinese Civil War late in 1949 and North Korea invaded South Korea the next year. Senator Joseph McCarthy exploited the fear of communism and questioned why Truman had failed to oppose the Chinese communists sufficiently and why he waged a limited war in Korea if the world were in such crisis. Secretly, Truman authorized covert activities that broke with U.S. law and violated widely shared public principles. Truman rationalized: the ends justified the means.

President Eisenhower voiced similar themes. In his first inaugural address, with Vice President Nixon sitting nearby, Eisenhower concluded that the "forces of good and evil are massed and armed and opposed as rarely before in history." Later in his speech he added, "Freedom is pitted against slavery; lightness against the dark." As Truman had done, Eisenhower enumerated some of the noble principles upon which U.S. foreign policy was based. He promised that "we shall never use our strength to try to impress upon another people our own cherished political and economic institutions." Four years later in his second inaugural address, he warned that "rarely has this earth known such peril as today."[14]

Kennedy and Johnson, although differing from their two predecessors in age and political careers, presented the same crisis analysis of the world. In his inaugural address, Kennedy welcomed the responsibility "of defending freedom in its hour of maximum danger." On the day of his assassination, his prepared but undelivered speech warned of "the ambitions of international communism."[15] Johnson made the familiar promise that "no nation need ever fear that we desire . . . to impose our will, or to dictate their institutions," and he characterized Americans as "the guardians at the gate" of freedom in the world, an indispensable role because "there is no one else."[16]

At times, presidents explained to the public the complexities of U.S. involvement in world affairs, but like most politicians of the late 1940s, 1950s, and 1960s, post–World War II presidents portrayed the United States primarily as the "free world" champion of peace and democracy pitted against an enemy without principles. And because this enemy never rested in its aggression, the "free world" faced constant crises. Fortunately for the world, the presidents believed, the United States shouldered a leadership position for completely unselfish reasons.

In ways essentially removed from public awareness, however, these four presidents pursued covert activities of a character that contradicted their public pronouncements. To cover up their covert operations, presidents insisted that their agencies and aides provide them with "plausible deniability." They denounced, meanwhile, other nations that attempted similar activities. During these four presidencies, a culture of bureaucratic secrecy developed, in part by withholding records under the claim of national security. Congress avoided close oversight of record classification or of intelligence operations.

President Truman launched the first important, post–World War II, covert political operation from a fear that Italian voters would elect a communist government in April 1948. Beginning in 1947, but increasingly in January 1948 when polls projected a communist victory, he committed the United States to a plan that would produce a different election result. Truman funneled millions of dollars to the Christian Democratic and conservative democratic Socialist Parties and encouraged American corporations and labor unions to do the same. A massive propaganda campaign highlighted the benefits of American aid and reduced the issues to a series of simplicities: totalitarianism or democracy, the Soviet Union or the United States, atheism or Christianity. None of these or other measures, overt or covert, guaranteed the desired results. The United States, therefore, sent equipment and military advisers to Italy's domestic security forces and drafted contingency plans for military intervention in case an Italian civil war erupted. Italian voters gave the American-backed Christian Democrats a stunning victory. American leaders celebrated.[17]

In August 1953 the CIA succeeded in helping to overthrow the government in Iran. That government, in the judgment of Eisenhower and the CIA, had become too independently nationalistic and too susceptible to communist influence. Under the direction of Kermit Roosevelt, the grandson of one American president and cousin to another, CIA agents arranged and financed riots, propaganda, and recruitment of key leaders for a new government. The United States immediately sent it financial aid and committed itself to support of the unreservedly pro-American shah, whom the CIA had helped restore to power.

Encouraged by the success in the Middle East, the Eisenhower administration once again turned to the CIA to mount a similar, and equally successful, operation in Guatemala. The objective was to remove an elected but reform-minded government. In essence, the United States helped establish a dictatorship in place of a democracy on the unsubstantiated charges of a possible communist takeover.

During the 1950s and 1960s, the CIA secretly disbursed millions of dollars to subsidize the Japanese Liberal Democratic Party and its members. The party leaders denied the existence of the support that helped them stay in power until corruption contributed to their downfall. Only in autumn 1994 did the American public learn about "the breadth and depth of the support."[18]

In April 1961 one covert operation became public when the CIA-directed attempt to overthrow the Cuban government failed at the Bay of Pigs on the Cuban coast. Eisenhower had approved the training of Cubans living in exile in the United States to prepare them for the overthrow, although American law forbade such training. Kennedy authorized that operation although it violated the charter of the Organization of American States that the U.S. Senate had ratified. The scholar Trumbull Higgins titled his book about the Bay of Pigs affair *The Perfect Failure.*

In 1962 President Kennedy approved a CIA plan to influence the outcome of the presidential election in Brazil. Two years later President Johnson directed the CIA to block covertly the election of Salvador Allende as president of Chile. In his first year in office Nixon continued Johnson's policy and approved funding to prevent Allende from winning the 1970 election. Nixon also encouraged American corporations to provide funding, and Anaconda, International Telephone and Telegraph, and Kennecott did. This time, however, despite massive American spending, Allende won. With ample precedent, Nixon then ordered the CIA to undermine the Allende government.[19]

American covert activities during the Cold War included more than rigging or influencing elections in Italy, Brazil, Japan, and Chile and overthrowing elected governments in Iran, Guatemala, and Chile. Kennedy had ordered the invasion of Cuba in 1961, and Johnson ordered the invasion of the Dominican Republic in 1965. These examples illustrate the readiness of presidents to order operations at total variance with American values and with some of their public statements. The cases of Italy and Chile also illustrated how corporate leaders were willing, in the national interest, and in secrecy, to finance rigged elections. To the extent to which they knew, the vast majority of politicians accepted these actions as unfortunate necessities.

Truman, Eisenhower, Kennedy, and Johnson formulated and explained their actions to the American public as a two-sided conflict between good and evil. The document that perhaps best rationalizes this approach was the Doolittle Report; General James Doolittle had chaired the committee that wrote it. In 1954 Eisenhower directed Doolittle "to conduct a study of the covert activities of the C.I.A." According to the Doolittle Report, "We are facing an implacable enemy whose avowed objective is world domination. . . . There are no rules in such a game." To fight it, the report continued, the United States "must learn to subvert, sabotage, and destroy our enemies by more clever, more sophisticated, and more effective methods than those used against us."[20] The report, a guide to top policy makers, remained classified and unknown to Americans for years.

When Nixon became president he understood well the foreign policy of his four predecessors and their core belief that anticommunism sanctified exaggerations, rigged elections, and cover-ups. An astute politician, Nixon had observed American presidents since 1946, and, indeed, for eight years as vice president stood ready to replace one should the need arise. He knew how the system worked.

President Nixon and his aides believed the nation faced a crisis at home that imperiled national and world security. Intercontinental ballistic missiles had eradicated the distinction between national and world safety, and these men believed Nixon's leadership was critical. Despite lack of evidence to support his position, the president remained convinced that communists were behind the anti-Vietnam protests. While talking to John Ehrlichman on September 8, 1972, Nixon called his Democratic presidential opponent, George McGovern, a "Communist sonofabitch."[21] Within the White House, the objective of ensuring Nixon's reelection justified strong measures, because, as his adviser and speechwriter Patrick Buchanan told him in March 1971, if he lost, "we all go, and maybe the country with us."[22] With Nixon's approval, Buchanan and others set about to prevent that loss. A year later Buchanan reported to Attorney General John Mitchell and Nixon's chief of staff, H. R. Haldeman, that "our primary objective to prevent Senator Muskie from sweeping the early primaries . . . and uniting the Democratic party behind him for the fall, has been achieved." Buchanan recommended as their next step that they assist George McGovern in his bid for the Democratic nomination "in every way we can." Looking back, William Safire, one of three Nixon speechwriters, admitted the obvious when he wrote, "Watergate was essentially an abuse of the power of the government in order to affect an election." Charles Colson later explained Watergate as the result of White House officials believing illegal actions were "necessary for the president to survive and [they] covered their own misdeeds while rationalizing it all as being in the interests of the country."[23]

Nixon's two closest political associates left vivid accounts of their reasoning that the end justified illegal means in winning the election of 1972. In February of that year Haldeman declared on national television that the critics of Nixon's Vietnam policy "now are consciously aiding and abetting the enemy of the United States." These critics included former vice president Hubert Humphrey and Senators Edmund Muskie, Ted Kennedy, and George

McGovern. Haldeman believed that "the President's critics are in favor of putting a Communist government in South Vietnam."[24] Haldeman's belief that the leading Democratic candidates for their party's presidential nomination were traitors thus validated his illegal activities during the 1972 campaign and his later obstruction of justice and perjury.

On July 10, 1973, when John Mitchell testified before the Senate Watergate Committee, he explained why he withheld information about the Watergate break-in from the police and the FBI; why he failed to report information about Donald Segretti's dirty tricks campaign that Mitchell called "the White House Horrors"; and why he did not report information about individuals who he knew had committed perjury to cover up these crimes. One committee member reminded Mitchell that during the 1972 campaign he knew that Magruder, Haldeman, Ehrlichman, and persons "all around" the president were "involved in crime, perjury, accessory after the fact, and you deliberately refused to tell" Nixon. The senator then asked the former attorney general, "Would you state that the expediency of the election was more important than that?" Mitchell replied, "Senator, I think you have put it exactly correct. In my mind, the reelection of Richard Nixon, compared with what was available on the other side, was so much more important that I put it in just that context." The next day Mitchell testified again and repeated the logic behind his perjury and obstruction of justice: "The most important thing to this country was the reelection of Richard Nixon and I was not about to countenance anything that would stand in the way of that reelection."[25] Mitchell apparently missed the irony that CREEP and Nixon's aides maneuvered covertly to have the Democratic Party nominate McGovern.

Mitchell's testimony articulated the dominant philosophy of the Nixon reelection campaign. Second only to the president with responsibility to enforce the law, Mitchell preferred, and helped plan, an unfair election rather than accept the prospect of voters electing a Democratic president in an honest election. Nor were Nixon's aides alone in their philosophy. Top executives in eighteen of the nation's best-known corporations made illegal campaign contributions to give Nixon a secret, unfair advantage. Once a corporate leader or a presidential aide accepted the basic premise that a Nixon defeat would damage the national interest, the other activities justifiably followed. The atmosphere that Cold War presidents created while conducting foreign policy and, more important, internal secret policy made Watergate possible.

In addition to national interest in the broader world perspective, the loose ethics of American political campaigns helps to explain the manifestations of Watergate. The Nixon White House often blurred the line between criminality and accepted campaign tactics. The tape of June 23, 1972, that Nixon fought so hard to keep, the tape that indeed was the smoking gun that his defenders insisted investigators must produce, recorded a conversation between Haldeman and the president. On the tape Nixon and his chief of staff discussed having the CIA director Richard Helms tell the FBI director L. Patrick Gray to stay away from investigating the Watergate break-in. Then, Nixon said, "All right, fine. How do you call him in — I mean you just — well, we protected Helms from one hell of a lot of things." One implication is obvious. Helms and the CIA had carried out activities that exceeded his and the agency's authority, and Nixon had covered them up.

For Nixon, a cover-up of unauthorized operations was nothing new when he and his aides embarked on the Watergate cover-up. Indeed, Jeb Stuart Magruder later remembered the cover-up as "immediate and automatic; no one ever considered that there would not be a cover-up." Haldeman did not view a political burglary as anything exceptional. To Nixon's speechwriter Ray Price, Haldeman later recalled "the unimportance of it in our minds at the time it happened" and added that Watergate was "really only one of maybe fifteen things we were honing in on that day."[26] A burglary, even in the headquarters of the opposition party, and its subsequent cover-up seemed so commonplace to Nixon and his various appointees that they completely underestimated its potential for disaster.

Americans have tolerated campaign activities that sometimes transgress accepted norms of decency and violate the spirit and, at times, the letter of the law. Three examples illustrate this point: Lyndon Johnson won his first Senate seat with voter tabulations manipulated to provide him with a winning margin; until the 1965 Voting Rights Act, local jurisdictions and states across the South routinely denied their black citizens the right to vote; and in 1952 the Republican Party platform maintained that "successive Democratic Administrations . . . have shielded traitors to the Nation in high places." The burglary did not shock Americans, which was one reason George McGovern could never turn it into an important issue during the 1972 campaign. Although the break-in, combined with the earlier dirty tricks, strained the outer limits of acceptability, they would not have driven Nixon from office when disclosed, unless he personally had orchestrated most of them. The public, moreover, would have accepted a cover-up, and even misinformation or lies, if a president could demonstrate that such actions had served the national interest. Nixon and his aides believed his reelection was indispensable to the national interest and hence justified the use of the CIA to block the investigation of the Watergate burglary and all other aspects of the cover-up. Americans interpreted the matter differently; they saw it as an attempt to promote and protect Nixon's political career.

At several instances between June 1972 and July 1973, Nixon could have taken decisive actions to defuse Watergate. After the break-in he could have declared his own innocence and fired Mitchell, Magruder, Haldeman, and Ehrlichman. No one ever contemplated such a measure because the break-in fell within accepted political campaign behavior.

In January 1973 Nixon and his advisers should have recognized that Judge John Sirica threatened the continuation of the cover-up when he indicated he wanted to learn who ordered and financed the burglary. Carl Bernstein and Bob Woodward had kept the story in the news, and their on-going investigations also threatened the continuation of the cover-up. The landslide victory in November, the Vietnam agreement, and the highly favorable public opinion polls, however, had dulled the political instincts of Nixon and his close circle of assistants. Moreover, Nixon realized that President Kennedy, with assistance from the press, had successfully covered up aspects of his personal life and that President Johnson had survived years in office despite a serious credibility gap. In January 1973 the concept of a presidential resignation lay outside the political thinking of Americans.

In July 1973, when Alexander Butterfield disclosed the existence of the taping systems, Nixon had his last chance to resolve the Watergate affair and remain in office. He might have survived had he burned the tapes, admitted administrative laxity, feigned some ignorance, and pointed out he had fired the close aides involved. Without those tapes, there would have been no Saturday Night Massacre, no missing conversations, no eighteen-minute erasure, and no smoking gun. Nixon believed that he would not have to surrender the tapes — no other president had been forced to disclose White House communications. Presidential libraries continued the principle that presidential records were the personal property of the president.

Nixon underestimated the public's reaction to the steadily increasing information, revealed bit by bit, relating to the break-in and cover-up. His reaction to the break-in and his automatic acceptance of the cover-up reflected an insensitivity to the idealism that most Americans expect of their president. Even when his presidency collapsed, Nixon did not appreciate the meaning of Watergate.

On August 5, 1974, when he released to the public the transcript of the June 23, 1972, tape, Nixon admitted having lied and having obstructed justice by attempting to misuse the CIA, but he believed those actions did not justify "impeachment and removal of a President." In his resignation speech three days later, he explained that some of his judgments had been "wrong," but he had made them in what he "believed at the time to be the best interests of the Nation." The next day, in his remarks before leaving the White House, he again admitted that "we have done some things wrong in this Administration. . . . Mistakes, yes. But for personal gain, never."[27]

A month later President Ford pardoned Nixon for all crimes he "committed or may have committed" as president. In accepting the pardon, Nixon again admitted he had been "wrong in not acting more decisively and more forthrightly in dealing with Watergate, particularly when it reached the stage of judicial proceedings." In his memoirs, Ford recounted that Nixon's acceptance statement "hadn't been as forthcoming as I had hoped. He didn't admit guilt and it was a good deal less than a full confession." Ford's pardon and Nixon's failure to admit guilt troubled the country. Three days later the Senate adopted a resolution opposing any future pardon to a Watergate participant until after a trial and after the completion of all appeals. The Gallup Poll reported that public approval of Ford plunged from 71 to 49 percent.[28]

Nixon perhaps expressed his most penetrating self-analysis of his role in Watergate during spring 1977, when the author David Frost, a British television producer and program host, interviewed the former president for twenty-eight and three-quarter hours. When Frost pressed him about a decision to "do something illegal," Nixon replied, "Well, when the President does it, that means it is not illegal." The justification in such instances, Nixon continued, was "national security or, in this case, because of a threat to internal peace and order of significant magnitude." Later, he maintained that he never obstructed justice, "because I did not have the motive required for the commission of that crime."[29]

In 1977, as throughout the entire Watergate affair, Nixon believed he had acted within the American presidential political system because he used his power to protect and promote the national interest; he acknowledged only "mistakes and misjudgments." Nixon and his assistants interpreted the anti-Vietnam campaign and the 1960s' cultural revolution as threats to national stability and to U.S. leadership in the world. To counter these perceived national threats, he instinctively reacted according to prevailing political presidential values. In this respect, Watergate constituted a chapter in the history of what Arthur M. Schlesinger Jr. has called "the imperial presidency." The reaction of the nation to President Johnson's imperial presidency should have served as a warning to Nixon, but it did not.

Nixon made two glaring mistakes. First, he operated on the belief that foreign and domestic affairs and policies were inseparable and could be dealt with in the same manner. His predecessors repeatedly expressed such beliefs, and historians consistently emphasize the relationship between domestic conditions and foreign affairs. When Nixon related the domestic mood and activities to the nation's image and role in the world, therefore, he acted within the intellectual framework of post–World War II history. His mistake was the unsubtle application of that belief in specific instances, such as the burglary of the office of Daniel Ellsburg's psychiatrist, the suborning of testimony to protect the cover-up, and the attempt to have the CIA block the FBI investigation of the Watergate break-in. In these instances the vast majority of Americans, it turned out, did not see the connection between domestic and foreign affairs.

Nixon's second glaring mistake was his systematic lying between the beginning of the cover-up and the resignation. This lying, when exposed, combined with his persistent refusal to release the tapes that most Americans believed would reveal the truth about Watergate, led to Nixon's resignation. The country's earlier post–World War II presidents had lied to the public, but none ever did so in such detail, so often, and over such a long period of time. Nixon strained the nation's patience; the cover-up lasted too long. Americans believed that if Nixon really wanted to end the Watergate controversy, as he insisted he did, he would have released the tapes. His citing of abstract principles sounded unconvincing. Common sense defeated Nixon.

The struggle over the tapes, the Justice Department investigation, the Senate investigation, the trial of burglars, and the media investigation kept Watergate constantly in the news. Almost all the findings of these investigative activities undermined Nixon's previous positions. In response, he acknowledged he should have been more aware of activities conducted on his behalf and promised renewed commitment to get at the truth. With each episode he lost credibility.

During 1973 and 1974, Nixon faced other problems, unrelated to the cover-up, that further lessened his credibility. One was Vice President Spiro Agnew's resignation and plea in federal court of no contest to charges of income tax evasion and of accepting bribes during his governorship of Maryland. Another problem stemmed from Nixon's questionable tax deduction for the donation of his vice presidential papers to the National Archives. Still another was the amount of money the federal government spent to improve his Florida and California houses. These headline issues, combined with the steady conviction of White House aides for their part in the primary campaigns, the illegal fund-raising, the break-in, and the cover-up, created the appearance of an administration out of touch with morality and honesty. In the public's eyes, Nixon had no reserve of integrity to draw upon in his appeal for public support.

Watergate was Nixon's personal disgrace. More important, it was a political, a constitutional, and a societal crisis. Through all of Watergate wound a thread of irony. On August 8, 1968, in his speech accepting the Republican presidential nomination, Nixon had declared, "If we are to restore order and respect for law in this country, there's one place we're going to begin: we're going to have a new Attorney General of the Untied States of America."[30] After winning the election, he appointed his 1968 campaign manager and former New York law partner John Mitchell, who later became the first attorney general in the nation's history to serve a prison sentence. For his conspiracy, obstruction of justice, and perjury in the Watergate affair Mitchell received a two-and-a-half to eight-year prison sentence. After nineteen months he accepted parole. In another touch of irony, Senator Howard Baker intended to protect Nixon by stopping Watergate at the door to the Oval Office. His striking question, what did the president know and when did he know it, while initially working well, eventually promoted the idea of Nixon's guilt, as evidence was uncovered documenting the president's knowledge of the cover-up. Once the nation learned of the existence of the tapes, Nixon's repeated refusal to release them steadily eroded his credibility. The public understood that their release would have told what Nixon knew and when he knew it. Judge Sirica's actions also contributed to the thread of irony. "Maximum John" was exactly the type of law-and-order judge Nixon favored. He had emphasized the law and order theme in his 1968 campaign for the presidency while assailing the permissiveness of the liberal Warren Court. President Eisenhower, moreover, had appointed Sirica to his judgeship.

Up to a point, Nixon's actions were not aberrations. The Watergate break-in and the dirty tricks campaign fit within the context of internal security policies with which Nixon and his aides were familiar. By itself, exposure of the dirty tricks would not have led to Nixon's, or any other president's, resignation. Executives at American Airlines, Goodyear Rubber, and sixteen other corporations secretly and illegally contributed funds to give Nixon an unfair advantage in the 1972 campaign. They, like the president and his aides, assumed that the ends justified the means. In 1964 and 1968 President Johnson tapped the office and plane telephones of the Republican presidential candidates. In 1972 the Committee to Re-elect the President did the tapping instead of the FBI. Nixon expected the director of the CIA to cover up for him in return for past protection. With the CIA's budget both generous and removed from congressional debate, the protection Nixon gave apparently related to Helms's acting beyond his constitutional authority.

Above all, Watergate was a predictable, though unique, expression of the contours of American politics, the imperial presidency, during the Cold War. The president, constitutionally empowered to conduct foreign affairs and to command the armed forces, came to dominate politics during a bipolar era when either of two nations could destroy much of the world. Each president through that time believed covert activity necessary, and each relied on oversimplification, exaggeration, and crisis analysis as an operational philosophy. Throughout this period the influence of the National Security Council, the CIA, the FBI, and the White House staff steadily increased. So did surveillance.

At home, intelligence agencies instituted programs that included wiretapping for political reasons, character assassination, instigation of violence, and dissemination of false information. In 1956 the FBI director J. Edgar Hoover established, without authorization from either of his two superiors, the attorney general or the president, the program COINTELPRO. Initially, the objective of this counterintelligence operation was to disrupt the Communist Party, but during the 1960s Hoover extended its scope to include other dissenting groups: the Ku Klux Klan, the Socialist Workers Party, the Black Panther Party, and the Students for a Democratic Society. In 1971 Hoover terminated COINTELPRO after a dissident stole related FBI documents and leaked them to the media. The fear of congressional and public reaction motivated Hoover's decision.

In 1967 the CIA compromised its legal authority and instituted several programs, CHAOS for example, that focused on domestic dissent. Two years later, another intelligence organization, the National Security Agency, established MINARET to gather information about protest groups. The FBI, the CIA, and the NSA surrounded their illegal operations in secrecy and worked on the assumption that foreign governments financed protests in the United States.

In planning the 1972 campaign, Nixon's aides adopted measures "to affect an election," as William Safire later wrote. Nixon's top campaign managers approved disruption of primary campaigns and elections, dissemination of false information, and intelligence gathering. To block investigation of the failed June 1972 burglary, Haldeman immediately thought of assistance from the CIA. Nixon's aides instinctively covered up their illegal campaign activities. Ultimately, they explained that the reelection of the president was in the national interest, and that justified whatever steps they deemed necessary.

The patterns of their thinking and their activities mirrored those of U.S. officials during the Cold War. In an atmosphere of oversimplification, exaggeration, and crisis analysis, a noble end justified illegal means. To an extent, Watergate was an expression of foreign policy at home. None of this excuses or defends Nixon's actions or those of his aides. Domestic conditions and foreign policy, indeed, are interrelated, but Watergate clearly demonstrated that Americans will accept executive actions in other countries that they will not accept at home. Nixon and his aides went beyond the pale of public acceptance with the illegal Plumbers and their burglaries, the obstruction of justice, the subornation of testimony and commitment of perjury, and the abuse of federal agencies. For their inadequate sense of limits and their lack of respect for due process at home, Nixon and his aides paid a price. Nixon lost his presidency and accepted a pardon from his successor; eighteen of his aides went to prison. An analysis of Nixon's role in Watergate framed in the context of the Cold War demands a broader and deeper indictment than merely that of his being the first president to resign from office.

Chronology

1970

July 14   Nixon approves Huston Plan.

July 28   Nixon withdraws approval of Huston Plan because of opposition
             by FBI director J. Edgar Hoover and Attorney General John
             Mitchell.

1971

June 13   *New York Times* begins printing of Pentagon Papers.

June 30   Supreme Court rules Pentagon Papers do not threaten national
             security.

September 3–4 Plumbers burglarize office of Daniel Ellsberg's psychiatrist.

1972

January 17   Harris Poll. If elections held today for whom would you vote:
             Nixon, 42 percent; Muskie, 42 percent

January 27   John Mitchell, John Dean, G. Gordon Liddy, and Jeb Stuart
             Magruder meet in attorney general's office and discuss Liddy's
             proposed intelligence-gathering plan that includes burglary.

January 31   Gallup Poll: Nixon, 43 percent; Muskie, 42 percent.

February 4   Mitchell, Dean, Liddy, and Magruder meet again to consider
             revised plan with a lower budget.

March 1   John Mitchell becomes director of the Committee to Re-elect the
             President (CREEP).

April 27   Edmund S. Muskie withdraws from campaign to win Democratic
             Party's nomination for president.

May   Plumbers attempt three times to break into Democratic National
             Committee headquarters in the Watergate complex. The third
             time they are successful, photocopying documents and installing
             telephone taps. Plumbers fail in two attempts to break into
             headquarters of George McGovern. They break into the embassy
             of Chile in hopes that FBI will consider all break-ins as the work of
             the CIA.

June 17	Police arrest five burglars in the headquarters of the Democratic National Committee.
June 21	John Mitchell reports publicly that neither the White House nor CREEP is connected to the break-in.
June 23	Nixon and his chief of staff formulate plan to have the CIA call off the FBI investigation of the June 17 break-in. Nixon's taping system records the conversation.
August 29	Nixon states "categorically" that the White House is not involved with the break-in.
September 15	Federal grand jury indicts the five Watergate burglars and E. Howard Hunt and G. Gordon Liddy.
October 10	The *Washington Post* reports that CREEP and the White House control a secret fund that financed a campaign of political sabotage, including the June 17 break-in.
November 7	Republican ticket of Nixon and Vice President Spiro Agnew wins reelection with 60.8 percent of the popular vote.

1973

January 10–30	Trial of Watergate burglars under Judge John J. Sirica. Five of the indicted plead guilty, and jury convicts McCord and Liddy.
January	Gallup Poll: 68 percent approve of Nixon's "handling his job as President."
February 7	Senate votes seventy-seven to zero to establish a select committee to investigate 1972 campaign.
March 23	Judge Sirica reads McCord's letter in which he reports that higher-ups approved break-in, committed perjury during the investigation, and pressured those indicted to plead guilty.
April 30	In a nationally televised speech President Nixon announces the resignations of H. R. Haldeman, John D. Ehrlichman, and Attorney General Richard Kleindienst and the firing of John Dean.
May 17	Senate Watergate Committee starts its hearings on television under the chair of Sam Ervin (D-N.C.).
May 18	Attorney General Elliot Richardson names Harvard Law School professor Archibald Cox as special prosecutor.
June 22–25	Gallup Poll: 98 percent of Americans had "heard/read about Watergate."
June 25–29	Dean testifies before Watergate Committee.
July 16	Presidential aide Alexander Butterfield reveals the existence of a taping system in the White House, Camp David, Executive Office Building, and Lincoln Sitting Room.
July 16–25	Senate Committee and Cox subpoena tapes of some conversations. Nixon refuses, citing executive privilege.

July	Harris Poll: job rating of Senate Watergate Committee: 62 percent positive.
August 29	Judge Sirica rules Nixon must turn over the tapes. Nixon appeals.
September	Harris Poll: "If you had to do it over again, for whom would you vote for President in 1972 — McGovern or Nixon?" McGovern, 38 percent; Nixon, 36 percent; neither, 11 percent; not sure, 9 percent; and other 6 percent.
October 10	Vice President Agnew resigns and pleads no contest to charge of income tax evasion. Two days later the president nominates Congressman Gerald L. Ford for vice president.
October 20	Nixon orders Cox fired. Attorney General Elliot Richardson and Deputy Attorney General William Ruckelshaus resign. Media calls events the Saturday Night Massacre.
October 23–24	Members of Congress introduce twenty-two bills for impeachment investigation.
November 4	Senator Edward W. Brooke (R-Mass.) calls for the president to resign.
November 10	In response to reaction to Saturday Night Massacre, the president names Leon Jaworski as new special prosecutor.
November 21	Judge Sirica and public learn that the tape of June 20 contains an eighteen-and-a-half-minute gap.

1974

January 15	Panel of six technical experts reports that the gap on the June 20 tape was the result of five separate manual erasures.
February 6	House of Representatives votes 410 to 4 to begin formal impeachment inquiry.
March 1	Federal grand jury indicts seven Nixon aides for conspiracy to cover up crime, including Mitchell, Ehrlichman, and Haldeman. The jury names Nixon an unindicted coconspirator but withholds this information from the public.
April 11	House Judiciary Committee votes thirty-three to three to subpoena forty-two tapes. Nixon refuses to release them.
April 30	On national television Nixon announces the release of 1,308 pages of edited transcripts of tapes requested by the House Judiciary Committee, but he will not release the tapes.
May 9	Republican leader in the House John J. Rhodes announces that Nixon should consider resignation.
May 24	Special Prosecutor Jaworski appeals to Supreme Court for ruling on his subpoena for the president to release to him sixty-four recorded conversations.
July 24	The Supreme Court rules eight to zero that the president must release the tapes Jaworski subpoenaed.

July 27	House Judiciary Committee passes its first impeachment article twenty-seven to eleven for obstruction of justice. Six Republicans vote for the article.
July 29	Judiciary Committee passes its second impeachment article twenty-two to ten for abuse of power.
July 30	Judiciary Committee passes a third impeachment article twenty-one to seventeen for defying House subpoenas.
July 31	For his crimes of perjury and conspiracy John Ehrlichman receives a prison sentence.
August 2	For his crime of cover-up John Dean receives a prison sentence.
August 5	Nixon releases the subpoenaed tapes, including the smoking gun tape of June 23, 1972.
August 6	Every Republican member of the House Judiciary Committee, all of whom are lawyers, state that they will vote to impeach the president. Only two members of the House announce they will vote against impeachment.
August 8	In an evening address to the nation President Nixon announces he will resign the next day. Gallup Poll: 65 percent of Americans support impeachment.
August 9	Nixon resigns, and at 12:03 P.M. Gerald Ford takes the presidential oath.

Notes

1. PATTERNS FROM THE BEGINNING

1 Paul K. Conkin, *The New Deal,* 2d ed. (Arlington Heights, Ill.: Harlan Davidson, 1975), 1.

2 Stephen E. Ambrose, *Nixon: The Triumph of a Politician, 1962–1972* (New York: Simon and Schuster, 1989), 248, 271.

3 *Report to the President by the Commission on CIA Activities within the United States* (Washington, D.C.: Government Printing Office, 1975), 134.

4 For the Hoover-Nixon relationship here and later, see Richard Gid Powers, *Secrecy and Power: The Life of J. Edgar Hoover* (New York: Free Press, 1987), chapter 13, "Nixon and Hoover," and Ambrose, *Nixon: The Triumph of a Politician,* 234–236, 361–362, 368, 448–449.

5 Stanley I. Kutler, *The Wars of Watergate: The Last Crisis of Richard Nixon* (New York: Knopf, 1990), 119–121; Ambrose, *Nixon: The Triumph of a Politician,* 235, 272–274, 448–449; Frank J. Donner, *The Age of Surveillance: The Aims and Methods of America's Political Intelligence System* (New York: Knopf, 1980), 248–251; and J. Anthony Lukas, *Nightmare: The Underside of the Nixon Years* (New York: Viking, 1976), chapter 3, "Leaks and Taps."

6 *The Public Papers of the Presidents of the United States, 1970 Richard Nixon,* 6 vols. (Washington, D.C.: Government Printing Office, 1970–1975), 407 (hereafter *Public Papers of the President,* with appropriate year).

7 Ibid., 406.

8 Ambrose, *Nixon: The Triumph of a Politician,* 350–353, 355–357; William Safire, *Before the Fall: An Inside View of the Pre-Watergate White House* (New York: Ballantine, 1977), 257–272.

9 Safire, *Before the Fall,* 381.

10 U.S. Congress, Senate, Select Committee on Presidential Campaign Activities of 1972, *Watergate and Related Activities, Phase I: Watergate Investigation, Hearings,* Ninety-third Cong., 1st sess., 1973, 3: 1321 (hereafter *Watergate Hearings*).

11 Ibid., *Final Report,* 4–6; Donner, *The Age of Surveillance,* 263–268, 284–285; Kutler, *The Wars of Watergate,* 96–101; William C. Sullivan, with Bill Brown, *The Bureau: My Thirty Years in Hoover's FBI* (New York: Norton, 1979), 211–217, 251–257; Athan Theoharis, *Spying on Americans: Political Surveillance from Hoover to the Huston Plan* (Philadelphia: Temple University Press, 1978), 13–39.

12 Kutler, *The Wars of Watergate,* 116–119; Donner, *The Age of Surveillance,* 249–252; and Lukas, *Nightmare,* chapter 4, "Plumbers."

13 Theoharis, *Spying on Americans,* 38–39.

14 Richard M. Nixon, *RN: The Memoirs of Richard Nixon* (New York: Grosset and Dunlap, 1978), 640. On the smoking gun tape of June 23,1972, Nixon commented, "We protected Helms from one hell of a lot of things."

2. CONTEXT OF THE BREAK-IN

1 Richard M. Nixon, *Six Crises* (New York: Doubleday, 1962), 412.

2 Stephen E. Ambrose, *Nixon: The Triumph of a Politician, 1962–1972* (New York: Simon and Schuster, 1989), 565, 30, 320.

3 William Safire, *Before the Fall* (New York: Ballantine Books, 1977), 124.

4 Henry A. Kissinger, *White House Years* (Boston: Little, Brown, 1979), 264; Tom Wicker, *One of Us: Richard Nixon and the American Dream* (New York: Random House, 1991), 423.

5 *Public Papers of the President, 1973,* 330.

6 Box 89, President's Office File, Nixon Presidential Materials Project, National Archives, College Park, Md.

7 Safire, *Before the Fall,* 135.

8 See Mort Allin to George Bell, February 10, 1971, box 1, Patrick Buchanan Papers, Nixon Presidential Materials Project, National Archives, College Park, Md. (hereafter Buchanan Papers). Nixon "withdrew" from the files Allin's letter to Bell of January 28 that accompanied the original list.

9 In the index to his diaries, which cover the period from January 21, 1969, to April 30, 1973, Haldeman lists nineteen references to Price, twenty-one to Safire, but forty-three to Buchanan. See H. R. Haldeman, *The Haldeman Diaries: Inside the White House* (New York: G. P. Putnam's Sons, 1994).

10 Buchanan to Nixon, March 24, 1971, box 4, Buchanan Papers.

11 Buchanan to Magruder; Magruder to Mitchell, July 28, 1971, box 1, Buchanan Papers.

12 Box 2, Buchanan Papers.

13 Interview in Gerald S. Strober and Deborah H. Strober, *Nixon: An Oral History of His Presidency* (New York: HarperCollins, 1994), 322.

14 Magruder interview, in ibid., 254.

15 Theodore H. White, *The Making of the President, 1972* (New York: Atheneum, 1973), 274.

16 *New York Times,* February 8, 1972; Haldeman later claimed that Nixon specifically told him to make this point. See Ambrose, *Nixon: The Triumph of a Politician,* 511. Haldeman's diary, however, does not support this later claim.

17 Buchanan to Nixon, March 24, 1971, box 6, Buchanan Papers.

18 U.S. Congress, Senate, *Hearings before the Select Committee on Presidential Campaign Activities, Ninety-third Cong., 1st sess.,* October 3, 1973, 10: 3987 (hereafter *Campaign Hearings*).

19 Box 9, Buchanan Papers.

20 *Campaign Hearings,* 10: 4280, 4292–4293.

21 White, *The Making of the President, 1972,* 275; Safire, *Before the Fall,* 829.

22 Buchanan and Khachigian to Mitchell and Haldeman, April 12, 1972, in *Campaign Hearings,* 10: 4186; also in box 6, Buchanan Papers.

23 Haldeman, *Diaries,* 449.

24 *Campaign Hearings,* 11: 4616, 4663–4667.

25 For dirty tricks, see J. Anthony Lukas, *Nightmare* (New York: Viking, 1976), chapter 6; *Campaign Hearings,* 10: 3980–4053, and 11: 4376–4402, 4403–4432.

26 See Strober and Strober, *Nixon,* 273–280.

27 Ibid., 254.

28 *Campaign Hearings,* 10: 4266; *Final Report,* 202–203.

29 *Washington Post,* December 7, 1992.

30 Stanley I. Kutler, ed., *Abuse of Power: The New Nixon Tapes* (New York: Free Press, 1997), 20.

31 See Lukas, *Nightmare,* chapter 5.

32 John Dean, *Blind Ambition: The White House Years* (New York: Simon and Schuster, 1976), 84, and Magruder, *An American Life: One Man's Road to Watergate* (New York: Atheneum, 1974), 195.

33 Mitchell later denied that the group discussed specific targets.

34 *Campaign Hearings,* 4: 1612.

35 G. Gordon Liddy, *Will: The Autobiography of G. Gordon Liddy* (New York: St. Martin's Press, 1980), 232; John Sirica, *To Set the Record Straight: The Break-in, the Tapes, the Conspirators, the Pardon* (New York: Norton, 1979), 44.

36 *New York Times,* January 18, 1972, and January 31, 1972.

37 Box 401, H. R. Haldeman Papers, Nixon Presidential Material Project, National Archives, College Park, Md.

38 Box 9, Buchanan Papers.

39 Quoted in Raymond Price, *With Nixon* (New York: Viking, 1977), 336.

3. THE COVER-UP

1 Jeb Stuart Magruder, *An American Life* (New York: Atheneum, 1974), 240.

2 John Dean, *Blind Ambition* (New York: Simon and Schuster, 1976), 121.

3 J. Anthony Lukas, *Nightmare* (New York: Viking, 1976), 238; *Washington Post,* June 19, 1972.

4 Magruder, *An American Life,* 247, 243–245.

5 *Washington Post,* June 20, 1972.

6 Dean, *Blind Ambition,* 112; *Watergate Hearings,* 9: 3621.

7 *Watergate Hearings,* 6: 2490.

8 *Public Papers of the President,* 1972, 690–691.

9 Transcript of June 23, 1972 tape, in Stanley I. Kutler, ed., *Abuse of Power* (New York: Free Press, 1997), 67, 69.

10 Ibid., 70.

11 *Watergate Hearings,* 9: 3462, 3541.

12 Ibid., 2: 543.

13 Ibid., 544, 579–580.

14 Ibid., 6: 2502.

15 Kutler, *Abuse of Power,* 252.

16 *The Presidential Transcripts* (New York: Dell, 1974), 106.

17 *Watergate Hearings,* 9: 3651.

18 Magruder, *An American Life,* 264.

19 *The Presidential Transcripts,* 105. Kutler did not include this passage in *Abuse of Power.*

20 *Washington Post,* August 29, 1972.

21 *Public Papers of the President, 1972,* 828–829.

22 Ibid., 957–958.

4. DISCLOSURES

1 Carl Bernstein and Bob Woodward, *All the President's Men* (New York: Simon and Schuster, 1974), 71, 72, 139, 131.

2 Woodward told Bernstein and, after Nixon's resignation, the *Washington Post's* editor Ben Bradlee.

3 The several quotations are from Bernstein and Woodward, *All the President's Men,* 130, 131, 195, 317, 333.

4 Gladys Engel Lang and Kurt Lang, *The Battle for Public Opinion: The President, the Press, and the Polls During Watergate* (New York: Columbia University Press, 1983), 26–29.

5 Ibid., 29–32.

6 *Washington Post,* September 16, 1972; John Dean, *Blind Ambition* (New York: Simon and Schuster, 1976), 133.

7 *The Presidential Transcripts* (New York: Dell, 1974), 36, 37, 40.

8 *Public Papers of the President, 1973,* 185–186.

9 March 15, 1973.

10 Dean, *Blind Ambition,* 184.

11 *The Presidential Transcripts,* February 28, 1973, 63.

12 Ibid., March 21 and 22, 1973, 117, 127, 176, 170.

13 John J. Sirica, *To Set the Record Straight* (New York: Norton, 1979), 96–97.

14 George D. Aiken, *Aiken: Senate Diary, January 1972–January 1975* (Brattleboro, Vt.: Stephen Greene Press, 1976), 173, 174.

15 Dean, *Blind Ambition,* 220, 240.

16 *The Presidential Transcripts,* April 14, 1973, 275, 278, 279.

17 Ibid., 287, 293; Dean, *Blind Ambition,* 224.

18 *The Presidential Transcripts,* 444–445.

19 Ibid., 425; see also 513–514.

20 Ibid., 525.

21 Ibid., April 17, 1973, 533, 525–526.

22 *Public Papers of the President, 1973,* 298–299.

23 *The Presidential Transcripts,* April 27, 1973, 666, 667, 676.

24 *Public Papers of the President, 1973,* 328–332.

25 May 1, 1973.

26 May 8, 1973.

27 May 2, 1973.

28 May 3, 1973.

29 May 1, 1973.

30 May 1, 1973.

31 May 2, 1973.

32 Quoted from J. Anthony Lukas, *Nightmare* (New York: Viking, 1976), 363.

33 Both from May 3, 1973.

5. THE SENATE COMMITTEE, TESTIMONIES, AND BUTTERFIELD DISCLOSURE

1 Gladys Engel Lang and Kurt Lang, *The Battle for Public Opinion* (New York: Columbia University Press, 1983), 62–63, 65.

2 *Watergate Hearings*, 1: 254–260, May 22, 1973.

3 *Public Papers of the President, 1973*, 533–536.

4 Ibid., 551, 547–555.

5 May 25, 1973.

6 *Watergate Hearings*, 2: 785, 186.

7 Ibid., 3: 915, 943, 958, 959, 998–1000.

8 Ibid., 4: 1466.

9 *Public Papers of the President, 1973*, 636–639.

10 *Watergate Hearings*, 4: 1666, 1653, 1664; 5: 1832, 1834, 1835.

11 Lang and Lang, *The Battle for Public Opinion*, 77.

12 *Watergate Hearings*, 5: 2074, 2090.

13 Richard M. Nixon, *RN: Memoirs* (New York: Grosset and Dunlap, 1978), 902.

6. THE STRUGGLE FOR THE TAPES

1 *Watergate Hearings*, 5: 2178.

2 Ibid., 6: 2478–2479.

3 *Public Papers of the President, 1973*, 670.

4 *Watergate Hearings*, 7: 2659.

5 August 3, 1973, 821.

6 *New York Times*, July 25, 1973.

7 *San Francisco Examiner and Chronicle*, July 29, 1973.

8 *Washington Post*, July 29, 1973.

9 August 3, 1973.

10 July 31, 1973.

11 July 20, 1973.

12 July 24, 1973.

13 July 29, 1973.

14 July 18, August 3 and 9, 1973.

15 Page 821.

16 *Public Papers of the President, 1970*, 406.

17 *Watergate Hearings,* 7: 2510–2522.

18 Samuel Dash, *Chief Counsel: Inside the Ervin Committee — The Untold Story of Watergate* (New York: Random House, 1976), 195.

19 Fred D. Thompson, *At That Point in Time: The Inside Story of the Senate Watergate Committee* (New York: Quadrange/New York Times, 1975), 98.

20 *Watergate Hearings,* 7: 2863.

21 Ibid., 2867, 2871, 2881, 2882.

22 Dash, *Chief Counsel,* 195.

23 *Watergate Hearings,* 8: 3091.

24 Ibid., 3232.

25 *Papers of the President, 1973,* 329.

26 Ibid., 691–697.

27 Ibid., 716.

28 Ibid., 710–725.

29 *Time,* August 27, 1973, 11–13.

30 *Congressional Record,* September 13, 1973, vol.119, part 23, 2945.

31 *The Harris Survey Yearbook of Public Opinion* (New York: Louis Harris and Associates, 1976), 203, 152.

32 *Watergate Hearings,* 9: 3664.

33 Ibid., 10: 3900–3901.

34 *Papers of the President, 1973,* 718, 735.

35 *New York Times,* September 30, 1973.

36 *Time,* October 22, 1973, 14–15.

37 October 11, 1973.

38 Both from October 11, 1973.

39 October 22, 1973.

40 *Honolulu Star–Bulletin,* October 23, 1973; all other newspapers, October 22, 1973.

41 *Papers of the President, 1973,* 898–899, 897, 901, 904, 905.

42 *The Harris Survey Yearbook of Public Opinion, 1973,* 186, 188.

43 November 2, 1973.

44 November 5, 1973.

45 November 14, 1973.

7. FROM THE SATURDAY NIGHT MASSACRE TO THE TAPE TRANSCRIPTS

1 Pages 20–21.

2 November 9, 1973.

3 *New York Times,* November 1, November 9, and December 12, 1973; *Time,* November 19, 20–21, 1973.

4 *New York Times,* November 10, 1973.

5 November 11, 1973.

6 *Public Papers of the President, 1973,* 921, 940–941.

7 *New York Times,* November 12 and 14, 1973.

8 *Papers of the President, 1973,* 949, 956, 959.

9 Quoted in Stanley I. Kutler, *The Wars of Watergate* (New York: Knopf, 1990), 430.

10 November 28, 1973.

11 *New York Times,* December 1, 1973.

12 *Public Papers of the President,* 1973, 1005, 1006, 1007.

13 December 10, 1973.

14 December 14, 1973.

15 Richard Ben-Veniste and George Frampton Jr., *Stonewall: The Real Story of the Watergate Prosecution* (New York: Simon and Schuster, 1977), 205, 210; Leon Jaworski, *The Right and the Power: The Prosecution of Watergate* (New York: Reader's Digest Press, 1976), 54.

16 *Christian Science Monitor,* December 26, 1973.

17 December 23, 1973.

18 January 11, 1974.

19 All quotations from January 10, 1974, except for the Albuquerque and Phoenix newspapers, which came out January 11, 1974.

20 All quotations from January 17, 1974.

21 *New York Times,* January 21, 1974.

22 Ibid., January 23, 1974.

23 January 24, 1974.

24 *New York Times,* January 23, 1974.

25 *Public Papers of the President,* 1974, 55.

26 Ben-Veniste and Frampton, *Stonewall,* 189–194.

27 Jaworski, *The Right and the Power,* 99.

28 Ibid., 88.

29 Quoted from the report reproduced in *Impeachment of Richard M. Nixon, President of the United States: The Final Report of the Committee on the Judiciary, House of Representatives* (New York: Viking Press, 1975), 10, 11, 12.

30 *Public Papers of the President,* 1974, 202, 204.

31 February 25, 1974.

32 Both quotations from February 20, 1974.

33 *Public Papers of the President, 1974,* 208; *Louisville Courier–Journal,* February 27, 1974.

34 Ben-Veniste and Frampton, *Stonewall,* 211–263; Jaworski, *The Right and the Power,* 99–108.

35 *Public Papers of the President,* 1974, 231–232, 236, 240.

36 *Roanoke Times, Memphis Commercial Appeal, Salt Lake Tribune, Chicago Tribune,* March 8, 1974.

37 March 14, 1974.

38 Both quotations from March 14, 1974.

39 *Public Papers of the President,* 1974, 261–277.

40 Ibid., 279–282.

41 *Los Angeles Times,* March 20, 1974.

42 *Public Papers of the President,* 1974, 284–298.

43 Ibid., 389–397.

44 *New York Times,* May 4, 1974; *Time,* May 13, 1974, 14.

45 May 5, 1974.

46 All newspaper quotations are from the first week of May.

47 *New York Times,* May 2 and 4, 1974.

48 May 10, 1974.

49 May 5, 1974.

8. THE CONSENSUS AND THE RESIGNATION

1 *Public Papers of the President, 1974,* 451.

2 Bill Gulley, with Mary Ellen Reese, *Breaking Cover* (New York: Simon and Schuster, 1980), 227.

3 December 14, 1972, box 8, Buchanan Papers; Haldeman to Dean, February 10, 1973, box 205, Haldeman Papers.

4 *Public Papers of the President, 1974,* 479.

5 House of Representatives, *Hearings before the Committee on the Judiciary,* Ninety-third Cong., 2d sess. (Washington, D.C.: Government Printing Office, 1974), 1: 34, 70 (hereafter *Hearings, Judiciary*).

6 William Rehnquist had excused himself from the case on grounds of his past association with the administration.

7 Richard M. Nixon, *RN: Memoirs* (New York: Grosset and Dunlap, 1978), 1001–1002, 1019, 1042, 1049.

8 *New York Times,* July 24, 1974.

9 Nixon, *RN: Memoirs,* 1050.

10 U.S. House of Representatives, *Impeachment of Richard M. Nixon, President of the United States: Report of the Committee on the Judiciary,* H. Doc. 93–1305, Ninety-third Cong., 2d sess., August 20, 1974, 3, 8.

11 Nixon, *RN: Memoirs,* 1057, 1059.

12 Stanley I. Kutler, ed., *Watergate: The Fall of Richard M. Nixon* (St. James, N.Y.: Brandywine Press, 1996), 44, 45.

13 *Public Papers of the President, 1974,* 621, 623.

14 All quotations from editorials on August 6 or August 7, 1974.

15 August 8, 1974.

16 All of the editorial comments appeared during the period August 6 to August 9, 1974.

17 July 31, August 6, 1974.

18 *Washington Post,* August 6, 1974.

19 Henry Kissinger, *Years of Upheaval* (Boston: Little, Brown, 1982), 1203.

20 Gerald R. Ford, *A Time to Heal: The Autobiography of Gerald R. Ford* (New York: Harper and Row, 1979), 21.

21 Kissinger, *Years of Upheaval,* 1204.

22 Nixon, *RN: Memoirs,* 1071.

23 Barry M. Goldwater, with Jack Casserly, *Goldwater* (New York: Doubleday, 1988), 279, 280.

24 Kissinger, *Years of Upheaval,* 1202.

25 Ibid., 1207.

26 *Public Papers of the President, 1974,* 627, 628.

27 Ibid., 631.

9. ENDS AND MEANS

1 Melvin Small, *The Presidency of Richard Nixon* (Lawrence: University Press of Kansas, 1999), 310, 311.

2 For a book that deals with this point, see Robert H. Johnson, *Improbable Dangers: U.S. Conceptions of Threat in the Cold War and After* (New York: St. Martin's, 1994). See also the review by Walter Nixon in *American Historical Review* 101 (April 1996): 591–592.

3 Patrick J. Maney, *The Roosevelt Presence: A Biography of Franklin D. Roosevelt* (New York: Twayne, 1992), 201.

4 Small, *The Presidency of Richard Nixon,* 310.

5 John F. Kennedy, *The Strategy of Peace,* ed. Allan Nevins (New York: Harper and Row, 1960), 160.

6 Bruce Russett, *Controlling the Sword: The Democratic Governance of National Security* (Cambridge: Harvard University Press, 1990), 1, 7; see also 144.

7 For a survey of these relationships, see Melvin Small, *Democracy and Diplomacy: The Impact of Domestic Politics on U.S. Foreign Policy, 1789–1994* (Baltimore: Johns Hopkins University Press, 1996); his bibliographic essay is especially rich.

8 Henry Kissinger, *Years of Upheaval* (Boston: Little, Brown, 1982), 1122.

9 Henry Kissinger, *White House Years* (Boston: Little, Brown, 1979), 986n.

10 Kissinger, *Years of Upheaval,* 415.

11 Knowledge of the Chilean embassy burglary became known with the release of additional Nixon tapes in February 1999. See *New York Times* and *Washington Post,* both from February 26, 1999.

12 Richard M. Nixon, *RN: Memoirs* (New York: Grosset and Dunlap, 1978), 512.

13 Harry S. Truman, *Public Papers of the President, 1947,* 178, 180, and *Public Papers of the President, 1949,* 112.

14 Dwight D. Eisenhower, *Public Papers of the President, 1953,* 1, 4, 5, and *Public Papers of the President, 1957,* 61.

15 John F. Kennedy, *Public Papers of the President, 1961,* 2, and *Public Papers of the President, 1963,* 892.

16 Lyndon B. Jonson, *Public Papers of the President, 1965,* 1: 397, and 2: 794.

17 James E. Miller, "Taking Off the Gloves: The United States and the Italian Elections of 1948," *Diplomatic History,* 7 (winter 1983): 35–55.

18 *New York Times,* October 9, 1994.

19 U.S. Congress, Senate, "Covert Action in Chile, 1963–1973," *Staff Report of the Select Committee to Study Government Operations with Respect to Intelligence Activities* (Washington, D.C.: Government Printing Office, 1975).

20 Stephen E. Ambrose, *Eisenhower: The President* (New York: Simon and Schuster, 1984); 189; Athan Theoharis, *Spying on Americans* (Philadelphia: Temple University Press, 1978), 229.

21 Stanley I. Kutler, ed., *Abuse of Power* (New York: Free Press, 1997), 137.

22 Buchanan to Nixon, March 24, 1971, box 1, Buchanan Papers.

23 Charles Colson, "Law Isn't Enough," *Washington Post,* July 30, 2002.

24 *New York Times,* February 8, 1972.

25 *Watergate Hearings,* 4: 1666, and 5: 1834.

26 Jeb Stuart Magruder, *An American Life* (New York: Atheneum, 1974), 240; Raymond Price, *With Nixon* (New York: Viking, 1977), 336.

27 *Public Papers of the President, 1974,* 623, 628, 631.

28 Gerald Ford, *A Time to Heal* (New York: Harper and Row, 1979), 169–170, 172, 178, 180.

29 David Frost, *"I Gave Them a Sword": Behind the Scenes of the Nixon Interviews* (New York: William Morrow, 1978), 164, 242.

30 Stanley I. Kutler, ed., *Watergate: The Fall of Richard M. Nixon* (St. James, N.Y: Brandywine Press, 1996), 3.

Bibliographical Essay

The Watergate affair generated a rich body of primary sources. Although Richard M. Nixon was addicted to secrecy, his administration, ironically, left more internal documents than any other administration. The Nixon Presidential Materials Project at the National Archives in College Park, Maryland, includes approximately 4,000 hours of taped recordings; only a minority of hours are now open to researchers and the public. The historian Stanley I. Kutler has edited transcripts of some of the tapes as they have become available; see his *Abuse of Power: The New Nixon Tapes* (New York: Free Press, 1997). For another volume of documents, some of which include transcripts of tapes, see Kutler, ed., *Watergate: The Fall of Richard M. Nixon* (St. James, N.Y.: Brandywine Press, 1996). Bruce Oudes likewise has edited a large collection of documents from the Nixon Presidential Materials Project; see *From the President: Richard Nixon's Secret Files* (New York: Harper and Row, 1989).

For Watergate, two sets of hearings of the Ninety-third Congress, 2d session, are indispensable: the twenty-seven volumes of the Senate Watergate Committee Hearings and the thirty-nine volumes of the House of Representatives Judiciary Committee Hearings. The final report of each set of proceedings is excellent. Scholarly Resources has published an index for each set of hearings. In 1975 the Viking Press published the final report of the House committee, *Impeachment of Richard M. Nixon: President of the United States.*

The Public Papers of the Presidents of the United States, Richard Nixon, 6 vols. (Washington, D.C.: Government Printing Office, 1970–1975) contains every public statement the president made. The transcripts of the news conferences are especially useful. Particularly handy is *Watergate: Chronology of a Crisis*, 2 vols. (Washington, D.C.: Congressional Quarterly, 1974).

For a valuable source, see Gerald S. Strober and Deborah Hart Strober, *Nixon: An Oral History of His Presidency* (New York: HarperCollins, 1994). In 1974 the *New York Times* published the transcripts of the tapes that the White House released to the House Judiciary Committee. Late in his life Nixon spent hours talking with Monica Crowley, who published his remembrances and opinions: see *Nixon Off the Record* (New York: Random House, 1996) and *Nixon in Winter* (New York: Random House, 1998). Eleanora W. Schoenebaum edited a practical volume, *Profiles of An Era: The Nixon/Ford Years* (New York: Harcourt Brace Jovanovich, 1979).

Watergate has attracted a multitude of books, with no end in sight. The best remains Stanley I. Kutler, *The Wars of Watergate: The Last Crisis of Richard Nixon* (New York: Knopf, 1990). Kutler based his authoritative study on the Nixon archival material then open to researchers and also on interviews and placed the events into a historical context; he concluded that Nixon's personality and the events of the 1960s led to Watergate.

Stephen Ambrose has published a massive three-volume biography of Nixon; the second volume, *Nixon: The Triumph of a Politician, 1962–1972* (New York: Simon and Schuster, 1989), covers the early stages of the cover-up. The third volume, *Nixon: Ruin and Recovery, 1973–1990* (New York: Simon and Schuster 1991), offers a narrative of the basic events of Watergate without the analytical richness and breadth of Kutler's book. Although he treats Nixon harshly regarding Watergate, Ambrose provides a sympathetic portrait of Nixon's postpresidential years.

Biographies of Nixon provide examinations of his earlier career that shed light on his political personality and practices. See especially Ambrose, *Nixon: The Education of a Politician, 1913–1961* (New York: Simon and Schuster, 1987), and Roger Morris, *Richard Milhouse Nixon: The Rise of an American Politician* (New York: Henry Holt, 1990). Morris ends his book in 1953. Herbert S. Parmet, *Richard Nixon and His America* (Boston: Little, Brown, 1990) devotes scant treatment to Watergate. Jonathan Aitken, *Nixon: A Life* (Washington, D.C.: Regnery, 1993), rests on weak research and offers unsound conclusions. In his unfavorable portrait of Nixon, Anthony Summers, *The Arrogance of Power: The Secret World of Richard Nixon* (New York: Viking, 2000), devotes more than 100 pages to Watergate, with an emphasis on Nixon's instability. The journalist Richard Reeves, *President Nixon: Alone in the White House* (New York: Simon and Schuster, 2001), ends his study in April 1973. The liberal *New York Times* columnist Tom Wicker presents a sympathetic treatment of Nixon in *One of Us: Richard Nixon and the American Dream* (New York: Random House, 1991). Wicker concludes that Watergate was inevitable in the context of the times.

Fred Emery, *Watergate: The Corruption of American Politics and the Fall of Richard Nixon* (New York: Random House, 1994), is a full-length treatment of Watergate that clearly documents Nixon's criminality. During the Watergate years Emery served as the Washington bureau chief of the *Times* (London) and wrote in conjunction with what became a five-part BBC Watergate series. Emery's book lacks the extensive research base and broad historical perspective of Kutler's *The Wars of Watergate* and does not go beyond that model study's essential interpretive themes.

Two books worth consideration are David Frost, *"I Gave Them a Sword": Behind the Scenes of the Nixon Interviews* (New York: William Morrow, 1978), and Robert Sam Anson, *Exile: The Unquiet Oblivion of Richard M. Nixon* (New York: Simon and Schuster, 1984). Two books that reveal fundamental conspiracies in the Watergate affair include Len Colony and Robert Gettlin's *Silent Coup: The Removal of a President* (New York: St. Martin's Press, 1991) and Jim Hougan's *Secret Agenda: Watergate, Deep Throat and the CIA* (New York: Random House, 1984). Also see Victor Lasky, *It Didn't Start with Watergate* (New York: Dial Press, 1977).

A sample of the studies that examine the legacy of Watergate include Ronald E. Pynn, ed., *Watergate and the American Political Process* (New York: Praeger, 1975); Donald W. Harward, ed., *Crisis in Confidence: The Impact of Watergate* (Boston, Little, Brown, 1974); and Michael Schudson, *Watergate in American Memory: How We Remember, Forget, and Reconstruct the Past* (New York: Basic Books, 1992).

Essential for understanding the background of the atmosphere that produced the Huston Plan is Athan Theoharis, *Spying on Americans: Political Surveillance from Hoover to the Huston Plan* (Philadelphia: Temple University Press, 1978). Four specialized studies require note: Leo Rangell, *The Mind of Watergate: An Exploration of the Compromise of Integrity* (New York: Norton, 1980); Philip B. Kurland, *Watergate and the Constitution* (Chicago: University of Chicago Press, 1978); David Rudenstine, *The Day the Presses Stopped: A History of the Pentagon Papers Case* (Berkeley: University of California Press, 1996); and Leonard Garment, *In Search of Deep Throat: The Greatest Political Mystery of Our Time* (New York: Basic Books, 2000).

With the exception of John Mitchell, the principal participants in the Watergate break-in and its cover-up wrote memoirs: Richard M. Nixon, *RN: The Memoirs of Richard Nixon* (New York: Grosset and Dunlap, 1978); H. R. Haldeman, with Joseph DiMona, *The Ends of Power* (New York: New York Times Books, 1978); John Ehrlichman, *Witness to Power: The Nixon Years* (New York: Simon and Schuster, 1982); John Dean, *Blind Ambition: The White House Years* (New York: Simon and Schuster, 1976); Charles W. Colson, *Born Again* (Old Tappan, N.J.: Chosen Books, 1976); G. Gordon Liddy, *Will: The Autobiography of G. Gordon Liddy* (New York: St. Martin's Press, 1980); Jeb Stuart Magruder, *An American Life: One Man's Road to Watergate* (New York: Atheneum, 1974); and James W. McCord Jr., *A Piece of Tape: The Watergate Story — Fact and Fiction* (Rockville, Md.: Washington Media Services, 1974).

Presidential aides not directly involved in the crimes of Watergate also wrote memoirs. The most useful include Raymond Price's *With Nixon* (New York: Viking, 1977); Herbert G. Klein's *Making It Perfectly Clear* (Garden City, N.Y.: Doubleday, 1980); and Alexander M. Haig Jr.'s, with Charles McCarry, *Inner Circles: How America Changed the World — A Memoir* (New York: Warner Books, 1992). After the resignation of Haldeman, Haig served as chief of staff for the remainder of the Nixon administration.

Members of Nixon's cabinet also published their memoirs, in which they touched, in varying degrees, on Watergate. The one with which to start is Richard Kleindienst, *Justice: The Memoirs of Attorney General Richard C. Kleindienst* (Ottawa, Ill: Jameson Books, 1985). For his perjury, Kleindienst received a suspended sentence. See also William E. Simon, *A Time for Truth* (New York: McGraw-Hill, 1978); Elliot Richardson, *The Creative Balance: Government, Politics, and the Individual in America's Third Century* (New York: Holt, Rinehart, 1976); and Maurice Stans, *One of the President's Men: Twenty Years with Eisenhower and Nixon* (Washington, D.C.: Brassey's, 1995).

For an understanding of the Senate Watergate Committee, start with Samuel Dash, *Chief Counsel: Inside the Ervin Committee — The Untold Story of Watergate* (New York: Random House, 1976). The minority counsel, Fred D. Thompson, also wrote an account, *At That Point in Time: The Inside Story of the Senate Watergate Committee* (New York: Quadrangle/New York Times, 1975). For a favorable biography of Howard Baker, the ranking Republican member of the committee, see J. Lee Annis Jr., *Howard Baker: Conciliator in an Age of Crisis* (Lanham, Md.: Madison Books, 1995). Paul R. Clancy's *Just a Country Lawyer: A Biography of Senator Sam Ervin* (Bloomington: Indiana University Press, 1974) is a sympathetic treatment of the North Carolinian who became a national folk hero as chair of the Senate committee.

Several solid books cover the special prosecutors. The journalist James Doyle, who served as press secretary and special assistant, wrote *Not above the Law: The Battles of Watergate Prosecutors Cox and Jaworski: A Behind-the-Scenes Account* (New York: William Morrow, 1977). Ken Gormley's *Archibald Cox: Conscience of a Nation* (Reading: Addison-Wesley, 1997) is an excellent full biography of the first prosecutor. The second prosecutor, Leon Jaworski, wrote *The Right and the Power: The Prosecution of Watergate* (New York: Reader's Digest Press, 1976) and, with Mickey Herskowitz, *Confession and Avoidance: A Memoir* (Garden City, N.Y.: Anchor Press/Doubleday, 1979). Two former assistant special prosecutors, Richard Ben-Veniste and George Frampton Jr., wrote a careful study, *Stonewall: The Real Story of the Watergate Prosecution* (New York: Simon and Schuster, 1977). The political scientist Katy J. Harriger offers a comprehensive review of the office in *Independent Justice: The Federal Special Prosecutor in American Politics* (Lawrence: University Press of Kansas, 1992).

Judge John Sirica, who played an indispensable role in the Watergate affair, recorded his experiences in *To Set the Record Straight: The Break-in, the Tapes, the Conspirators, the Pardon* (New York: Norton, 1979).

Journalists who covered Watergate wrote several superb studies. The team of Bob Woodward and Carl Bernstein wrote two best-sellers. *All The President's Men* (New York: Simon and Schuster, 1974) appeared early in 1974 before the Watergate drama had played to its end. Their by-line articles helped the *Washington Post* win the Pulitzer Prize for its coverage of Watergate. *The Final Days* (New York: Simon and Schuster, 1976) appeared two years later and again offered a well-written narrative based largely on interviews. J. Anthony Lukas, whose honors include a Pulitzer Prize and the Page One Award of the New York Newspaper Guild, published *Nightmare: The Underside of the Nixon Years* (New York: Viking, 1976), which equals in brilliance the volumes by Woodward and Bernstein. Theodore H. White, the veteran journalist who wrote the classic *The Making of the President — 1960*, placed Nixon and Watergate in a broad perspective in *Breach of Faith: The Fall of Richard Nixon* (New York: Atheneum, 1975). Barry Sussman, city editor of the *Post* at the time of the June 1972 break-in, published *The Great Coverup: Nixon and the Scandal of Watergate* (New York: Crowell, 1974) immediately after the resignation; in 1992 he published a third edition with the same title (Arlington, Va.: Seven Locks Press, 1992). Clark R. Mollenhoff, another Pulitzer Prize–winning journalist, spent 1969 and 1970 in the White House as deputy counsel and special counsel to the president before returning to journalism; see his *Game Plan for Disaster: An Ombudsman's Report on the Nixon Years* (New York: Norton, 1976). Another solid study is Jonathan Schell's *The Time of Illusion* (New York: Knopf, 1976). Elizabeth Drew, *Washington Journal: The Events of 1973–1974* (New York: Random House, 1975), and Mary McCarthy, *The Mask of State: Watergate Portraits* (New York: Harcourt Brace Jovanovich, 1974), published articles they had written during 1973 and 1975. The staff of the *Washington Post* wrote *The Fall of a President* (New York: Dell, 1974), a collection of essays that includes two of the president's speeches, a chronology, the three articles of impeachment, and transcripts of the tapes Nixon released on August 5, 1974. Dan Rather and Gary Paul Gates's *The Palace Guard* (New York: Harper and Row, 1974) went to press before Nixon's resignation. John Osborne's, *The Last Nixon Watch* is a collection of articles published during 1974, most of them before Nixon's resignation (Washington, D.C.: New Republic, 1975). See also George V. Higgins, *The Friends of Richard Nixon* (Boston: Little, Brown, 1975); an attorney and sometime journalist, he wrote about Watergate in 1974 in the *Atlantic*. In his memoir, the CBS newscaster Daniel Schorr discusses his Watergate experiences, including position number seventeen on the enemies list, in *Clearing the Air* (Boston: Houghton Mifflin, 1977).

Other memoirs and biographies provide insights into Watergate. John Mitchell receives important treatment in Wizola McLendon's *Martha: The Life of Martha Mitchell* (New York: Random House, 1979). Julie Nixon Eisenhower's important study contains information and insights beyond the subject of her mother in *Pat Nixon: The Untold Story* (New York: Simon and Schuster, 1986). Thomas Powers, *The Man Who Kept the Secrets: Richard Helms and the CIA* (New York: Knopf, 1979), includes information about Haldeman, Ehrlichman, and Nixon. Solid autobiographies with relevant information about Watergate include those by Ben Bradlee, executive editor of the *Washington Post* from 1968 to 1991, *A Good Life: Newspapering and Other Adventures* (New York: Simon and Schuster, 1995); Barry M. Goldwater, with Jack Casserly, *Goldwater* (New York: Doubleday, 1988); Tip O'Neill, with William Novak, *Man of the House: The Life and Political Memoirs of Speaker Tip O'Neill* (New York: Random House, 1987); Gerald R. Ford, *A Time to Heal: The Autobiography of Gerald R. Ford* (New York: Harper and Row, 1979); and Lawrence F. O'Brien, *No Final Victories: A Life in Politics, from John F. Kennedy to Watergate* (Garden City, N.Y.: Doubleday, 1974). At the time of the June 17, 1972 break-in, O'Brien served as chair of the Democratic National Committee.

For the best history of the Nixon administration, see Melvin Small, *The Presidency of Richard Nixon* (Lawrence: University Press of Kansas, 1999); the bibliographical essay is exceptionally thorough.

Index

testimony before Senate
Committee, 107, 108
Vietnam critics guilty of treason,
29–39, 175–176
Halperin, Morton H., 10, 11
Hamilton, Edward J., 39
Harmony, Sally J., 94
Harriman, W. Averell, 11
Harris Polls, 26, 29, 41, 65, 83–84, 88,
100, 105, 111, 112–113, 121–122, 129,
158
Hearst, William Randolph Jr., 144, 145–
146
Helms, Jesse A., 105
Helms, Richard, 8, 9, 21, 51, 87, 93, 98,
159, 177, 181
Higby, Larry, 77, 100, 101
Higgins, Trumbull, 174
Hiss, Alger, 59
Hogan, Lawrence, 155, 156, 157
Honolulu Star–Bulletin, 118
Hoover, J. Edgar, 10, 16, 21, 34, 72
illegal programs, 182
Johnson's use of FBI to investigate
Nixon and Agnew, 8
Nixon disappointed, 8–9
objections to Huston Plan, 17, 20
Horner, Jack, 142
House Armed Services Subcommittee
on Intelligence, 93, 98, 99, 111,
120
House Banking and Currency
Committee, 60, 66
House Judiciary Committee, 121, 124,
133, 134, 135, 136, 138, 139, 140, 142,
143, 144, 146, 147, 148, 149, 150,
151, 156, 158, 161
formal impeachment debate, 156–
157
impeachment preliminaries, 152–154
positions of members toward
impeachment, 155, 162–163, 167
votes on impeachment articles 1
through 5, 157, 158
Houston News, 148
Hughes, Emmet John, 144

Hughes, Howard R., 132
Hughes, Philip S., 66–67
Humphrey, Hubert H., 22–23, 27, 31,
33, 175
Hunt, E. Howard, 35, 51, 52, 55, 56, 58,
61, 76, 79, 80, 82, 86, 89, 91, 112,
114, 121, 130
background, 18–19
change of plea to guilty, 69
cooperation with Senate
Committee, 113
demand for support money and
legal fees, 74, 95–96
and Fielding break-in, 19–20
and Plumbers, 19–20
shredding of files, 50
testimony on use of CIA equipment
in investigations, 98
and Watergate break-in, 38–39, 44–
46
Hunt, Dorothy (Mrs. Howard Hunt),
55, 69
Huston, Tom Charles, 16, 17, 99
Huston Plan, 16–17, 20, 21, 36, 92, 93,
123

ICI (Interagency Committee on
Intelligence), 16
IEC (Intelligence Evaluation
Committee), 21
Illegal corporate campaign
contributions, 174, 176, 180, 181.
See also American Airlines;
Anaconda; Ashland Oil; Braniff
Airlines; Goodyear Tire and
Rubber
Imperial presidency, 169, 179, 182
Imperial Presidency, The (Schlesinger),
169
Indianapolis News, 162
Inouye, Daniel K., 70–71, 99, 107
IRS (Internal Revenue Service), 7, 16,
97, 114, 130, 142, 149, 150, 157, 169
ITT (International Telephone and
Telegraph Corporation), 120,
130–131, 132, 133, 174

retreat from position of ultimate
authority over Special
Prosecutor, 92
and Saturday Night Massacre, 117–
118
sees abuse of power, 125
Rietz, Ken, 81–82
Ringer, Gordon, 133
RN: The Memoirs of Richard Nixon, 5
Roanoke Times, 145, 161, 162
Rockefeller, Nelson A., 15, 29, 116
Rodino, Peter, 134, 135, 154, 157
building the impeachment case,
134–135
formal debate on articles of
impeachment, 156
hearings, 149
minimizing partisanship, 153, 155
no criminal charges if Nixon
resigns, 164–165
seeking the tapes, 150
Rodham, Hillary, 135
Rogers, William P., 24, 77, 83, 106
Romney, George, 82
Roosevelt, Franklin D., 5, 14, 138., 169
Roosevelt, Kermit, 173
Roosevelt and the Isolationists, 1932–1945
(Cole), 169
*Roosevelt Presence, The: A Biography of
Franklin Delano Roosevelt*
(Maney), 169
Roper Poll, 147
Rosenfield, Harry M., 44
Ruckelshaus, William D., 118
Russett, Bruce, 169–170

Safire, William, 24, 25
dismissing impact of dirty tricks, 32
FBI taps telephone, 12
as Nixon speechwriter, 16
Watergate an abuse of power to win
election, 175, 182
Saginaw News, 136, 137
Salt Lake City Desert News, 131
Salt Lake City Tribune, 103, 118, 161
Sanchez, Manolo, 15

Sanders, Donald G., 100, 101
San Diego Union, 161
Sargent, Francis W., 125
Saturday Night Massacre, 103, 123, 134,
144, 178
impact on Nixon, 119–120, 121, 122,
147
label for series of events, 118, 170
press reaction, 118–119, 120, 124
Saxbe, William B., 121, 125, 130, 140
Schlesinger, Arthur M. Jr., 169, 179
Schlesinger, James R., 86, 105–106
Schorr, Daniel, 30
Scott, Hugh
and attempts to discredit Dean, 96
and calls for full disclosure, 126
with information that will clear
Nixon "entirely," 132
meeting with Nixon on August 7,
1974, 164
negative characterization of tape
transcripts, 144
Scripps-Howard Papers, 110
Sears, John P., 11–12
Seattle Times, 140
Sedan Chair I and II, 33
Segretti, Donald, 30, 36, 55–56, 73, 74,
95, 99, 137, 142, 176
assessment of impact, 33
Bernstein-Woodward story reveals
activities, 64
dirty tricks operations, 30–33, 113–
114
guilty plea and prison sentence, 112,
125
hired to conduct covert dirty tricks,
30–31, 72, 87, 114
testimony before Senate
Committee, 113–114
Senate Appropriations Subcommittee,
93
Senate Banking and Currency
Committee, 58
Senate Committee. *See* Senate Select
Committee on Presidential
Campaign Activities

firing Liddy, 54
fund raising, 35, 36, 41, 53
maintaining no connection with dirty tricks, break-in, or cover-up, 95
possible violation of 1972 Federal Campaign Expenditures Act, 67
State Department. *See* Department of State
St. Clair, James D., 135, 153, 155
as head of Nixon's legal team, 130, 150, 153, 154, 157–158
meetings with Jaworski and Haig, 149
and Nixon's tape statements, 134, 140, 143, 148, 157–158
Stennis, John, 117, 147, 156
Stephenson, Dennis P., 40
St. Louis Globe–Democrat, 25, 161
St. Louis Post–Dispatch, 161
St. Petersburg Times, 119
Strachan, Gordon C., 55, 74, 78, 99, 138
Cox recommends reduced charges for guilty pleas, 98
Fielding and Watergate break-ins, 39, 48, 95
grand jury interviews and indictment, 80, 137
role in hiring Segretti, 30, 99
shredding of files, 49, 50
testimony before Senate Committee, 106
Students for a Democratic Society, 182
Sturgis, Frank A., 39
Sullivan, William C., 16
Supreme Court. *See* U.S. Supreme Court
Sussman, Barry, 44, 45, 61
Symington, Stuart, 87
Syracuse Herald–Journal, 86, 161

Talmadge, Herman E., 70–71, 98, 99, 107
Tapes
erased eighteen-and-a-half minutes, 127, 128, 131, 178

June 23, 1972, "smoking gun," 141, 143, 148, 155, 157, 158, 159, 160, 162, 163, 164, 165, 167, 176–177, 178
potential for quick answer to cover-up, 103
summary of year-long struggle, 156
Thompson, Fred D., 71, 101, 106–107
Time, 69, 95, 110, 111, 116, 120, 123, 124, 146
Timmons, William E., 66, 154, 155, 163, 164–165
Titus, Harold, 78
Toledo Blade, 131
Topeka Daily Capital, 144, 145, 161
Truman, Harry S., 98, 171–172, 173, 174
Tulsa Daily World, 160
Tydings, Joseph M., 34

Ulasewicz, Anthony T., 9, 13, 18, 36, 55, 97, 106, 113
University of California, Berkeley, 30, 134
University of Maryland, 61
University of Southern California, 35, 54
University of Texas Law School, 104, 150
University of Washington, 18
U.S. Court of Appeals for the District of Columbia, 150
upholding Sirica, 116, 138
urging Nixon and Cox to settle out of court, 112
U.S. Supreme Court, 17, 133, 147, 150, 154
decision regarding control over tapes, 155–156, 158, 167

VanderLann, Robert, 136
VanderVeen, Richard, 136
Vesco, Robert L., 86, 96
Veterans of Foreign Wars, 109
Vietnam, 9, 10, 11, 13–14, 17, 23, 26, 27, 29–30, 41, 50, 58, 59, 65, 69, 77, 82, 90, 102, 119, 135, 151, 164, 170, 175, 176, 178